ULTRAVIOLENT
MOVIES

ULTRAVIOLENT MOVIES

FROM SAM PECKINPAH TO QUENTIN TARANTINO

Revised and Updated

Laurent Bouzereau

Citadel Press
Kensington Publishing Corp.
www.kensingtonbooks.com

CITADEL PRESS books are published by

Kensington Publishing Corp.
850 Third Avenue
New York, NY 10022

All Kensington titles, imprints, and distributed lines are available at
special quantity discounts for bulk purchases for sales promotions,
premiums, fund raising, educational, or institutional use. Special book
excerpts or customized printings can also be created to fit specific
needs. For details, write or phone the office of the Kensington special
sales manager: Kensington Publishing Corp., 850 Third Avenue, New
York, NY 10022, attn: Special Sales Department, phone 1-800-221-2647.

Kensington and the K logo Reg. U.S. Pat. & TM Office
Citadel Press is a trademark of Kensington Publishing Corp.

First printing 2000

10 9 8 7 6 5 4 3 2 1

Printed in the United States of America

Design by Andrew B. Gardner

Library of Congress Cataloging-in-Publication Data

Bouzereau, Laurent.
    Ultraviolent movies : from Sam Peckinpah to Quentin Tarantino /
Laurent Bouzereau. Rev. and updated.
        p.   cm.
    "A Citadel Press book."
    ISBN 0-8065-2045-0 (pbk.)
    1. Violence in motion pictures.   I. Title.
PN1995.9.V5B68   1996
791.43′653—dc20   95-48086
                                                     CIP

Contents

Preface

It happened in Manhattan, where I lived for six years. In 1989, late on a hot and muggy summer afternoon. I was on my way to the subway station and crossing Madison Avenue at Thirty-fourth Street, when I saw a middle-aged driver try to make a right turn. His car nearly hit a young bicycle messenger who was riding in the same direction. The driver immediately stopped his car and got out to see if the bicyclist was harmed. It seemed to me that the man was not truly at fault but was ready to apologize. The young messenger, on the other hand, was outraged; he threw his bike on the sidewalk, and as the driver approached him, he rummaged in his backpack's front pouch, frantically looking for something. Before the man had a chance to say anything, the kid pulled out a wrench and hit him over the head with it. Time seemed to stop; it was as if every passerby had been attacked. We were all stunned. The man stood for a moment, completely in shock; then, as blood started trickling down his face, he collapsed. The kid stared at his victim without moving. It wasn't long before the police and an ambulance arrived.

That is the most violent event I have ever witnessed, and the vision of that poor man getting hit so senselessly with the wrench still haunts me. At times, I even wonder whether I really saw all of this or only dreamed it.

On another occasion, I was on line in the freezing cold in Park City, Utah, waiting to get into a restaurant. I was attending the Sundance Film Festival and was chatting with a young director who had a movie in competition. It was impossible not to notice a scar that ran from the top of his nose down his left cheek. An insensitive journalist (as if there are any other kind) who was on line with us and had joined the conversation asked the director what had happened to his face. He explained that leaving the subway in New York, he had gotten into an argument with a bum; before he knew it, the bum had taken a razor out of his coat pocket. "All I remember," the director said, "was seeing a rain of blood." The bum had slashed him so quickly that at first the victim had not felt any pain.

At this point in his story, all I remember was that it was cold and I was starving. Suddenly I felt my face turning completely white. Slowly sounds became muffled. I kept thinking about "the rain of blood." While the journalist and the director carried on their conversation, not paying any attention to my nausea, I managed to stumble inside the restaurant. I sat down and put my head between my legs (I still wonder what people must have thought I was doing) and slowly regained my senses.

Despite my own personal revulsion to blood, understand that when my publisher called me and asked if I'd be interested in writing a book on violent movies, I simply couldn't say no!

Whether it's on the streets or on the news, violence is everywhere. While few except criminals and psychopaths enjoy violence, many of us love it in films. Although you must believe me when I say that I'm not of a violent nature, it's fair to assume that using some of that "good old ultraviolence" on some of my least favorite people has definitely crossed my mind. So I agree with psychiatrists who claim that watching violent movies can be a cathartic experience. Of course, there is also the possibility that screen violence might have the reverse effect on certain individuals and inspire them to act out in real life some of the mayhem seen in movies. Films take us to worlds we would never imagine. In order to be commercially successful, they offer sensations that we don't necessarily experience in our everyday life. Watching violence in the safety of a theater or of our own home can be as thrilling as a roller-coaster ride. Through movies, we test our ability to face certain fears. Saying, "Hey, I can watch anything; it doesn't affect me," can be as satisfying as beating up the neighborhood bully. While screen violence has never seemed more graphic, it has been the center of controversy ever since a cowboy faced the camera with his gun and shot at the audience in *The Great Train Robbery* in 1903. In the late sixties, when the old Hollywood Production Code was replaced by a new ratings system, it became possible to depict sex and violence in more explicit ways. However, the Motion Picture Association of America (MPAA) still wields power and today never fails to punish some of our most daring filmmakers who have decided to challenge the ratings board—as well as the audience—with shocking images of sex and violence.

Although many films are featured in the pages that follow, this book is not about all the violent movies ever made; it's about those films that have had the most impact and defined—or redefined—screen violence. While writing this book, I was interested in the various aspects of screen violence: I wanted to find out about the anatomy of screen violence and how it was filmed. There are many styles and different ways of filming people getting killed or tortured, and before one can understand the effect and impact violence might have on an audience, one, I assume, must know how it's done. I then became intrigued by the response to ultraviolent movies from the censors, the critics, and the public. For many films I have included behind-the-scenes stories (sometimes told by the directors themselves) about making some of these movies. These stories include both bad and beautiful filmmaking.

While my focus is primarily on the filmmaker's art, I have paid particular attention to their responsibility to their audience and to society. I have also included cases where on-screen violence has incited riots and copycat behavior from its viewers.

My intention in this book is never to celebrate violence or to seem insensitive to the problems of murder, mayhem, and bloodshed in the real world. At the same time, the presentation of ultraviolence has become such an intrinsic part of contemporary cinema that it cries out to be explored, dissected, even celebrated, when it is depicted in a thought-provoking and original manner.

After all, many of the most beautifully crafted films of the last generation can only be considered ultraviolent. While we all wish for a world without killing and violence, I am not so sure I would want to live in a culture that had no room for *A Clockwork Orange, Bonnie and Clyde, The Godfather, Scarface,* or *Taxi Driver.*

Acknowledgments

I wish to thank my agent Kay McCauley, my editor at Carol Publishing, Kevin McDonough, and Alvin H. Marill and Margaret Wolf. Also, very special thanks to Michael Arick, Clive Barker, Joyce Brouwers, Wes Craven, Sean S. Cunningham, David Dodds, Don Mancini, Maitland McDonagh, Greg Nicotero and KNB EFX Group, Inc., Oliver Stone, the staff of the Margaret Herrick Library at the Motion Picture Academy, and as always, my family, my parents, Micheline and Daniel, and my sisters, Cécile and Géraldine. The list could go on but it would probably be as long as this book . . . So, to all of you my friends here in the States and those back in France, thank you for your support, friendship, and for putting up with me!

ULTRAVIOLENT MOVIES

1

They Wrote the Book...

The glamorous world of crime . . . (*left to right*) Gene Hackman, Estelle Parsons, Warren Beatty, Faye Dunaway, and Michael J. Pollard in Arthur Penn's *Bonnie and Clyde*. (Warner Bros.—Seven Arts)

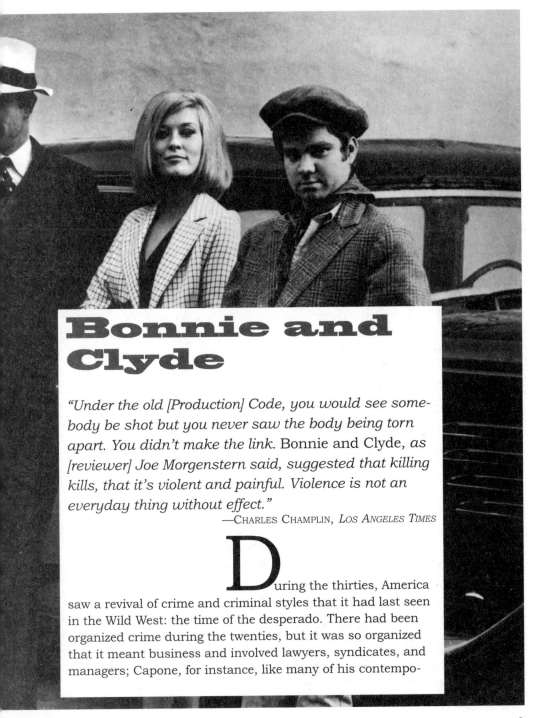

Bonnie and Clyde

*"Under the old [Production] Code, you would see some-
body be shot but you never saw the body being torn
apart. You didn't make the link.* Bonnie and Clyde, *as
[reviewer] Joe Morgenstern said, suggested that killing
kills, that it's violent and painful. Violence is not an
everyday thing without effect."*
—CHARLES CHAMPLIN, *LOS ANGELES TIMES*

During the thirties, America
saw a revival of crime and criminal styles that it had last seen
in the Wild West: the time of the desperado. There had been
organized crime during the twenties, but it was so organized
that it meant business and involved lawyers, syndicates, and
managers; Capone, for instance, like many of his contempo-

raries, was a businessman. But as the Great Depression deepened, a very different kind of criminal emerged, the desperado, whose appeal was closer to that of folk heroes like Jesse James than that of the dapper gangsters played by George Raft.

In *Bonnie and Clyde*, Clyde Barrow (Warren Beatty) meets Bonnie Parker (Faye Dunaway) in 1931 as he is about to steal her mother's car. They are both in their early twenties. Bonnie becomes more interested in Clyde than in the family car and decides to follow him to a life of robbing stores, gas stations, and banks. After a series of ridiculous raids, Bonnie and Clyde hook up with C. W. (Michael J. Pollard), who becomes their car heister. Later on, they add to the group Clyde's brother, "Buck" Barrow (Gene Hackman), who has just been released from prison, along with his wife, Blanche (Estelle Parsons), who wrongly believes that because he has served time, Buck is through with crime.

The gang's raids continue from Texas across Missouri and Kansas, Nebraska and Iowa. The violence escalates, and murder is soon added to Bonnie and Clyde's list of crimes. Their reputation as desperadoes grows, and their love relationship continues to blossom despite Clyde's impotence. En route, they capture one of their pursuers, Sheriff Hamer (Denver Pyle); they humiliate him, but they don't kill him. During an escape, Buck is mortally wounded, and Blanche is captured. Bonnie, Clyde, and C. W. find refuge with C. W.'s father, Malcolm (Dub Taylor), in Louisiana. In order to reduce his son's sentence, Malcom makes a deal with Sheriff Hamer, who has tracked down the gang, thanks to Blanche, and helps the police set a trap for Bonnie and Clyde. The couple ride into an ambush; the actual police records show that a thousand rounds of amunition were used to kill them when they were shot down in 1934. Their end as portrayed on the screen was as bloody in real life, with one difference: In the film, they're shown riddled with bullets before they have a chance to surrender, whereas in fact, Hamer and his posse did not start shooting until the couple made an attempt to fight.

In real life, Bonnie and Clyde were not as glamorous as their on-screen portrayal. Clyde was sadistic. Even as a child he liked to torture animals, and by the time he and Bonnie hooked up with their young recruit, Clyde had already murdered at least two men. Clyde was not as attractive as Warren Beatty, was somewhat effeminate, and leaned toward homosexuality. The

New York Times called him "a snake-eyed murderer who killed without giving his victims a chance to draw." The real Bonnie was no Faye Dunaway. She was tiny and boyish. As in the film, she was a waitress and liked to write poems. But she was also a married woman who had a number of lovers as well. It was reported that Bonnie and Clyde were physically offensive. They stank. In a zippered compartment down his right trouser leg Clyde concealed a shotgun which he could draw as rapidly as a pistol. He did so on numerous occasions, since the gang killed at least fifteen people in their crime spree. Whether or not Bonnie smoked cigars is uncertain. She once told a wounded police chief that she and Clyde had kidnapped that the famous photo taken of her with a cigar was only a joke. "Tell the public I don't smoke cigars," she supposedly confided in him. "It's the bunk."

The character of C. W. was created after William Daniel

Gene Hackman and Estelle Parsons are arrested after a brutal struggle. (Warner Bros.— Seven Arts)

Jones, a seventeen-year-old car thief who was chosen not only because of his mechanical skills but also to fulfill Bonnie's insatiable sexual desires. He eventually escaped, was captured in Texas, and in his confession, begged for a life sentence; behind bars, he felt he would at last be safe from the pair that had kept him in bondage for months. After Buck's death and the arrests of Blanche and Jones, Bonnie and Clyde looked for other confederates; they selected their old friend and common lover Raymond Hamilton, who was serving terms totaling 263 years. At the prison they machine-gunned the guards, leaving one dead body behind them and several others wounded. They escaped with Raymond and an added bonus, a youngster named Henry Methvin. It was Methvin's father who, in real life, betrayed Bonnie and Clyde in exchange for the protection of his son.

Released in 1967, the film, directed by Arthur Penn from a script by Robert Benton and David Newman, portrays Bonnie and Clyde as victims of their time.

The film's power arises from the fact that we, the audience, follow the story from the antiheroes' point of view. At first, even their acts of violence are bumbling, which enhances the sympathy we feel for them. But as the violence becomes increasingly graphic, we tend to distance ourselves from the couple. But the

film's pièce de résistance was the last scene, the bloody shoot-out and ultraviolent killing of Bonnie and Clyde. In the script by Robert Benton and David Newman, that legendary sequence was described as follows:

Exterior—Roadside—Day

We see alternately, the bodies of CLYDE and BONNIE twisting, shaking, horribly distorted; much of the action is in slow motion. CLYDE is on the ground, his body arching and rolling from the impact of the bullets. BONNIE is still in her seat: her body jerking and swaying as the bullets thud relentlessly into her and the framework of the car.

Exterior—The Car on the Verge

BONNIE's body slews out sideways, head first. A final burst and her head and shoulders drop down onto the running board. CLYDE's body rolls over on the ground dead, then lies still. The firing stops. Utter silence. It has been a massacre. BONNIE and CLYDE never had a chance to return the gunfire.

Bonnie and Clyde depicted violence in a way that had never been shown before in films. (Warner Bros.— Seven Arts)

The death of Bonnie and Clyde was perfectly choreographed by Arthur Penn. The carnage is haunting; this brief moment of ultra gore got mixed reactions from the critics and the public alike. Penn wanted to get the spasm of death on film, and he used four cameras, each one set at a different speed (24, 48, 72, and 96 frames per second). Different lenses were also used to get the shock value of a "ballet of death," in Penn's words. "There's a moment in death when the body no longer functions," he declared, "when it becomes an object and has a certain kind of detached, ugly beauty. It was that aspect I was trying to get."

Penn wanted two kinds of death: Clyde's had to be rather like a ballet, and Bonnie's had to have a physical shock about it. There is a sense of realism about that scene that is both captivating and repulsive, especially when a piece of Beatty's head comes off. In directing Dunaway for that crucial ending, Penn simply told her "to enact the death, to fall and follow the laws of gravity." The actress was sort of trapped behind the wheel of the car; one of her legs was tied to the gear shift so that she could feel free to fall but would not tumble out of the car. "We shot it three or four times," Penn said, "to get this feeling and changed speed and lenses constantly to get this sort of change of space and time."

Interestingly, Faye Dunaway's character in *Chinatown* (1974) met a similar fate at the end of that film when she gets shot through the head while attempting to drive away in her car. Dunaway and *Chinatown* writer Robert Towne did not want that violent and extremely graphic ending, but director Roman Polanski did, and it's interesting to notice how Dunaway's murder in *Chinatown* is similar in impact to her death in *Bonnie and Clyde*.

When thinking out the death scene in his mind's eye, Arthur Penn knew he could have done the killing in a gross and vulgar way, where you would see the bodies being torn apart. Instead, he decided to move away from what had really happened and to create an aura of unreality about the death of Bonnie and Clyde. What he achieved was a mythical, balletic ending. Still, the deaths are extremely bloody and graphic. "Very bloody and very painful," Penn told André Labarthe and Jean-Louis Comolli of the French publication *Les Cahiers du Cinéma*.

My own experience—it's not very broad—is that blood always surprises me, the amount of blood—too much. It recalls

"There's a moment in death when the body no longer functions, when it becomes a certain kind of detached, ugly beauty. It was that aspect I was trying to get."—director Arthur Penn (Warner Bros.—Seven Arts)

Shakespeare's line "Who would have thought the old man to have had so much blood in him?" In film, when you show death, it should have that shock effect. But at the end of *Bonnie and Clyde*, we didn't do the same kind of death; we were trying to change the character of death, to make their deaths more legendary than real.

The film's performances and production values were roundly praised by the critics. Its sympathetic portrayal of ruthless killers and its final bloodbath scene garnered mixed reactions. Henry Miller, the famous and controversial author, wrote a venemous article entitled "Make Love Not Gore":

> I had intended to sit down and let loose a stream of vitriol the morning after I saw *Bonnie and Clyde*, which is now three weeks ago, alas, and in the meantime I have cooled off somewhat. Nevertheless, I am still furious, more toward the public which acclaims the film and enjoys it than toward the producer and director, though I hold them fully responsible for this monstrous piece of entertainment.

Miller advocated something else to replace violence on the screen: ". . . what a relief it would be to see some real warmhearted fucking on the screen."

On the other hand, critic Pauline Kael was outraged by the attacks that were made against the violence depicted in the film: "But the whole point of *Bonnie and Clyde*," she wrote in her *New Yorker* review, "is to rub our noses in it [violence], to make us pay our dues for laughing. The dirty reality of death—not suggestions but blood and holes—is necessary." Kael also criticized people who claimed that the glamorous Faye Dunaway and Warren Beatty might induce people into imitating their acts: "Would having criminals played by dwarfs or fatties discourage them?"

Newsweek critic Joseph Morgenstern wrote in his review of *Bonnie and Clyde* that the film was about the story of two robbers which turns into a "squalid shoot 'em for the moron trade" because it doesn't know what to make of its own violence. Two weeks later, he apologized and declared that his initial reaction to the film had been inaccurate and grossly unfair.

Morgenstern wrote:

I had become so surfeited and preoccupied by violence in daily life that my reaction was as excessive as the stimulus. There are indeed a few moments in which the gore goes too far, becomes stock shockery that invites standard revulsion. And yet, precisely because *Bonnie and Clyde* combines these gratuitous crudities with scene after scene of dazzling artistry, precisely because it has the power both to enthrall and appall, it is an ideal laboratory for the study of violence, a subject in which we are matriculating these days.

Time magazine took a similar turnabout on their evaluation of the film, "But producer Beatty and director Arthur Penn have elected to tell their tale of bullets and blood in a strange and purposeless mingling of fact and claptrap that teeters uneasily on the brink of burlesque." Yet, a few weeks later, *Time* reversed itself and called the film "not only the sleeper of the decade but also, to a growing consensus of audiences and critics, the best movie of the year." The magazine also had this to say about the controversial and ultraviolent climax of the film: "The bloody ending is as inevitable as the climax of a Greek tragedy; yet to most audiences it comes as a shock, and there is usually a hushed, shaken silence to the crowds that trail out of the theaters." It's important to mention also that *Time* made *Bonnie and Clyde* the first film ever featured on its cover.

In addition to the violence, audiences were also sensitive to the fact that, in the film at least, Bonnie and Clyde emerged as heroes. The film became so controversial that Arthur Penn felt he had to speak up.

He told *Variety*:

Our purpose was first to engage the audience with the comedy, and then to snap them around quickly, with the effect of heightening and distilling the violence, of making it more acute. And though some people say we weren't successful, we seem to have got what we wanted. When I've seen the picture with an audience, they laughed when they were supposed to laugh. And when they weren't supposed to, they were completely silent.

Penn went on to explain that the Depression era was a time

of extremes, of the wildest comedies against a background of crisis. He cited *Nothing Sacred* (1937), a successful comedy about a cynical Vermont girl, played by Carole Lombard, who uses the false reports of her imminent death to become the toast of the town.

Warren Beatty, who not only starred in *Bonnie and Clyde* but also produced it, felt he had to come to the defense of his film as well. Beatty was especially disappointed by the *New York Times* review by Bosley Crowther, which accused *Bonnie and Clyde* of being a glorification of violence. The truth is that possibly not since Alfred Hitchcock's *Psycho* (1960) had a movie been so controversial and generated so many debates about violence and the power a film can have over its audience. "Maybe Crowther thought when the audience cheered, it was cheering for violence," Beatty declared. "See, there are several scenes in which we carefully develop one emotion in the audience, and then— zing!—we cut very fast to the opposite emotion. So you're sitting there laughing and suddenly you look at the screen and what you're laughing at isn't very funny at all."

Arthur Penn expressed the fact that violence is part of the American character. Historically, it began with the western, the frontier. "America is a country of people who act out their views in violent ways," he argued at the time the film was released, "Let's face it: Kennedy was shot. We're in Vietnam shooting people and getting shot. We have not been out of a war for any period of time in my lifetime. Gangsters were flourishing during my youth. I was in the war at age eighteen. Then came Korea; now comes Vietnam. We have a violent society. It's not Greece, it's not Athens, it's not the Renaissance. It is the American society, and I would have to personify it by saying that it is a violent one. So why not make films about it." Penn also declared: "I don't like to fight, but I'm intrigued by watching people fight and seeing it happen."

Obviously, most critics and the public, even if they did not necessarily want to admit it, felt the same morbid fascination driving them to see *Bonnie and Clyde*. While the controversy lived on about whether or not it glamorized violence, there was no argument about its brilliance and about the great performances in the film. With *Bonnie and Clyde*, Faye Dunaway, Warren Beatty, Gene Hackman, and even Gene Wilder, in a small but memorable role in the film, were suddenly thrust in the limelight. As a result of all this attention, the movie received

11

ten Academy Award nominations. "Some critics have called *Bonnie and Clyde* a glorification of violence," Warren Beatty said. "We wouldn't have gotten ten nominations if the people in our business felt that way. My director, Arthur Penn, and I felt each scene of violence made a moral point."

The impact of the film on the audience almost turned into a rage when a "Bonnie and Clyde Happening" was set at the Century City Shopping Center on Saturday, March 16, 1968, complete with a "fabulous" Bonnie and Clyde fashion show moderated by the film's costume designer and Academy Award nominee Theadora Van Runkle; a Bonnie and Clyde auto show; a Bonnie and Clyde dance contest judged by Gene Hackman; a Bonnie look-alike contest; and flagpole sitters! An ad read: "See grudge match between two flagpole sitters—Bonnie and Clyde, at 2:15 P.M. up they go!" Winners were promised Bonnie beret prizes, free record albums of the film's soundtrack, tickets to the Academy Awards, etc. The fifty stores were riddled with fake bullet holes, and the Bonnie and Clyde collection of tommy guns used in the film was put on display!

People went nuts over these two infamous criminals. One has to wonder if Oliver Stone's mid-nineties vision of the media and Mickey and Mallory, the (anti)heroes of *Natural Born Killers*, were not inspired by the Bonnie and Clyde fever of the late sixties. The film influenced fashion: Faye Dunaway put on her costumes again for a fashion spread in *Life* and appeared on the covers of *Newsweek* and *Look*, while Warren Beatty was on the cover of *Harper's Bazaar*. Michael J. Pollard was offered $1,000 by a leading San Francisco department store to appear at a fashion show for teenagers, and it was reported that the young actor had emerged as a sex symbol. TWA and Pontiac made commercials using Bonnie and Clyde, and the fever even spread to Europe, especially to France, where sex symbol Brigitte Bardot devoted a large part of her annual TV show to the film, wearing the Bonnie fashion and immediately causing a style revolution in Paris. *Bonnie and Clyde* also became a record rage, from the soundtrack of the film and recordings about the bandits by Brigitte Bardot and Mel Torme to an interview-album entitled *To Tell the Truth*, recorded by Bonnie Parker's sister, who disapproved of the film. "The Ballad of Bonnie and Clyde" became a top-forty hit, and the jangling bluegrass sounds of Flatt and Scruggs used in the film's score became a popular musical metaphor for chase scenes. In several European countries, some of the songs featuring excessive violence in sounds were even censored by radio stations.

Bonnie and Clyde captivated the public and even received recognition from the National Catholic Office for Motion Pictures, which named it Best Film of the Year for Mature Audiences. The group hailed Penn's movie as "a genuine folk epic challenging the individual viewer to recognize within himself the seeds of meaningless violence which are just below the surface of easy conscience." The worldwide success and acceptance of the film, after all, showed that its scenes of ultraviolence were intelligently used and made, in fact, an important moral statement.

Bonnie and Clyde allowed directors to show us more, to depict violence as it should be depicted, although, as we will see, some films have indeed pushed it beyond the boundaries of good taste. When *Time* wrote, "In the wake of *Bonnie and Clyde*, there is an almost euphoric sense in Hollywood that more such movies can and will be made," nobody knew just how far violence in film would go.

The Wild Bunch

"Listen, killing is no fun," director Sam Peckinpah declared. "I was trying to show what the hell it's like to get shot." The film Peckinpah is referring to here is his controversial and megaviolent Western *The Wild Bunch* (1969). It was shocking because it was so innovative in technique, especially in the way Peckinpah choreographed the action sequences; shots were repeated, and scenes were filmed at different speeds. But most of all, just as in *Bonnie and Clyde*, what was shocking about *The Wild Bunch* was that the bad guys were the heroes. Even children were shown doing sadistic things and enjoying it. While Peckinpah admitted he disliked violence and wanted to show his distaste for it on-screen, he also wanted to top *Bonnie and Clyde* and with *The Wild Bunch*, he succeeded.

The Wild Bunch opens as five ruffians dressed as U.S. cavalrymen enter a small Texas border town, circa 1913. Pike Bishop (William Holden) is the leader, followed by Dutch Engstrom (Ernest Borgnine), the Gorch brothers, Lyle (Warren Oates) and Tector (Ben Johnson), Crazy Lee (Bo Hopkins), and Angel (Jaime Sanchez.) As the group enters the railroad building, a ring of gunmen perched on the rooftops prepares to shoot. These men are working for railroad executive Pat Harrigan (Albert Dekker) and his lieutenant, Deke Thornton (Robert Ryan), who is under the constant threat from Harrigan that he'll be returned to jail if he doesn't follow orders. Pike and his wild bunch realize that they're surrounded, and the carnage begins. The hired guns ignore Harrigan and Thornton's order to stop shooting, and as the slaughter escalates, Pike and most of his men ride out of town with the railroad company's money bags.

What's left of the bunch—two have died—gathers at a small ranchero run by an old gunslinger named Sykes (Edmond O'Brien), only to realize that the bags they stole were filled with worthless washers. With the bounty hunters at their heels, the bunch hooks up with Mapache (Emilio Fernandez), a bandit who has stolen Angel's girlfriend. When Angel shoots the young woman, Mapache thinks he tried to assassinate him. Pike fortunately intervenes and saves the young man's life. The furor settles, and Mapache offers Pike a job; he wants the bunch to hijack a munitions train for gold. Pike accepts; not only does he succeed, but he also manages to elude Thornton and Deke's bounty hunters each time they close in on him. It turns out there's more to this hunt; it's also a personal vendetta. Pike and Deke were once friends, and during an ambush, Deke got caught, but Pike managed to escape.

Pike soon discovers that Mapache wants the amunitions without compensation, and he threatens to blow up the convoy; Mapache is amused by Pike's temerity and agrees to pay. The bandit-general invites the bunch for a celebration during which Pike wants to make a move to free Angel, now Mapache's prisoner. Pike is tricked into thinking Mapache will free Angel; the general slashes his throat, and a bloodbath ensues. Everyone is slaughtered. Thornton rides in with his bounty hunters and collects the bodies of the men the railroad wants. The bounty hunters ride off to claim their reward and Thornton stays behind. Sykes shows up with a group of Mexicans; sacks of gold, which had been exchanged for arms, are tied to their saddle. All along, Sykes and Thornton had been silent partners.

When Sam Peckinpah was rehearsing *The Wild Bunch*, the special-effects crew staged a demonstration of the kinds of

explosions and gunfire effects they had in mind. Peckinpah was furious with the results: "That's not what I want! That's not what I want!" He took a real gun loaded with real bullets and fired several times into the air. "*That's* the effect I want!" Peckinpah had made his point; from that day on, the special-effects crew decided to use bigger squibs (electronically wired charges which suggest bullets and bullet holes) that would blow pieces of raw meat off the actors for stronger effects.

Working with Peckinpah on *The Wild Bunch*—or on any of his other films—was a lot like working for Pike Bishop. Peckinpah fired people left and right. When he heard that Warners thought that the dailies looked great, he took even longer to set up his shots. The cast and crew were perfectly chosen to produce one of the most violent and controversial films ever made. Emilio Fernandez, Mapache in the movie, was a former Mexican director, known as El Indio, who had not made a film since he

Sam Peckinpah's *The Wild Bunch.* (*left to right*) Ben Johnson, Warren Oates, William Holden, and Ernest Borgnine. (Warner Bros.)

15

had shot his producer. He was also famous for once having fired at a newspaperman. He was acquitted, however, and only had to pay to dry-clean the powder burns on the reporter's coat! He lived in a castle in Mexico with a harem of fifteen women.

The characters portrayed in Peckinpah's film were ruthless, violence-hungry men, and it seems that the violence during production inspired morbid behavior from the crew members as well. "There was a graveyard near where we were shooting that had been looted," reported stuntman Joe Canutt. "Our only entertainment was going into the graveyard and standing the corpses on end and having our pictures taken with them. One of the guys would put a stiff up against the wall and we'd take the picture."

But by far the most sensational story came from actor William Holden, who told the *Hollywood Citizens News* from Parras, in the heart of Mexico, where he was on location, the wild and weird tale of the ghost of a headless horseman who was haunting the site. It seemed that three hundred Mexican extras were asking Warners for an additional "stunt pay" just for sleeping in an ancient, deserted bodega-winery being used for the setting of some of the dramatic action. "Stunt pay" is the extra fee that stunt actors get from daredevil tricks because the work might involve great risks and hazards. In any case, the extras claimed they saw the ghost of the Marquis de Aguayo, who had been dead for over 220 years! According to the legend, the marquis returned to the winery, suspecting that his wife was cheating on him. He shot her on the spot, in a room which was used as the wardrobe department by the production.

After butchering his wife, the marquis went berserk and killed the rest of his family as well as all the laborers who worked for him; his horse ran amok and severed the madman's head from his body against a tree. The ghost of the marquis returns at night, still searching for his head. Thus, the Mexican extras wanted "stunt pay" for their trouble. A strange parallel can be made between the legend and an actual subplot in *The Wild Bunch*. In the story, William Holden, as Pike, is seeing a married woman. They're caught by her husband, who shoots her and wounds Pike.

Some of the film's extras were members of the Mexican army; the prop department soon found out that the bandoliers the soldiers were wearing contained *real* bullets. "I had this image," said editor Louis Lombardo, "that, in the heat of the moment, if one of them put a real bullet in, I'd have a hole in my head." Whether or not all these elements contributed to the violence that we saw on the screen is anyone's guess. One thing is for sure: No one on the set of *The Wild Bunch* lacked "motivation" for his character.

One of the most imaginative touches in *The Wild Bunch* was that of James Dannaldson, who imported 12,000 red harvester ants into Mexico as well as a dozen scorpions for the opening sequence. As the bunch rides into town, kids are feeding scorpions to a nest of ants, which foreshadows the extreme cruelty that is yet to come. The opening scenes of carnage were extremely dangerous for the actors and stunt players because of the precision that Peckinpah demanded. At one point, William Holden jumps out of the express office, climbs onto his horse, and tramples over a woman as her shawl catches in his stirrup. Peckinpah wanted a shot taken directly overhead showing the horse and Holden's stunt double with the woman beneath the hooves to accentuate the fact that it was not only men who were being killed. Stuntman Whitey Hughes dressed as a woman for the long shot, but for a closer one, the director used the Mexican stuntwoman Yolanda Ponce. The stuntman riding the horse didn't see that he already had passed over her and backed up. His horse put a hoof in the middle of her back, cracking her tailbone. Fortunately, she recovered from the injury. Peckinpah made a point of using her in many of his later films.

Actor Bo Hopkins, who played Crazy Lee, was also hurt when a charge embedded in a bench went off and he caught a sliver in his eye. There's a scene during which a whole bridge collapses, with the bounty hunters on horseback falling into the water. Initially, Peckinpah wanted to use a lot more explosives, but his stunt director, Joe Canutt, confronted him and explained just how dangerous that could be. Eventually, Canutt reorchestrated the scene for maximum safety.

The final bloodbath sequence set new standards in film violence. According to special-effects specialist and property master Phil Ankrum, more (blank) ammunition was used for the battle sequence—some ninety thousand rounds—than was used during the entire Mexican revolution of 1913! One of the reasons for this excessive use of firearms and bullets was the presence of "Brownie," a 1909 machine gun rented from a Hollywood prop house for the film's production. For that final sequence, effects men also used over three thousand squibs.

"The Battle of the Bloody Porch" set new standards in screen violence. (Warner Bros.)

The final shoot-out was known among the crew and cast members as the Battle of the Bloody Porch because it required that they "kill" so many people. The shooting of this sequence took *only* eleven days. At first, Peckinpah had no clue as to how he was going to film the climactic ending, so he decided to cover each shot from all possible angles. He would first film the action in the foreground, then move to the middle ground, and end in the background. The editing of that scene was crucial, and Peckinpah, by using slow motion and repeating certain shots, broke new ground in the depiction of screen violence. There are approximately thirty-seven hundred editing cuts in *The Wild Bunch*, more than in any other film shot in Technicolor.

During the shooting of the Battle of the Bloody Porch, uniforms had to be cleaned, and squibs had to be recharged; the tiny explosives were, in fact, condoms filled with stage blood, which were hidden underneath costumes and sent geysers of gore flying from the bullet wounds. The raw meat laid over the condom gave the impression that tissue was being torn by bullets. After an extra was shot, the wardrobe department would take his squibbed costume and give him a new one for the next

18

take. But the extras began dying too fast. "So we set up these giant heaters—big lights—and mixed this fantastic colored paint," recalled wardrobe head Gordon Dawson. "Now, when a guy'd be shot and come to us, we had a regular assembly line going!" Actors and extras would first get hit with a bucket of water—to wash away the gore. Then they'd basically get recharged with new squibs after green tape had been applied to conceal the bullet holes. While the guys were drying off under the big lights, someone would "age" the costumes with paint to make them look worn out. "Towards the end," Dawson remembered, "we were reloading guys in five minutes, which was a hell of a lot faster than the way we started. I had started *The Wild Bunch* thinking I was pretty well prepared to do it, but Sam [Peckinpah] really threw one at us with that scene."

James Dannaldson (who had provided the production with ants and scorpions) captured over fifty vultures and made weighed boots for the predators to make sure that they stared down at William Holden and Ernest Borgnine after the two

actors were brutally shot to death. This final sequence was just as powerful and as brutal as it was envisioned in the script, by Walon Green and Sam Peckinpah, based on a story by Green and Roy N. Sickner. When the smoke clears, it seems we can almost smell the blood. The script described in minute detail the aftermath of the bloodbath, which Peckinpah wanted to be as realistic as the battle itself. The script called for the sound of millions of flies to accompany the scenes of vultures flying over the corpses. Unfortunately, that particular sound effect never made it into the film, and as a result, Peckinpah always felt that something crucial was missing from the sequence.

The first sneak preview of *The Wild Bunch* took place in Kansas City, Missouri, on May 1, 1969. About four hundred teachers were in town attending a convention, and that day, they elected to see the film. "The worst potpourri of vulgarity, violence, sex and bloodshed I've ever seen put together," said one viewer's card. "The whole thing is sick!" said another. One member of the test audience wrote: "Would suggest you rename it *Bath of Blood*. Of course, this would then indicate to future moviegoers that the pic is a horror picture." Still another said: "It is sickening to see so much violence, unnecessary bloodshed, and to see innocent children and women killed for no reason." The test audience even hissed at the screen. The only comment Peckinpah could make after the screening was that he wanted to redub all the sound effects, especially the gunfire, to make them more potent.

A second test screening took place in Long Beach, California. Again, all the odds were against Peckinpah; *The Wild Bunch* was being shown back-to-back with *The Killing of Sister George*, which had been rated X, meaning that no one under seventeen was admitted. Peckinpah was so furious that he got into a fistfight with Max Bercutt, Warners' publicity chief.

Before the new rating system was put in place in 1968, scripts had to be submitted to the Production Code office before filming began, in order to get an early evaluation of potential problems. The ratings board had concerns about the violence in *The Wild Bunch* even before the cameras started rolling. Geoffrey Shurlock, vice president and director of the Production Code Administration at the time, wrote to Ken Hyman of Warners: that basically the film, in its present form, was so bloody and filled with so many crudities of language that it couldn't be approved under the Production Code.

When the film finally was shown to the board, the censors still maintained their resistance to giving it anything but an X. Peckinpah trimmed down the blood-splattered close-up of Angel's throat being slit and took out a scene during which actor Ben Johnson bares a woman's breast for costar Warren Oates and compares the size of her nipple to that of his thumb. It took seven visits to the Motion Picture Association of America (MPAA) to finally get an R rating. "I actually cut out more than Warners requested," Peckinpah declared. "I cut parts of the violence after we got our [R] rating because I thought they were excessive to the points I wanted to make. I not only want to talk about violence in the film, but I have a story to tell, too, and I don't want the violence, per se, to dominate what is happening to the people."

The film was censored in Canada. Alberta totally rejected it, citing the film's "repugnant barbarity, extreme brutality, wallowing in gore" and went on to say it makes "*A Fistful of Dollars* look like *Mary Poppins*." In Toronto, the film could be shown but four and a half minutes had to be taken out. Sam Peckinpah and Phil Feldman, his producer, went on television claiming that censorship "was a venereal disease: it creeps on you and then spreads fast." Finally, Peckinpah and Feldman recut the film and only took out 24 feet, whereas the Canadians had initially removed 404 feet!

Unfortunately, *The Wild Bunch* was not a box-office success, so Warners decided to edit down the film. The studio eventually cut about seven minutes of the film, bringing the running time from about 152 to 145 minutes. The cuts were made by producer Phil Feldman under Warners' supervision without Peckinpah's input. *New York Times* critic Vincent Canby made a good point when he wrote that "the 'lifts' definitely reduce the humanity that runs through the movie in ironic counterpoint to the vividly overstated violence."

Critical notices were generally mixed to positive. Journalist Jonas Mekas, however, wrote a particularly nasty article entitled "Why Do People Like Morbid Movies?" in the *New York Times*: "The other evening I went to see *The Wild Bunch*. On the screen, the blood was splashing, like never before. This side of the screen, there was the most boorish audience I had ever seen. A married couple with whom I went to see the movie had to change their seats three times. Such were the manners and behavior of their neighbors. The movie ended, we left the theatre, and for hours, I couldn't get rid of the images of the gratuitous violence on the screen, and the atmosphere of the theatre. I felt low. I had gone to the theatre in a good mood. I left it tired, depressed, low and drained."

The Catholic Film Office (CFO) gave *The Wild Bunch* an A-4 rating (morally unobjectionable for adults with reservations). The CFO claimed it would be easy to dismiss such a film "as simply another celluloid bloodbath." But as with *Bonnie and Clyde*, they felt that westerns that showed people getting shot as a bloodless, almost painless action was in part responsible for violence in society—not the other way around! *The Wild Bunch* aimed to demythologize the Old West and to depict it as it really was. "But because Peckinpah may appear to have made his statement about America's violent past with a butcher knife rather than a scalpel," they stated, "the film can only be recommended to a select audience. It could help thoughtful viewers to understand who we are and where we have come from in a way that, considering the history of the western genre, is singularly healthy."

The Wild Bunch became well known, as Charles Champlin (*Los Angeles Times*) put it, as "not so much a movie as a bloodbath." He wrote, "Peckinpah's argument, if I understand him, is that violence is a primal instinct in each of us—man and boy, mother and child. And he suggests, in his gory dramatic terms, that we have not merely a capacity for violence but a joy in violence, a blood lust." In fact, Peckinpah saw violence in himself and in others and had found through his films a way to channel it to positive effect; not everyone agreed with him. In the film, death is ugly, bodies explode, flesh is torn, blood pours. "The squeamish, the weakhearted, or the simply tenderhearted are quite seriously warned away," Champlin suggested.

The most heated debate over the violence in *The Wild Bunch* took place during a near-raucous press conference. After a particular screening, the press became violent about the film's violence. During the conference, the movie's creators met with the critics to discuss and justify their intentions, since at that particular time in Hollywood history, *The Wild Bunch* had gained the reputation as the most violent American movie ever made. Producer Phil Feldman defended the film: "We tend to look away from our violence, as we look away from hunger in America. But these things must be looked at squarely." "But do the ends justify the means?" someone asked. "Truth is not beautiful," Feldman replied. "The entertainment industry has a right and duty to depict reality as it is. If audiences react against the reality that is shown, it may prove therapeutic." Peckinpah, who showed up when the press conference had already started, made a very short statement and declared he didn't even want to be there. "I think we deserve an answer to the simple question as to whether Mr. Peckinpah enjoys violence," one voice asked. Peckinpah, reluctantly, answered: "All right—my idea was that it would have a cathartic effect. No, I don't like violence. In fact, when I look at the film myself, I find it unbearable. I don't think I'll be able to see it again for five years. . . . I tried to emphasize the sense of horror and agony that violence provides. Violence is no game."

Critics were also upset at the fact that Peckinpah juxtaposed children with people being killed. Yet Peckinpah never shows a child being gunned down. "I'm constitutionally unable to show a child in jeopardy," the director said blankly. Another issue came up: If Peckinpah wanted to make a statement about violence, why not make a film about Vietnam? Peckinpah said he felt that the western was a universal frame within which it was possible to comment on contemporary issues. Richard Lederer, Warners' vice president of advertising and publicity, told the angry critics that the campaign that had been designed for the film did not mislead people; *The Wild Bunch* was a violent movie, and the studio wanted everyone to know that up front. "We don't want the wrong people seeing this film."

Also present at the press junket were William Holden and Ernest Borgnine. Both were shocked by the reactions to the film's violence. "I just can't get over the reaction here," Holden said. "Are people surprised that violence really exists in the world? Just turn on your TV set any night. The viewer sees the Vietnam war, cities burning, campus riots; he sees plenty of violence. Against this background, the pendulum in motion pictures has swung in one direction. Let us hope that it swings back on matters of sexual morality and violence." And Ernest Borgnine: "I must say that when I received the script I didn't read into it all of these controversial things. We who made the film knew it was violent and even felt repulsed at times, but we felt that we were achieving something. So many significant things are now being read into it that perhaps there is a moral suggestion here."

Twenty-four years after *The Wild Bunch* first came out, several film historians and director Martin Scorsese began lobbying for a new release of the film on 70 mm. In February 1993,

Warners announced its plans to release the uncut version of the film. That one had actually been released widely in Europe and had also been available on videotape since 1986. Warners' new generation of "suits" resubmitted the film to the ratings board, and to everyone's surprise, the version that had received an R rating in 1969 was slapped an NC-17 for graphic violence. Suddenly, rereleasing the film with an NC-17 didn't make any sense, since most exhibitors wouldn't want to show it.

"Along with *Bonnie and Clyde*," wrote critic Peter Rainer, "*The Wild Bunch* is the great, essential American film from the sixties because it confronted point-blank the audience's fear and fascination about violence, and it did so in the ways of an artist. People who condemn the film for being upsetting are superbly beside the point." Maybe what the MPAA was doing was trying to legitimize the NC-17 rating (which is viewed as an X rating and which, in people's minds, used to signify pornography) by giving it to a classic film like *The Wild Bunch*; or, more simply, Peckinpah's film was paying the price for having set new standards in screen violence. "In the last decade," explained MPAA's president Jack Valenti, "there has been a public outrage . . . and the judgment of the ratings board, which is comprised of parents, is that the degree, the intensity, and the persistence of violence is beyond the ken of young children." Curiously, this was the same man who, in 1969, had defended Peckinpah's cut.

On the eve of a screening that was to be followed by a debate against the NC-17 rating of *The Wild Bunch*, the MPAA told Warners that they were giving the film an R. Despite all the controversy, *The Wild Bunch* was rereleased in March 1995, ready, perhaps, to influence a new generation of directors. When it originally came out, its ultraviolence influenced such directors as Martin Scorsese, Oliver Stone, Francis Ford Coppola, Walter Hill, and Quentin Tarantino. So, in a way, Sam Peckinpah gets the credit, or the blame, for more than three decades of ultraviolent movies.

A Clockwork Orange

"There was me, that is Alex, and my three droogs, that is Pete, Georgie, and Dim; and we sat in the Korova Milkbar trying to make up our rassoodocks what to do that evening. The Korova Milkbar sold milk-plus, which is what we were drinking. This would sharpen you up and make you ready for a bit of the old ultraviolence."

—ALEX IN *A CLOCKWORK ORANGE*

Thus begins Stanley Kubrick's *Clockwork Orange* (1971). Set in England in the future, the film is about a young delinquent, Alex DeLarge (Malcom McDowell), whose "principal interests are rape, ultraviolence, and Beethoven"—or Ludwig van, as Alex likes to refer to him. We follow Alex and his three droogs through a night of crime, which includes an assault on a bum, a fight with a rival gang, and the savage rape of a woman in front of her husband, a writer and politician named M. Alexander (Patrick Magee), whom Alex brutalizes while chanting "Singin' in the Rain."

Alex still lives with his folks, and the following morning, he is visited by P. R. Deltoid (Aubrey Morris), a social worker who keeps a close eye on him and who warns him that his escapades are going to get him into a lot of trouble. Later, Alex has a quick orgy, some good old "in-out, in-out," as he calls it, with two girls he has picked up at a record store. That day, Alex's droogs rebel against him; they're not sure they want him as their leader anymore. However, he beats them up as a fast way to end the argument. In the evening, Alex breaks into the house of a woman (Miriam Karlin) who raises cats and collects phallic-shaped sculptures. He attacks her and smashes her face with one of her artworks. On his way out, his droogs smash a bottle of milk in his face and run away, leaving Alex to deal with the cops. The cat lady dies, and Alex is sent to prison for murder. There he volunteers to become a guinea pig for the Ludivico Technique, a behavioristic barrage of electrical impulses and snuff films that cripples him with nausea at the thought of sex, violence, or the

25

sound of Beethoven's Ninth Symphony that accompanies the treatment. Alex ultimately is sent back into the real world, transformed into a "clockwork orange" (an expression derived from old Cockney slang: "Queer as a clockwork orange") with no free will of his own and described now "as decent a lad as you would meet on a May morning" by the minister of the interior (Anthony Sharp) who, to win an upcoming election, becomes an advocate of the Ludovico Technique.

Rejected by his family, Alex wanders the streets and is attacked by the same bum he once savaged. He is rescued by two of his former droogs, who've since become cops. They decide to teach him a lesson and torture him. Beaten and battered, Alex reaches the house of M. Alexander, left a crippled widower since the night he and his wife were attacked. Alexander realizes who his unexpected guest is and decides to use him to overthrow the government by making him a victim of the Ludovico Technique. When his host blasts Beethoven from his stereo, Alex tries to commit suicide. His "victim status" brings him full circle, and he is recovered from the Ludovico Technique and returned to a life of ultraviolence with the blessing of the minister of the interior himself!

A Clockwork Orange was based on a 1962 novel by Anthony Burgess. Actually, to be more exact, the film is based on the American edition of the book; while it did not include the last chapter of the British edition, which showed our young protagonist bored with senseless violence and deciding to procreate rather than destroy, it did include a glossary of "Nadsat," the language used both in the book and the film, a combination of Russian and London teenage slang, poorly translated into contemporary patois. Screenwriter Terry Southern, who had collaborated in 1964 with Kubrick on *Dr. Strangelove*, had written an adaptation of the Burgess book. At the time, actor David Hemmings was coming out of Antonioni's *Blowup* (1966), and was quite hot. In fact, to the protest and outrage of singers such as the Beatles and Marianne Faithful, who felt the role should go to Mick Jagger, a talent agency wanted to package the film with Hemmings attached to play Alex.

Southern showed his script to Kubrick, who rejected it. A short while later, the British Board of Film Censors refused to clear the script, objecting to its violence and bad language. Southern dropped the option and discovered that Kubrick was interested. Although having no intention of harming Kubrick,

Southern told his agent, who couldn't resist the temptation to blab. When the owners of the rights to the book found out about Kubrick's serious interest, the price suddenly rose from $500 for a six-month option against purchase price of $5,000 to $5,000 against $150,000. This, of course, ruptured the relationship between Kubrick and Southern.

"The book isn't really about violence," Burgess declared. "It's about the curing of violence. That's what the title suggests: a mechanical, inflexible system imposed on a juicy, organic whole. It's about the danger of the state taking over and using regressive Pavlovian techniques in order to burn violence out." Readers of the book and film audiences alike did not quite catch that the story was about free will and about the necessity to be free even if freedom means breaking the moral law. Stanley Kubrick, who wrote the script, followed closely the

structure of the novel, although, again, he decided to ignore the final chapter, which he read when he was already far advanced in the production of his film. He admitted being shocked at Burgess's tacked-on "happy ending," which he felt did not even have the same satiric tone as the rest of the novel and which he suspected had been written under pressure from the publisher. Some of the changes, especially in regard to the ultraviolent elements of the story, between the first draft of the screenplay, dated May 15, 1970, and the film itself are rather insightful:

The beginning of the *Clockwork Orange* script, showing Alex and his droogs on a rampage, was originally longer. As in

Within weeks of the release of *A Clockwork Orange*, press accounts appeared of youth gangs on the prowl dressed like Alex and his droogs. (Warner Bros. Ltd.)

the film, we meet them in the bar, but initially Kubrick had planned on having it designed like an arena, with couples having sex. At first, Alex and his droogs attack an old schoolmaster, then rip his old books apart and pull out his false teeth. Alex stomps on the teeth, but they prove to be indestructible. In the

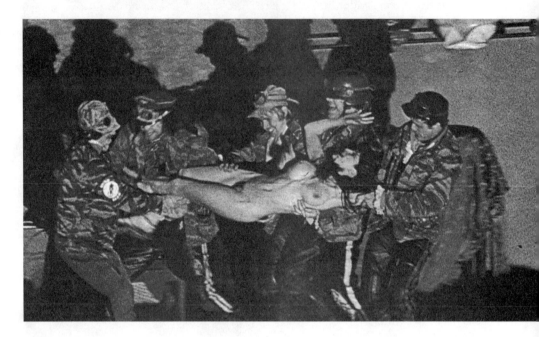

Billyboy and his four droogs get ready to perform a little of the old "in-out, in-out" on a weepy young "devotchka." (Warner Bros. Ltd.)

third act of the story, when Alex comes out of jail, he goes to a public library, looks at violent picture books, and gets sick; the old professor—not a bum as in the movie—tries to help him but then recognizes Alex and, with his colleagues, turns on his one-time attacker. As in the film, Alex is saved by his former droogs, who have become cops.

Kubrick also has a scene in the first draft showing Alex and his gang going to a club and trying to rip off some old ladies, but they are interrupted by policemen. The attack on M. Alexander is slightly different; first, the droogs wear masks of Elvis, Gandhi, and Lenin, and Alex has one of Churchill. As in the novel, Alexander is writing a book entitled *A Clockwork Orange*, and Alex reads excerpts from it while beating him up. During rehearsals, Malcom McDowell improvised the scene and began crooning "Singin' in the Rain." Kubrick loved the idea and finally used it not only in that scene but also as the way Alex betrays himself with Alexander toward the end of the film. In the original script, just as in the novel, after Alex is rescued by Alexander, he says, ". . . but I'm not ordinary, nor am I *dim*." Suddenly, Alexander remembers Dim being the name of one of the droogs and recognizes Alex as his attacker.

In the initial script, Alex does not have sex with the two girls he picks up at the record store; he takes them first to a pasta parlor and then watches them jump up and down on his bed while listening to music.

The visit at the cat lady's house was also different. In the script, she has a walking stick and tries to defend herself with it. There were no phallic sculptures in the script, and so Alex cracks her down with a silver bust of Beethoven. In the film, it's the cat lady herself who tries to defend herself with the Beethoven bust. Outside, his droogs attack Alex with a chain, not a milk bottle, as in the movie.

During his shock treatment, Alex is also shown films of Japanese soldiers cruelly laughing as they torture captured marines. This particular clip did not make it into Kubrick's movie. Finally, whereas in the film Alex is put onstage in front of an audience to show the effect the treatment has had on him, in the first draft of the script he is put to test in another room before a hidden camera. People watch his reactions on a big screen next door.

"I'd say my intentions with *A Clockwork Orange*," Stanley Kubrick said, "were to be faithful to the novel and to try and see the violence from Alex's point of view, to show that it was great fun for him, the happiest part of his life, and that it was like some great action ballet. It was necessary to find a way of stylizing the violence just as Burgess does by his writing style. The ironic counterpoint of the music [Kubrick only used published music] was certainly one of the ways of achieving this. All the scenes of violence are very different without the music." Indeed, with *A Clockwork Orange*, Kubrick made an effort to break from conventional ways of filming; there were slow-motion shots (when Alex attacks his droogs to show them who's the boss), fast motion (when Alex has sex with the two girls), and handheld camera shots (when Alex attacks the cat lady). For the point-of-view shot of Alex falling through the window, Kubrick put a camera in an insulated box, which he then tossed out the window; six takes were required to get the lens to land first and to achieve the desired effect. Kubrick's innovative style was almost as shocking as the subject matter of the movie itself.

Kubrick told British reporter Penelope Houston:

> The first section of the film that incorporates most of
> the violent action is principally organized around the
> Overture of Rossini's *Thieving Magpie*, and, in a very
> broad sense, you could say that the violence is turned
> into dance, although, of course, it is in no way any
> kind of formal dance. But in cinematic terms, I
> should say that movement and music must inevitably
> be related to dance, just as the rotating station and
> the docking Orion spaceship in [*2001: A Space
> Odyssey*–1968] moved to "The Blue Danube." From
> the rape on the stage of the derelict casino, to the
> superfrenzied fight, through the Christ figures cut, to
> Beethoven's Ninth, the slow-motion fight on the
> water's edge, and the encounter with the cat lady
> where the giant white phallus is pitted against the
> bust of Beethoven, movement, cutting, and music are
> the principal considerations—dance?

Like *Bonnie and Clyde* and *The Wild Bunch*, Kubrick's film
was told from the point of view of the antihero. To make matters
worse, Alex narrates the story directly to the audience, calling
for our sympathy toward his most brutal actions. In a sense,
and as Kubrick has said many times, Alex is like Richard III. He
is a character you like and fear at the same time; you're repulsed
and attracted to him. His candor, wit, strange intelligence, and
sense of logic, combined with the fact that all the other characters are lesser people and in many ways worse than he, make
him almost a hero. "Alex's adventures are a kind of psychological
myth," Kubrick said. "Our subconscious finds release in Alex,
just as it finds release in dreams. It resents Alex being stifled
and repressed by authority, however much our conscious mind
recognizes the necessity of doing this." He explained that Alex is
the symbol of the natural man in the state in which he is born,
unlimited and unrepressed. The Ludovico treatment symbolizes
the conflict between the structures imposed by our society and
our primal natures. "This is why we feel exhilarated when Alex is
'cured' in the final scene," Kubrick said. The director's philosophy assumes that man is born bad and society makes him
worse and that human nature is closer to an animal's instinct.

The Ludovico Technique is yet another fascinating aspect of
A Clockwork Orange. It uses film clips to permanently produce
in Alex disgust for ultraviolence and sex. He is forced to watch
newsreel footage of Nazis, snuff films of a woman being raped,
clips of a man being beaten up. "So far, the first film was a very
good professional piece of *sinny*, like it was done in Hollywood,"
Alex comments in a voice-over
narration. "The sounds
were real horrorshow. You
could slooshy the
screams and moans very
realistic, and you could
even get the heavy
breathing and panting of
the tolchocking malchicks
[boys] at the same time."
Later, Alex concludes: "It
was beautiful. It's funny
how the colors of the real
world only seem really
real when you viddy them
on the screen." Ironically,
what Kubrick is saying is
that the more we, the
audience, are exposed to
screen violence, the more

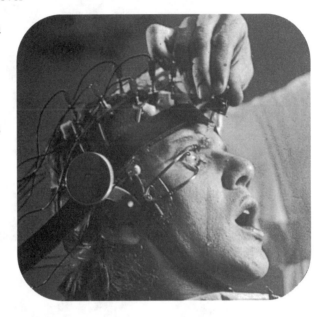

we'll be disgusted by it. Like Alex, we might enjoy it at first
because it only *seems* real; but the more we watch, the more it
begins to resemble reality. Curiously, the movie had the opposite
effect on many people who saw it.

Malcom
McDowell
gets the
Ludovico
treatment
and is forced
to watch
some real
"horror-
shows."
(Warner
Bros. Ltd.)

"A Clockwork Orange *is a brilliant nightmare.*"

—*VARIETY*

"*[It] is violent, crude, cold, profoundly gloomy, now and
again blackly funny and, as a piece of moviemaking,
alternately dazzling and curiously static and overlong.*"

—CHARLES CHAMPLIN, *LOS ANGELES TIMES*

"*Stanley Kubrick's ninth film,* A Clockwork Orange*,
which has just won the New York Film Critics Award as
the best film of 1971, is a brilliant and dangerous work,*

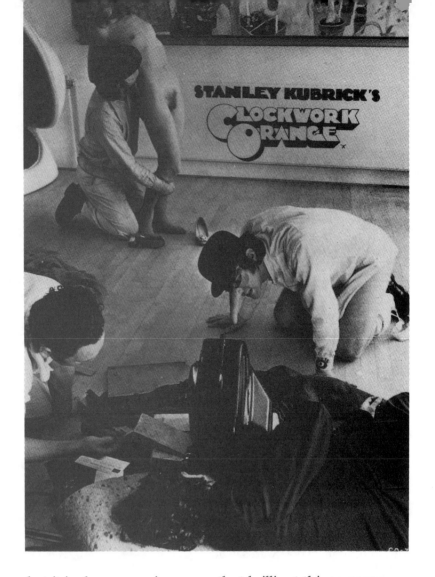

but it is dangerous in a way that brilliant things some-times are."

—Vincent Canby, *New York Times*

"Enough brutality of an instructive nature is contained in Orange *to provide a manual for the needs of every street gang and knuckle society in the U.S."*

—Clayton Riley, *New York Times*, in his article
". . . Or 'A Dangerous, Criminally Irresponsible Horror Show?'"

A Clockwork Orange was disorienting to critics; they didn't really know how to evaluate the film. It was obviously getting extreme reactions. Was the violence gratuitous? Should we view Alex as a hero? Was the message of the film dangerous? One of the most negative reviews came from Pauline Kael, who had defended *Bonnie and Clyde* and *The Wild Bunch*. "The numerous rapes and beatings have no ferocity and no sensuality," she wrote in the *New Yorker*. "They're frigidly, pedantically calculated, and because there is no motivating emotion, the viewer may experience them as an indignity and wish to leave." She goes on to criticize Kubrick for playing with violence in an intellectual way and also raises a broader argument over the cumulative effects of movie brutality on audiences. Without advocating censorship, Kael wrote: "At the movies, we are gradually being conditioned to accept violence. The directors used to say they were showing us its real face and how ugly it was in order to sensitize us to its horrors. You don't have to be very keen to see that they are now in fact desensitizing us. They are saying that everyone is brutal and the heroes must be as brutal as the villains or they turn into fools."

Actually, *Clockwork*'s violence was too close to us, exposing our fears in a way that had never been shown before. The story is set in the near future, and was therefore perceived as a warning to us to "Do something!" and that message only was a threat. The violence in the Penn and Peckinpah movies was set in the past and did not concern us directly, but with *A Clockwork Orange*, whether or not we liked it, Kubrick was disturbing us, making us responsible for something that had not happened yet.

And how was the audience reacting? The conflicting *New York Times* reviews of *A Clockwork Orange* (Vincent Canby liked it; Clayton Riley hated it) left readers equally divided.

Another reason the film was so controversial was that it had been given an X rating by the MPAA for its graphic violence as well as its explicit sexual depiction of Alex's fast-motion ménage à trois. In addition, a problematic shot took place during the aversion-therapy sequence in which footage of a gang rape is projected to Alex. Eventually, a few frames (a total of thirty seconds) were substituted by Kubrick several months after the release of the film. The director had initially refused to trim down those scenes to avoid the X, but finally changed his mind in view of broadening the booking of the film, even though he knew that under MPAA rules, in order to be rerated, a film had to be withdrawn from distribution for at least sixty days before the new R version could be released.

Clockwork was also hampered by advertising censorship. In Detroit, Cleveland, Cincinnati, San Diego, and other cities, certain newspapers were limiting ads to one-inchers, with a call-the-theater-for-film's-title teaser and no logo. Actresses Adrienne Corri (Mrs. Alexander) and Miriam Karlin (the cat lady), went on a press tour to protest the advertising ban. "The day they restrict ads for guns and for things that cause pollution I might see a possible reason for banning ads for pictures," declared Karlin. And about the ultraviolence in the film:

> They're all talking about this violence thing. I myself loathe violence. The film is antiviolence. You're not going to show Mary Poppins and say it's about antiviolence, are you? I think the film has been really badly sold on violence and sex. The kids come out saying, 'That's what we're revolting about, this plastic world.' Banning of the film is only another manifestation of this covering up cracks and not getting to the heart of the matter.

But Kubrick was not the only one being accused of concocting a piece of ultraviolent pornography. Author Anthony Burgess was living in America at the time the film was released and received daily phone calls from people who were reporting mayhem, violence, and rape and asking him if he felt responsible. Each time, he replied that no, he was not responsible for "mankind's inherent sinfulness." He said that all he had done in his book was reflect violence and maintained that art did not instigate violence. Meanwhile, the media was blaming Burgess and Kubrick for being the instigators of street violence. Burgess initially saw the film with Kubrick himself at a private screening. He was at first shocked and thought that some of the violence was a bit too overt, but it didn't really bother him. "When I went to see the film on its first public appearance in New York," Burgess recalled, "the people on the door wouldn't let me see it. They said I was too old. After having to persuade them that I wrote the damn thing, I found it really quite frightening, because the cinema was full of blacks standing up and shouting, 'Right on, man,' because they refused to see anything beyond a glorification of violence." In the book, Burgess had made an effort to temper what he called the pornographic impact by using a strange language. Of course, on the screen, the sex and the violence were clearly shown.

Reports came that in Indianapolis gangs of four, dressed in the manner of *A Clockwork Orange*, had raped nuns and pummeled senior citizens. In England, within weeks of the film's release, press accounts told of youth gangs, on the prowl, dressed like Alex and his droogs, wearing bowler hats, white overalls, and combat boots and sporting long false eyelashes on one eye. In one case, a young woman was raped by a teen gang who sang "Singin' in the Rain," just as Alex and his droogs did in the movie. In another case, a sixteen-year-old wearing a droog-like costume was convicted of a savage beating. Every outbreak of juvenile delinquency was dubbed as "a *Clockwork Orange*–style incident." Anthony Burgess said: "From the film of *A Clockwork Orange* youth did not learn aggression: It was aggressive already. What it did learn was a style of aggression, a mode of dressing violence up in a new way, a piquant sauce to season the raw meat of kicks, biffs, and razor slashings."

At that point, Kubrick began receiving death threats and decided to pull the film out of distribution in England. As late as 1993, *A Clockwork Orange* was still forbidden in England, and an exhibitor was sued for showing the film illegally.

When interviewed in 1993 about *A Clockwork Orange*, Burgess said that with the amount of ultraviolence he was seeing in films and especially on TV, he believed that art could be dangerous. ("There are no human beings in American detective series, merely cops and killers," he once wrote.) Kubrick, on the other hand, said: "Man isn't a noble savage. He is irrational, brutal, weak, unable to be objective about anything, where his own interests are involved . . . and any attempt to create social institutions to a false view of the nature of man is probably doomed to failure."

Taxi Driver

Listen, you screwheads, here is a man who wouldn't take it anymore, a man who stood up against the scum, the dogs, the filth; here is someone who stood up.

—TRAVIS BICKLE, *TAXI DRIVER*

In Martin Scorsese's *Taxi Driver* (1976), Travis Bickle (Robert De Niro) is a loner, an alienated, uncommunicative Vietnam veteran who has insomnia and decides to take a job as a taxi driver on the night shift. He takes his passengers anywhere; he doesn't care: "It don't make no difference to me." He occasionally joins other cabbies, including Wizard (Peter Boyle), and discusses his experiences. One day, he catches sight of Betsy (Cybill Shepherd), an attractive young campaign worker for presidential candidate George Palantine (Leonard Harris). He stares at Betsy from the street, but drives away when he spots Tom (Albert Brooks), her coworker. Later, he acquires a gun, rationalizing that it's for self-protection.

Travis begins pursuing Betsy and goes as far as volunteering his help for the campaign. He's turned down but gets a date with Betsy, who is cautious and intrigued by him. Travis takes her to a porn theater. Disgusted, Betsy storms out. His attempts to see her again are fruitless. The rejection contributes to his conviction that the world is ugly and corrupt; he buys more guns. He writes to his parents that he is on a secret mission for the government and is dating Betsy.

One night, Travis finds himself in the midst of a holdup. He pulls out a gun and shoots the perpetrator; the act earns him the nickname "killer" among his fellow cabbies. He then becomes involved with a fourteen-year-old hooker, Iris (Jodie Foster), and wants to save her from her pimp, Sport (Harvey Keitel), and from the old man (Murray Moston) who works with him. Travis shows up at a Palantine rally sporting a Mohawk haircut and with the intention of shooting the presidential candidate. He is spotted by Secret Service men but manages to escape. He finally snaps and goes on a wild shooting spree. He guns down Sport, the old man, and a cop who is with Iris. He tries to shoot himself, but he's run

36

out of bullets. Travis is hailed a hero in the press, and Iris is reunited with her parents. Back on the job one night, Travis finds Betsy jumping into his cab; she now shows him respect. Like the meter in his cab, Travis remains a time bomb, ticking away, ready to explode.

Film critic turned screenwriter Paul Schrader, who received a strict Calvinist education and did not see a movie until his late teens, was going through depression and living in his car early in his career. At the time, that career was going nowhere, although he had sold a number of scripts to major studios in the 1960s. At one point, Schrader realized that he had not talked to anyone in three weeks! He felt he was like a taxi driver, and that self-imposed loneliness gave Schrader the inspiration for *Taxi Driver*. This realization made him open the script with the following quote from "God's Lonely Man," a short story by Thomas Wolfe: "The whole conviction of my life now rests upon the belief that loneliness, far from being a rare and curious phenomenon, is the central and inevitable fact of human existence."

Schrader had only one disagreement with director Martin Scorsese on the film: He wanted the entire movie to be seen from Bickle's point of view. Scorsese wanted to gear away from Bickle twice; once to show Albert Brooks talking to the politician and a second time to show Sport and Iris together. Only the second found its way into the movie; Scorsese cheated, however, by using a shot of De Niro sitting in his cab outside Iris's building, as if he were watching them. So, in a way, we follow the whole story from Bickle's perspective, which makes it impossible for us not to identify with him.

Scorsese went as far as to say that Travis Bickle is like all of us, only he acts out his fantasies, which makes him crazy. He wants to change things; he is like a religious fanatic who wants to convert you even if it kills you. Bickle wants to turn the pure (symbolized by Betsy) toward corruption while he attempts—and succeeds in the end—to save the impure (Iris.) Bickle's nature is self-destructive, but at times he seems almost sympathetic. We feel sorry for him because, as Scorsese pointed out, there's a little bit of Bickle in every one of us. That Schrader came up with the story when he himself was going through depression makes the argument even more potent. Of course, Schrader and Scorsese took their character to an extreme; Bickle is someone who has no knowledge of others, not even celebrities. He lives in his own world and surrounds himself with the very things that repulse him; he acts on them with extreme violence.

A large part of the film's success is owed to Robert De Niro. He even became a cabbie in New York for a few days to prepare himself for the role. One night, a struggling actor jumped into the cab and immediately recognized De Niro, who had recently won an Oscar for *The Godfather, Part II* (1974). The actor's reaction was to sulk over the fact that even after winning an Academy Award, De Niro still had to drive a cab to make ends meet! De Niro borrowed a shirt, boots, and belt from Schrader for the film and asked the writer to read into a tape recorder Arthur Bremer's published diary. In 1972, Bremer shot and paralyzed Alabama's governor George Wallace. Stuntman Vic Magnota, who also portrayed a Secret Service photographer, had studied film with Scorsese and was a Vietnam vet. He showed Scorsese pictures of fellow soldiers in Saigon wearing Mohawk haircuts, when they were about to do something "special." One of the most memorable—and most brilliantly acted—sequences in the film takes place in Bickle's sordid apartment when Travis talks to himself in the mirror asking over and over; "Are you talking to me?" accenting different words each time. The script for that scene simply indicated: "He talks to himself." The monologue was completely improvised by De Niro. The "Are you talking to me" bit was in use at the time by a Greenwich Village comic as part of a skit. Funny it should end up in such a violent and gloomy film.

The city of New York also contributes a great deal to the film's atmosphere. Death and violence seem to be just around every corner. Schrader thoroughly researched his script. He even talked to real-life pimps to capture their dialogue and the nuances necessary to create Sport's character. Schrader wanted him to be black, but Scorsese was concerned it would be too racially inflammatory. It was bad enough that Bickle was extremely racist throughout the film, and so Harvey Keitel was cast to play Sport. Also for the sake of realism, Scorsese insisted on filming the assassination attempt of Palantine at Columbus Circle, where mobster Joe Columbo had been shot in 1971.

To convey Bickle's paranoia, Martin Scorsese said he wanted his camera to move very much as it does in horror films. Using influences from Jacques Tourneur (*Cat People*, 1942), Mario Bava (*Black Sunday*, 1961), Mark Robson (*Isle of the Dead*, 1945) and films of Michael Powell, Scorsese created a kind of Gothic tension that conveyed perfectly Bickle's growing anxiety. At times, we see Bickle mov-

ROBERT DE NIRO

TAXI DRIVER

A BILL/PHILLIPS PRODUCTION OF A MARTIN SCORSESE FILM

**JODIE FOSTER • ALBERT BROOKS • HARVEY KEITEL
LEONARD HARRIS • PETER BOYLE • CYBIL SHEPHERD**

DIRECTED BY MARTIN SCORSESE

ing in slow motion or literally floating toward someone. (At one point, after leaving Iris, Scorsese placed De Niro next to his camera on a dolly, and Bickle glides toward the old man.) Bickle moves slowly before he attacks; he is like an animal who operates on instinct. This "slowness" gives the later part of the movie an even greater shock value. The ultra-violence is, in the first part of the film, only in the dialogue and plays on a psychological level. Everyone talks about violence; a passenger in the cab, played by Scorsese himself, tells Bickle what he's going to do to his wife, who is cheating on him, using extremely violent terms. One morning, Bickle wipes blood from the backseat, leading us to believe that someone was killed or wounded in the cab earlier. We, the audience, never see any of this violence until De Niro shoots a burglar in a grocery store. The most gruesome part of that scene takes place after De Niro walks away, when the owner takes a crowbar and batters the corpse.

The killings of Sport, the old man, and the cop are extremely violent, brutal, and gory; they come in a payoff after two hours of mounting tension. From the script only, one could feel that the climax of the movie had to be horrifying:

> At the top of the stairs, TRAVIS spots THE OLD MAN sitting at the far end of the dark corridor. The OLD MAN starts to get up when TRAVIS discharges the

After watching *Taxi Driver*, John W. Hinkley Jr. became obsessed with Jodie Foster and later shot President Reagan in her name. (Columbia Pictures)

40

mighty .44 at him. Blaam! The hallway reverberates with shock waves and gunpowder.

THE OLD MAN staggers at the end of the corridor: His right hand has been blown off at the forearm.

And:

Just as TRAVIS draws back the knife, THE OLD MAN brings his huge left palm crashing down on TRAVIS: THE OLD MAN's palm is impaled on the knife.

Until finally:

TRAVIS fires the revolver, blowing the back of THE OLD MAN's head off and silencing his protests.

The stabbings, shootings, and mutilation effects were achieved by makeup wizard Dick Smith (*The Godfather*, 1972; *The Exorcist*, 1973; *Amadeus*, 1984, etc.). For the hand being blown off, Smith made the remaining portion of the hand out of rubber, fitted with tubes to pump blood. This part was worn over the actor's real hand. The removable palm and fingers were made out of wax. For the shot, the wax portion was blown away by explosive squibs placed between the rubber appliance, and blood was pumped through. The scene was so gruesomely realistic and violent that Scorsese had to find a way to tone it down in order to avoid an X rating. He remembered that John Huston had filmed *Moby Dick* (1956) with three-strip Technicolor stock, allowing him to fuse black and white and color together in a different ratio for each shot. The result gave the impression that the film had been hand-painted. In a way to settle with the MPAA, Scorsese diffused the color in that entire sequence; he had to do a visual trick (since the film stock was Eastmancolor, not Technicolor, as in *Moby Dick*) and had the choice to change the ratio from color to black and white in each shot. When there was too much blood, he used 30 percent color and 70 percent black and white; it was like playing with the color knob of a television. The result was convincing, and Scorsese was thrilled to have found a way to satisfy the ratings board without having to trim his film any more than he had to. Actually, the director would have loved to have shot the film in black and white or using the color-correction device throughout, but in the end, using black and white seemed uncommercial, and the color device was too expensive. Yet the climax of *Taxi Driver* remains one of the most graphic and ultraviolent scenes ever put on film. Even the sound effects and the absence of music in that scene contribute to the violence.

Composer Bernard Herrmann, famous for his collaborations with Alfred Hitchcock, suggested that there be no score accompanying the final bloodbath. Ironically, it was Herrmann who had suggested that Janet Leigh's murder in *Psycho* be accompanied by a score; Hitchcock had not initially wanted music.

Herrmann's moody, jazzy score in *Taxi Driver* creates a nice contrast to the images on the screen and is yet another aspect of the film that hooks us. In the final scene of the film, when Bickle drives off in his cab, Scorsese wanted to give the audience the feeling that he (Bickle) was a time bomb. Bickle seems to be catching his own reflection in his rearview mirror, and at that point a short musical sting comes on which confirms that Bickle's meter is on. Scorsese was not entirely satisfied with the sting that Herrmann had composed; finally, he played it backward and got the effect he wanted to convey the idea that Bickle would soon go off again. Herrmann died before the film opened, and Scorsese dedicated *Taxi Driver* to him.

As with most controversial films, critics were split on *Taxi Driver*. Many reviews acknowledged Scorsese's talents as well as De Niro's in his portrayal of Travis Bickle, but many were disturbed by the violence. Some found it "beautiful" and adequate, while others thought the violence—especially the final bloodbath—was gratuitous and exploitative: "Unfortunately, social comment does not come easily to him [Scorsese]," wrote Richard Schickel in *Time* magazine, "and the strain shows. It is a conflict he can resolve only in a violence that seems forced and—coming after so much dreariness—ridiculously pyrotechnical." John Simon of *New York* magazine took this argument even further: "The concluding violence (though Scorsese toned it down to avoid an X rating) is perhaps not so much excessively gruesome as lingered over with excessive enjoyment of the gruesomeness. Its almost slobberingly repetitive and protracted rehashing of images of blood and horror is ghoulish . . ."

On the other hand, Pauline Kael (*New Yorker*) had a better understanding of the film and of Travis Bickle; she explained in her review that violence is Bickle's only means of expressing himself.

> The violence in this movie is so threatening precisely
> because it's cathartic for Travis. I imagine that some

people who are angered by the film will say that it advocates violence as a cure for frustration. But to acknowledge that when a psychopath's blood boils over he may cool down is not the same as justifying the eruption. This film doesn't operate on the level of moral judgment of what Travis does. Rather, by drawing us into his vortex it makes us understand the psychic discharge of the quiet boys who go berserk.

De Niro, berserk. (Columbia Pictures)

The strongest criticism of the film's violence came from writer Thomas Thompson in a *Los Angeles Times* article he entitled "Worse Yet, the Audience Cheered. An Outburst of Gratuitous Movie Gore." At the beginning of his article, he recalled walking out on Sam Peckinpah's *Wild Bunch* and then switching the TV off when his teenage sons were watching *Magnum Force* (1973), the second Dirty Harry movie, and how his son argued that, as a writer, he should oppose censorship. When Thompson walked out on *Taxi Driver*, he declared that what truly horrified him most was that the audience seemed to enjoy the film's violence: "When the DiNiro [*sic*] character first assumed a menacing karate stance early in the film, many yelled support. Then, as he played with guns and embraced them as lovers, there was laughter. Not derision, mind you, laughter. And, unless I am very wrong it was the laughter of understanding and approval. Indeed, when the taxi driver began his slaughter in the whorehouse, the theatre erupted in applause and cheering."

Thompson declared that writers and directors should be concerned by what comes before and after a violent act, not with the act itself. He concluded his venomous article by quoting

43

Jodie Foster, who supposedly had told a reporter that she "thought that the violence was fun" and that it was her favorite part of the film. Thompson seemed to be missing the whole point of the movie simply by comparing *Taxi Driver* to *Magnum Force*. Maybe the fact that audiences were cheering at the violence in the film was showing just how valid and accurate the movie was. Scorsese's film was real; the violence was now at our doorstep.

"I was shocked by the way audiences took the violence," declared the director. "Previously, I'd been surprised by audience reaction to *The Wild Bunch*, which I first saw in a Warner Bros. screening room with a friend and loved it. But a week later I took some friends to see it in a theater, and it was as if the violence became an extension of the audience and vice versa. I saw *Taxi Driver* once in a theater, on the opening night, I think, and everyone was yelling and screaming at the shoot-out. When I made it, I didn't intend to have the audience react with that feeling. 'Yes, do it! Let's go out and kill.' The idea was to create a violent catharsis so that they'd find themselves saying, 'Yes, kill'; and then afterwards realize, 'My God, no'—like some strange Californian therapy session. That was the instinct I went with, but it's scary to hear what happens with the audience." Scorsese saw the final bloodbath as Travis's attempt to stop these people once and for all. For Paul Schrader, it was a kind of Samurai death with honor. Unfortunately, Bickle has no more bullets and can't give himself "le coup de grâce." If Schrader had directed that final sequence, Scorsese revealed, he would have wanted even more blood to give the scene a more surrealistic effect. "What I wanted," Scorsese explained, "was a *Daily News* situation, the sort you read about every day: 'three men killed by lone man, who saves young girl from them.' "

French director Jean-Luc Godard once said: "Every good film becomes successful for the wrong reasons." *Taxi Driver* became infamous when John Hinkley Jr. became obsessed with Jodie Foster after watching the film fifteen times and tried to assassinate President Ronald Reagan on March 30, 1981, outside the Washington Hilton. Prior to this, Hinckley, like Travis Bickle, had gone on a months-long gun-buying spree and had traveled cross-country on a lonely odyssey. He had written several letters to Jodie Foster, who was then attending Yale University. When she failed to respond to his love letters, Hinckley decided to assassinate Reagan to get her attention; "Jodie," Hinckley wrote in a letter that was found in his hotel room

before he left to shoot the president, "I'm asking you to please look into your heart and at least give me the chance with this historical deed to gain your respect and love. I love you forever."

Martin Scorsese only heard about the connection between *Taxi Driver* and the Reagan assassination attempt on Academy Award night, the day after the shooting. Scorsese had received a nomination for *Raging Bull* and arrived at the ceremony with his wife, Robert De Niro, and producer Harry Uffland. Scorsese was surprised when they were the first ones to be let into the auditorium. Then, later, when he went to the washroom, three men with a lot of hardware followed him. Still, Scorsese didn't make the connection; "A few years earlier, at the awards," Scorsese recalled, "when Jodie Foster and I were nominees for *Taxi Driver*, I had received a threatening letter: 'If Jodie Foster wins for what you made her do, you will pay for it with your life.' So we got the FBI then, and that night, when Billy Friedkin was directing the awards show, he let me in first. They showed me my FBI person, a woman in a gown, with a gun in her bag. Jodie didn't win, so that was that."

When Lillian Gish went onstage to give the award for Best Picture for 1980, an FBI agent told Scorsese that it was time to leave, and that the winner was going to be *Ordinary People*, not

Raging Bull. Scorsese still didn't know what was going on and didn't want to walk out on the venerable Miss Gish. Finally, he went backstage, and De Niro told him of the connection between *Taxi Driver* and the Reagan assassination attempt. De Niro had received the Oscar that night for Best Actor and had to make a statement to the press. He was immediately grilled about any responsibility he felt for the attempt on Reagan's life for his role as Travis Bickle. "That's a loaded question," he said. But the reporter who had asked the question wouldn't budge; finally, De Niro decided he had enough and walked out. As for Scorsese, he later found out that even his limo driver was from the FBI.

"We thought it was rather unfair, in the Hinckley trial, to show the film over and over." Scorsese declared, admitting that the event upset him deeply. "The film is a disturbing picture, but we made it as a labor of love. I really thought nobody would see that picture. Only Bob [De Niro] had a sense that the movie might be more successful than we thought. When he put on that Mohawk wig, he realized we had something special." Showing the picture at the trial was merely a way to find a rational way to explain why Hinckley had tried to kill the president and to point the finger at *Taxi Driver* and say, "That's what did it!" "Well, I'm a Catholic," Scorsese finally confessed about the shooting. "It's easy to make me feel guilty."

The FBI had received an anonymous letter a few months prior to the assassination attempt, saying that there was a plot to abduct Foster from her dormitory at Yale. Agents had questioned and warned the actress. Foster had received several letters from Hinckley, and it was her roommate who immediately established the connection when she heard on TV that Hinckley had tried to kill Reagan. Foster couldn't believe it was the same guy. During a press conference she was asked about the violence contained in the film: "I really am not here to answer questions about *Taxi Driver.* All I know is that it's one of the finest films I have ever seen. It's an important film." She was then asked if life was beginning to imitate art: "As far as I'm concerned, there was no message from *Taxi Driver,*" Foster replied. "It was a piece of fiction. . . . It's very relevant, but it's a piece of art. It's not meant to inspire people to do anything. It is a portrayal."

On the day Reagan was shot, screenwriter Paul Schrader was in New Orleans directing his remake of *Cat People.* The FBI showed up to question him; they wanted to know if Hinckley had been in touch with him. Schrader recalled that one day his office had received a letter from someone who wanted to meet Jodie Foster; his secretary had thrown it out, but Schrader suspected it was from Hinckley. "He recognized himself, and he identified with [the film]," Schrader said. "If you want to stop criminals from identifying with art, then you can do one of two things; demand that art not portray pathological minds or demand that it portray them superficially and inaccurately. Unless you are willing to put those kinds of censorship limits on art, those kinds of identifications will occur. Because the more accurate art is, the more likely the mind will plug into it. The connection here between Hinckley and *Taxi Driver* is one at a psychological level, not a violent level."

While Schrader agrees that certain things like child pornography are censorable, he felt that censoring a film like *Taxi Driver* because its violence might wrongly influence certain people was not really confronting the problem. Sick-minded people can be triggered by anything. "A few years ago," Schrader said, "they did a study about incitement to rape, and one of the things that cropped up most often was the old Coppertone suntan-oil ad [which featured Jodie Foster, as a toddler]—it had a little puppy tugging at a girl's swimsuit. It had just the right mixture for these rapists of adolescent sexuality, female nudity, rear entry, animals, violence."

Broadcast mogul Ted Turner claimed that he opposed censorship of any type but he decried the blood and gore in *Taxi Driver* and suggested that executives at Columbia Pictures, the film's distributor, should be as much on trial as John Hinckley. Schrader argued, saying that following this prescription against screen violence may have the opposite effect on real-life criminals. According to Schrader, if psychopaths can see themselves portrayed in films, maybe they can help themselves.

"What am I supposed to do about the Hinckley shooting?" Martin Scorsese declared. "Quit? Maybe my films do strike a nerve. That's what I'm supposed to do, isn't it? I can't and I won't be responsible for every person that walks into a theater where one of my films is playing. I have a hard enough time being responsible for myself." Although certain sources said that the director was thinking of not making any more films after the assassination attempt on Reagan, Scorsese never *stopped*; he went further, and many followed him.

2

Killer Couples

"Mass murder is wrong. But if I was a mass murderer, I'd be Mickey and Mallory." Juliette Lewis and Woody Harrelson in Oliver Stone's *Natural Born Killers*. (Warner Bros., photo by Sidney Baldwin)

T he censors weren't too happy when they read the script of a film called *Deadly Is the Female*, by MacKinlay Kantor and Millard Kaufman, based on a magazine story by Kantor entitled "Gun Crazy." The film was about a young man's mania for guns whose passion is capitalized on by an adventuress; the two take off together for a life of crime, robbing and killing people, and eventually both lose their lives. The censors felt the film violated several of the code's rules:

> Pictures dealing with criminal activities, in which minors participate, or to which minors are related, shall not be approved if they incite demoralizing imitation on the part of youth.

> No picture shall be produced which will lower the moral standards of those who see it. Hence the sympathy of the audience shall never be thrown to the side of crime, wrong-doing, evil or sin.

> Crimes against the law shall never be presented in such a way as to throw sympathy with the crime as against law or justice or to inspire others with a desire for imitation.

49

Deadly Is the Female (a.k.a. *Gun Crazy*), which was directed in 1949 by Joseph H. Lewis, did break all of the above rules, even despite the fact that the producers, Frank and Maurice King, made a lot of changes in the script to try and satisfy the censors. One can easily wonder what the censors of the time would have thought of David Lynch's *Wild at Heart* (1990), a wickedly violent comedy in which we followed a couple, Sailor

Dominic Gena's *Kalifornia* . . . Cool hand Brad. (Gramercy Pictures)

(Opposite) Bad to the bone . . . Laura Dern and Nicolas Cage in David Lynch's *Wild at Heart*. (Miramax Films)

and Lula (Nicolas Cage and Laura Dern), on the run in the Deep South through a maze of twisted, frightening events and characters. The film won the Palme d'Or at the Cannes Film Festival, which didn't necessarily please everyone, since the film's violence and overall tone were judged by many as over the top bad taste. Lynch knew when he made the film that some scenes would be a problem with the MPAA; the director even altered the movie after sneak previews. "There's a magic line, and if you cross it," he

said, "you're in bad trouble. The violence was going over the line and ruining everything." Still, one of the most upsetting moments in the film shows Cage smashing a man's head against the floor until he's dead, and at the end of the movie, the sleazy character played by Willem Dafoe gets his head blown off. That particular scene caused the film to receive an X rating and was eventually trimmed and disguised with a fire-and-smoke optical so that the head did not appear to leave the body.

Three years later came director Dominic Sena's small film entitled *Kalifornia*, about a couple (a writer and his photographer-girlfriend) who want to travel to mass-murder sites to write a photo book about them. When they advertise for a ride share they get more than they bargained for when they carpool with Brad Pitt and his trashy girlfriend, played by Juliette Lewis. As it turns out, Pitt's character is a murderer. Here again, the film was judged too violent, and both the sex and the intensity of certain scenes had to be toned down so that it could be released with an acceptable R rating. But none of these movies, not even the controversial *True Romance* (1993), which will be explored in another chapter, could prepare viewers for, or even compare to, Oliver Stone's *Natural Born Killers* (1994). Stone did more than take violence a step further; he took it to such an extreme that it may never be topped.

Natural Born Killers

"I wanted to have fun. And I really wanted to do a combination of a road movie, like Bonnie and Clyde *and* Easy Rider, *and a prison film, like* The Great Escape *and* Papillon.*"*

—OLIVER STONE ON *NATURAL BORN KILLERS*

"Mass murder is wrong. But if I was a mass murderer, I'd be Mickey and Mallory."

—A TEENAGER IN A MOCK-DOCUMENTARY SCENE FROM *NATURAL BORN KILLERS*

Mickey (Woody Harrelson) and Mallory (Juliette Lewis) are a perfect couple in the sense that they share the same passion—and talent—for violence and murder. Mallory lives with an abusive, foul, incestuous, and repulsive father (Rodney Dangerfield) and an idiot mother; she is rescued by Mickey, who shows up one day carrying fifty pounds of dripping raw meat. Together they beat Daddy to death and set Mom ablaze. And that's just the beginning. As they continue their rampage, the public and the media eat it up. Sleazy TV journalist Wayne Gale (Robert Downey Jr.) makes Mickey and Mallory cult heroes on his reality-based show *American Maniacs*. The couple is eventually arrested by a corrupt and homicidal cop named Jack Scagnetti (Tom Sizemore), who dreams of writing a book on Mickey and Mallory. In jail, the two are harassed by Scagnetti and by maniacal prison warden Dwight McClusky (Tommy Lee Jones), who wants to achieve media fame as the man who put them to death. Wayne Gale sets about doing the television show of the century by interviewing Mickey and Mallory behind bars. But Mickey manages to grab a rifle and instigates a riot in the prison. After shooting Scagnetti and leaving McClusky to be butchered by his inmates, Mickey and Mallory escape with Wayne Gale, who insists on going along. Free at last, Mickey and

Mallory kill Wayne while his video camera is rolling on him and escape. The film concludes with a quick montage of the John Wayne Bobbitt and Menendez brothers trials, O. J. Simpson, Tonya Harding, and with pulsing on the soundtrack for the end credits, Leonard Cohen's "Get ready for the future, it is murder."

Natural Born Killers (or *NBK* as it is known at Ixtlan, Oliver Stone's film company) is a hallucinatory trip, a satire on America's culture of violence and our country's obsession with true crime and its encouragement by the tabloid media. Based on a story by Quentin Tarantino, it had a script by Oliver Stone, David Veloz, and Richard Rutowski. As he did in *The Doors* (1991), Stone used a fast-cut style which mixes video, documentary film techniques, animation, rear projection images, black and white, and mock documentary reportage to draw the viewer into the interior world of Mickey and Mallory. The movie has approximately three thousand cuts; shot in about fifty-three days, it took Oliver Stone almost a year to edit, about twice the time it usually takes to cut most movies. The style of the film was crucial, and in a sense the innovative visuals made the violence bearable to watch. A completely original element is the sitcom parody (complete with laugh track) entitled *I Love Mallory*, which provides a flashback to Mallory's abuse-filled adolescence.

Stone shot the most violent scenes in a way which maximized the impact. "Most of the black and white was used for the violence," said director of photography Robert Richardson, referring to the opening—and bloody—diner sequence, "except for shots that provided pinpoints of color, such as the green pie, the record inside the jukebox, or blood on the table. If we had decided to shoot the initial fight sequence between Mallory and the cowboy entirely in color, it might have altered the rest of the sequence as it played out." Instead, Stone and his director of photography decided to isolate certain parts of the violence using highly grainy black-and-white film stock so that it would be a shock—almost as violent in terms of tone as the actual violence on the screen when juxtaposed to extremely strong, clean colors. "Specific shots were also intended to heighten the power of a kill," Richardson noted. "For example, we did one shot in which the bullet did not stop in front of the cook's head but actually continued to the point of impact. It just kept going and smashed into her brain, and the wall was shot in both black and white and color so that a postdecision could be made about how to temper the effect."

Filming violence is a science; there's a scene in *Natural Born Killers* when Mallory is in jail and she runs toward the door and smashes her head into it. Oliver Stone wanted to show the actual impact so that we, the audience, could actually feel Mallory's pain and the violence of her act. "I was using a fourteen-millimeter lens, handheld, and I had strapped a piece of foam rubber onto the camera so I could run up really close to the door," recalled Robert Richardson. "Once I felt the foam rubber absorbing the shock, I would stop my forward motion, because at that point I was only six inches from the door. But Oliver felt that he wasn't getting the actual hit, that I was pulling back at the last second—which was absolutely true!" Richardson was extremely reluctant to take the next step, but eventually Oliver Stone convinced him to go for it, and so he did. As a result, Richardson wound up breaking a finger, which put him out of commission. Second-unit cinematographer Phil Pfeiffer was next in line for the task. He tried his best and cut his eye. "He needed four stitches, and that was the end of the game, because we didn't have a third-string quaterback," Richardson concluded. "But Oliver got his shot."

The most intense and accomplished sequences in the film were shot on location at the Stateville Correctional Center at Crest Hill, Illinois. Cast and crew were surrounded by real incarcerated criminals, who spent much of the time yelling at them: "Go home, you movie motherfuckers!" *Village Voice* reporter Francine Russo, who visited the set, wrote that women who worked on the production were uneasy but did not find catcalls from the real-life inmates much different from those of a rowdy construction crew. The men, on the other hand, were "thrown off balance" when the prisoners called them "bitch" and when they became objects of sexual desire and hostility.

The energy in the prison scenes is almost too much to bear. Prison is not unfamiliar to Oliver Stone. "Yeah, I was there [in jail] briefly after Vietnam for federal smuggling charges . . . marijuana. The charges were dismissed. It gave me at a very young age a very strong vision of the lower depths of American society. A scary place. A very scary place."

It is not surprising that the prison scenes caused the most trouble when Stone submitted the film for a rating. Most of the heavy cutting he had to make took place in the jail sequence. After several trips to the MPAA, the film finally received an R "for extreme violence and graphic carnage, for shocking images, and for strong language and sexuality." As a guideline to their readers, the *Los Angeles Times* added to the MPAA's restriction: "Although the violence is not literally nonstop, it feels as though it is."

The film was controversial before it was released; the media frenzy over the O. J. Simpson case as well as the coverage of the Menendez, Bobbitt, and Harding trials were proving the film's message right. What Oliver Stone had meant as a satire had become a frightening reality. "When we set out to make *Natural Born Killers* in late 1992, it was surreal. By the time it was finished in 1994, it had become real. In that warped season, we saw Bobbitt, Menendez, King, Buttafuoco, and several other pseudo-celebrities grasp our national attention span with stories of violence, revenge, and self-obsession. Each week, America was deluged by the media with a new soap opera, ensuring ratings, money, and above all, continuity of hysteria."

Warner Bros., the film's distributor, was cautious in its marketing and insisted that Stone work at getting an R rating. "This movie speaks for itself," said Robert Friedman, Warners president of worldwide advertising and publicity. "The violence in this film is meant to be satirical. And we never intended to trivialize that message in this movie by sensationalizing it. We believe this movie really has something important to say." Oliver Stone knew he would get mixed reactions; his films always do. There are those who get it, and those who don't. "That old ultraviolence, American style, is served up in double-barreled salvos in Oliver Stone's semiautomatic treatise on our culture of killing," critic Duane Byrge wrote in the *Hollywood Reporter*. "A rewrite of

a Quentin Tarantino screenplay, *Natural Born Killers* is a relentless onslaught of murderous carnage culled from the bloody, cross-country rampage of two modern-day boneheads." On the one hand, there was *Newsweek*'s David Ansen, who said: ". . . fighting with fire, the movie cancels itself out. You leave it more battered than enlightened." On the other hand, there was Jack Kroll, who wrote, also in *Newsweek*: "If Oliver Stone didn't exist, American culture would have to invent him." Jim Hoberman of the *Village Voice* called *Natural Born Killers* "the most baroque film in American history," and Kenneth Turan of the *Los Angeles Times* felt that: ". . . if you don't find yourself on the film's often warped wavelength, the nonstop violence will sicken you."

Audiences had strong reactions. "This mediation on violence, tabloid media and the public obsession for both is an offensive assault by Stone, cartoon-quality bloodletting, carnage

Move over Bonnie and Clyde . . . here come Mickey and Mallory. (Warner Bros., photo by Sidney Baldwin)

on a grand scale, all designed as a hypersurreal meat cleaver to smash through our collective desensitization to violence by giving us a dose too large to handle," Jeff Softley, a Los Angeles writer who also directed a national energy-conservation campaign at the time, wrote in a venomous letter to the *Los Angeles Times*. The Coca-Cola Company was equally angry at the film; executives at the soft-drink headquarters in Atlanta were upset over the use of their polar-bear commercial intercut with images of ultraviolence. "It was all legally done; it was approved by the studio," Oliver Stone declared. "Personally, I think they should be proud of it. I think it's a very interesting usage of their commercial. It's part of the landscape, like Nixon's face."

Natural Born Killers was just as controversial overseas. It was pulled from its initial release schedule in the United Kingdom, where it ran into a storm of censorship trouble. In France, two high school graduates set off on a wild chase through Paris, killing three policemen and a taxi driver; although it was not established whether the couple had seen the film, promotional material for it was found in their apartment. They had underlined passages from the movie in a magazine; one of them read: "Everything becomes clear when you have a gun in your hand."

An Interview With Oliver Stone

For Oliver Stone, everything becomes clear when he is behind a camera. I first met him when he directed *Platoon* (1986), which remains the most realistic film ever made about Vietnam. Stone has created some of the most disturbing scenes of violence not only in his own movies but also in his screenplays directed by others; Who could forget the chain-saw sequence in Brian De Palma's *Scarface* (1983) or the tongue-biting scene in Alan Parker's *Midnight Express* (1978)? I met Oliver Stone a second time while he was in production on *Wall Street* (1987); he told me that three things kept him alive when he was struggling; "hate, rejection, and failure." While Stone has known failure—*Seizure* (1974), or *The Hand* (1981)—he has also won two Oscars and has come to be known as America's most ferocious contemporary director. In *Natural Born Killers* he experimented with a stylized, satiric, almost cartoonish violence that is guaranteed to shock. As Stone says himself, "Satire, if it's working, *should* be about shock."

58

EIN OLIVER STONE FILM

NATURAL BORN KILLERS

Laurent Bouzereau: You said that with *Natural Born Killers* you set yourself out to do a satire and that while making the film it suddenly became reality in the news.

Oliver Stone: Well, let me say that the picture is exaggerated and that's why I got a lot, again, misunderstood in a sense, but I call it a satire because the actions were larger than life. There was no intentions behind the questions of suffering; this is not a film about suffering like I had done about *Platoon* or *Born on the Fourth of July*, which were films about people who got hurt by violence. This was not about that; there are no victims in this movie, although people drop dead. It's sort of satiric. In a sense, it's like a fun-house mirror; you look into it and you see yourself distorted. It also has some truth in it; it's a way of understanding the world, and I always felt that America is so exaggerated that I have to exaggerate it even more to reflect back the kind of craziness that we have in our culture, not just the television culture

Stone's hallucinatory trip on America's culture of violence and our country's obsession with true crime. (Warner Bros.)

59

but also a culture of hype. The government is hyped; they sell huge amounts of weapons abroad and on the streets here. We have more and more prisons and a huge amount of the population in prison. We have many corrupt policemen. It's sort of like the world has gone crazy, and the movie is about our culture going to hell in a handbasket, and that is what is going on; that's the reality. But my treatment of it was not to take a real case like the Menendez brothers. . . . A good case might have been the Lorena Bobbitt . . . I mean the Tonya Harding case. . . . Lorena Bobbitt. . . . They kind of collide; I mean, a woman cutting off her husband's penis! When I was a kid, it would have been in the *National Enquirer*, but now in our culture it's making a huge amount of money for the networks. So was Tonya Harding; a stupid act of vandalism essentially set up a situation where the networks made a lot of money. The O. J. Simpson case is a ridiculous waste of time, waste of the national conscious, waste of money, but it must be making billions of dollars for the network[s]; it's a total preoccupation with trash and trivia. So if the culture is based on hype, superficiality, trivia, and because of the power of the media to enlarge any event and give it "significance," we live, I think, in an insane culture and, ultimately, a trivial one. The movie in a sense reflects that right back. It's a surface movie; it's about images. In our movie, images have now become our God. It's a movie of images; it's a prism.

LB: You reworked Quentin Tarantino's original draft of *NBK*. What are the major differences?

OS: His original draft was more about the film crew and the Wayne character, and Mickey and Mallory were just stick figures, they were supporting cast, and I really wanted to get into them. I also wanted a level of sociopolitical commentary that he didn't want to deal with.

LB: What is to you the most violent moment in *NBK*?

OS: Probably the riot. In the original cut, there wasn't any particular moment that was extremely gruesome, like in *Scarface* we had the chain-saw scene or the tongue-biting scene in *Midnight Express*. I mean, I've had violent images that really stood out. We didn't go for that here; we went for a faster film. It was a nervous film with a lot of cuts. But I've never seen in my experience such a great accumulation of energy and chaos as I saw in the riot sequence of *NBK*, at least in the version that was ultimately fucked with by the MPAA endlessly. They were so threatened by that scene because it was about the end of the world, the mutiny of the underclass. It was about the Jim Morrison phrase "The whole shithouse is burning." That's what it was about. And that scene for some reason sent the MPAA into a fit. At one point, they said to me literally; this is funny, but they said: "There's just such chaos; it's just anarchy. Just cut from the end of the interview [between Woody Harrelson and Robert Downey Jr.] and get them out of the prison. You don't need this riot." They never tell you what to cut; I was exasperated.

LB: Do you think it was the accumulation of violence that disturbed them?

OS: Energy is my feeling. There was something threatening about this movie; there was such a buildup of energy in this picture . . . and it was driving people nuts.

LB: Tell me about the cuts you had to make to get the movie from NC-17 to an R rating.

OS: The one-hundred-and-fifty trims and cuts were mostly in the riot scene and in the first scene, the cafe scene. We also had to recut the scene between Scagnetti and the hooker; in the original cut she had taken off her bra, but we had done coverage with her still having her bra, so we were able to substitute these shots. The MPAA didn't touch the Rodney Dangerfield scenes; they left that alone for some reason; that's bizarre. I don't know why. The killing of the parents they left alone for the most part. It was impact cuts that troubled them; my cutting style in the picture was very impactful; it was lots of different cuts. There'd be six shots, and they'd be very quick, but the MPAA would ask us to take three out or two out.

LB: What about the end of the riot scene with Tommy Lee Jones being literally ripped apart by the inmates. That's not in the theatrical cut of the film.

OS: That was a good scene. I loved that. He got nailed at the end and was ripped to shreds; that was the only solution, and we had his shoes coming off, his legs were coming out. . . . It was like Grand Guignol. It was funny, and his head got put out on a stick like in the French Revolution. The MPAA did not like that, so that was very muted in the final cut. Also, we had a shot, which was very funny, I thought, looking through Robert Downey

Jr.'s hand after he's been shot in the hand, and you saw the action through the hole in the hand. That was cut.

LB: I heard about a chain-saw scene.

OS: I cut that before we submitted the film to the ratings board. There was actually a courtroom scene and a chain-saw scene that I took out.

LB: Wasn't the courtroom scene with Ashley Judd?

OS: Yes. I knew that we would have a problem with that scene, anyway, because it was a very bloody scene and also very violent, but it was for me, in a sense, gratuitous. I didn't really need it.

LB: What happened in that scene?

OS: Mickey and Mallory go to trial. The judge questions one of the witnesses played by Ashley Judd, and Mickey and Mallory kill her.

LB: Do you think that your film lost part of its message because of the MPAA forcing you to recut it for an R rating?

OS: No. I think that ultimately the film is not about violence. The film is not about good or bad; it's about do you understand it or don't you. The film is very disturbing to me, too; it's also very ambivalent. There is no single message in this film, you know.

LB: Did you ever feel any kind of sympathy toward Mickey and Mallory?

OS: Yes, I did, absolutely. But some people don't.

LB: Do you feel sorry for them because they're victims of their parents?

OS: Well, they are creatures of the century, and you have to look beyond their badness and what their badness is about. It is genetic, it is environmental, but the century itself is polluted, and I tried to suggest that in the movie. I'm looking to under-stand. I think that any murderer has a reason, any murderer. That's not to excuse what they did; it's just to understand what they did. *"Tout comprendre, c'est tout pardonner"* [sic—"To under-stand everything is to forgive everything"]. *"Les Américains ne comprennent pas cela."* [sic—"Americans don't understand that"].

LB: Many people have asked you that question, but do you think that screen violence could actually influence certain people to kill or do acts of violence—like it happened when *A Clockwork Orange* came out?

OS: Each time I've examined that story it was never proven that those people had reacted to the film.

LB: In some cases, the perpetrators were dressed like Alex in the film, and in another case a guy beat up someone singing "Singin' in the Rain," like in *A Clockwork Orange.*

OS: And that's actually true? You see, the tabloids in England, which have accused me of ten murders, have no evidence. Scotland Yard, the FBI, cannot back what the tabloids say.

LB: Actually, Kubrick himself withdrew the movie from the theaters. I understand that he also received death threats.

OS: That's probably more likely because he is so paranoid.

LB: Tell me about England's position on *NBK.*

OS: The film was the subject of much controversy because the tabloids made it. The tabloids have acted exactly like our movie; they've made up a bunch of stuff and have linked to the film ten murders and are going on and on about how people are killing because they see the movie. People who kill are deeply disturbed, but they're disturbed before they see a movie. A movie can act as a spark, . . . but if it weren't the movie, it would be an argument with a sister, a brother, a wife, any kind of snub or insult. I mean, anybody can go over on anything.

LB: I feel there is a strong sense of censorship in America when it comes to sex and violence.

OS: Absolutely. We live in a culture that's Anglicized, as they say. And let's face it, there's much repression in the Anglo culture.

LB: Was Warner Brothers, the distributor of *NBK,* at all concerned about the violence in the film?

OS: They were very nervous. They ultimately backed the film, but until we got an R rating, they wouldn't release it; they wouldn't move forward. They insist on an R rating; the MPAA formed, as you know, an NC-17, which is acceptable to me. When the studio says they cannot sell a film with an NC-17, that's hypocritical, because they can sell it. If they told the exhibitors, "You cannot play our R-rated films unless you show our NC-17 movies," we would stop having problems. You have to work a little harder, but most people will judge the film, see it, and take it.

LB: Did you show the film to a test audience?

OS: Yes.

LB: What kind of audience did you recruit?

OS: We got a young, hip audience in Seattle and Chicago. Our scores were very mixed, as always. Radical films tend to do that, but what's important is that we got a very strong reaction, positive and against. It was coming from people who were laughing at the darker sections of the film; at that point, I realized that we were okay, because initially I was concerned that the film grammar was so advanced that it would be above the head of the audience. I was relieved that the audience was getting this film.

LB: Did you test-screen the R or the NC-17 version?

OS: The first one was the NC-17, and the second screening was the R-rated version.

LB: Do you find test screenings helpful?

OS: I always hated them because I was scared of them. Sometimes I think they can signal to the studio that a film is not as strong as they'd like it to be, and they cut back on their advertising, or it can signal problems to the press or to the exhibitors. So they can be very dangerous. On the other hand, on something like *NBK*, where you're dealing with something so radically new, you're finding out if you're in the same ballpark, if you're not missing completely. I tested *The Doors* because it was also an experimental and strange movie. On *JFK*, though, I knew what I wanted to say, and I didn't care if it didn't do well; the important thing for me was that I knew that audiences would want me to simplify the movie. Once you start simplifying a movie that's structured so finely as *JFK* was, it's going to crumble. I know that all my films will test mixed [test audiences will have mixed reactions]; it's inevitable because my films are disturbing, they're provocative. You see, my films are not made to be liked or disliked; they're made to be understood or not understood. I don't give a shit about opinion; opinion bores me. We have so much opinion in our society, we have nothing but critics, it's true.

What did you think of the movie? That's a stupid question. It's not about what you think of a movie. It's about did the movie get to your subconscious, did the movie affect your life, will the movie change you? None of these questions can be answered at the time you see a film; you have no concept of what a film does to you. The movie goes into the deepest, darkest part of you, and that's the beauty of a film. But it's not about what do you think of the movie; you know, there's too many movie critics in this country. It's disgusting. A movie is beyond liking or disliking. It's like Nietzsche said: "It's beyond good and bad."

LB: I see *NBK* as the *Clockwork Orange* for the nineties.

OS: In a sense, we're much more desensitized because there was one death or two deaths in *A Clockwork Orange*. We just go for it, so it does show a degeneration through time to mass murder, which was not a concept when *Clockwork Orange* came out. *A Clockwork Orange* was a great, influential film for me; so was Peckinpah's *The Wild Bunch*; so was Paddy Chayefsky's *Network* [1976].

LB: What do you think of the fact that *The Wild Bunch*, although it finally got an R, was recently slapped with an NC-17?

OS: I couldn't believe it. We're in such a regressive time. It's too bad.

LB: Do you have any thoughts about Brian De Palma's *Scarface*, Alan Parker's *Midnight Express*, Michael Cimino's *Year of the Dragon* [1985], which you wrote but did not direct? For example, would you have shown the violence differently?

OS: I would have done it differently, yes, but they were all well-made movies, and I understand, now especially, what a director goes through, and I understand how it's ultimately the director's movie. But certainly *Scarface* was much more realistic in its script form. I did a lot of research in the streets, but Brian, being who he is, and the fact that he likes Sergio Leone and that kind of operatic style, the film became something different and less realistic. *Midnight Express*, it wasn't exactly what was written, but it was a wonderful movie. *Year of the Dragon* was not ultimately that successful for me.

LB: Did you know that at the end of the book of the British version of *A Clockwork Orange*, which was never published in

America, Alex retires from violence and decides to have a family.

OS: I did not know that.

LB: I got the feeling you were aiming for a similar ending in *NBK*, with Mickey and Mallory talking about having children. Is that a hint of optimism?

OS: Oh, absolutely. When Mickey and Mallory killed the Indian, they changed; remorse set in. They ate the apple; they have conscience. The moment they have conscience, they can no longer kill out of malice.

LB: Do they feel guilt toward killing the Indian because he symbolizes some kind of purity and maybe the fact that he is untouched by civilization?

OS: He was touched by civilization; I always considered him a killer actually. I always thought like he had been corrupt but that he was living as a renegade outside society. It's like the Buddhist ideal; he's seen the world, and he stepped outside the world. He understood. So when they kill him, they change, and if you look at the film closely, the whole motivation for the second part of the movie is for them to get back together. They're not into killing per se; they just kill in order to get back together. At the end, they only kill Wayne because if they don't they won't have any freedom. Ultimately, they have to hide from the media; so they wipe out the media, they go underground, and they're happy, they have kids. So, yes, it is Romeo and Juliet, with a happy ending for the nineties. But a lot of people missed that. You see, the other thing that the film does which is very interesting, it provokes people because it's structured subjectively, it's some kind of virtual reality trip, you're in the mind of a killer, and you kill and you enjoy it. They have fun killing, and you enjoy it, and the audience, to some degree, has fun killing, and some people get very upset because they suddenly realize that they're enjoying it.

LB: You said that the film was cathartic for you. Can you explain that notion?

OS: I can't really explain it too well. The film makes you think about society, it makes you react, there is a revulsion that sets in; it's like when Alex in *Clockwork Orange* has his eyeballs pinned open and he has to watch horror images. That's sort of

what it's like. Doing that, it kind of sickens you; you pass through something, you burn off something, you cleanse yourself. There is no need after you see this movie to watch more violence on TV. I mean, it's sort of like saying, When is enough enough? You can walk away; you don't need this shit. Watch yourself watching. Look at yourself as a human being; why are you encouraging this violence with your eyes?

LB: TV has sort of legitimized violence.

OS: Yes. When Vietnam came into our living rooms, we got the bug; the virus is in us. Absolutely, and it's gotten bigger and bigger and bigger; it's more and more and more. We're gonna have an execution channel; we'll have it.

LB: When O. J. Simpson was in his car, holding a gun, he could have easily blown his brains out or shot someone and we would have seen it all on TV. Yet, on the other hand, the violence in *NBK* had to be trimmed down before it could be released.

"I wanted to have fun. And I really wanted to do a combination of a road movie, like *Bonnie and Clyde* and *Easy Rider*, and a prison film, like *The Great Escape* and *Papillon*"
—Oliver Stone (Warner Bros., photo by Sidney Baldwin)

OS: I've said that they're created censorship for fictional violence on TV. They sanitize TV violence to nothing; it doesn't mean anything. It has a perverse, obscene effect because it's hollow, but then you can turn to the news and they're selling violence around the clock. "Stay tuned, you'll see a mother get killed at three, a kid get killed at four, a grandmother at five. . . ." They make it exciting. "Stay tuned to the news." The news is writing the real violence, and they make some money off of it. Make the news nonprofitable; that would be an interesting possibility. But we're all attuned to violence. There's nothing wrong with watching violence. Forget about the politically correct people; think about the world and the world is violent; the nature of the world is extremely violent. We're born in an act of birth which is extremely violent; kids are very cruel. People forget that, so there is a natural-born fascination with watching what I call the approach of death because we all know that we're going to die. We're all in touch with that knowledge, and we're fascinated by it, we are.

LB: In your films, you have either the parody violence of *NBK* and *Scarface* or a violence set in reality like in *Platoon*. What kind of a director do you become when you do either one?

OS: More talented, more versatile; don't you think it's better to do more styles? What I've enjoyed doing with my career up to now has been the ability to really try different things like music in *The Doors*, realism in some things, investigation movie in *JFK*, tension thriller, and in *Heaven and Earth*, I was trying a more romantic, religious type of filmmaking; with *Natural Born*, I'm back to action. With *Talk Radio* [1988], I was into experimental film. . . . I've been really playing around with the medium, and it's given me versatility. My critics are always on me, but I haven't repeated myself that much.

LB: *Platoon*, for instance, was based on your own life experience in the Vietnam War. With *Natural Born Killers*, you went the opposite way in terms of realism.

OS: Part of the fun was making it all up and to have pure fiction. That was a relaxation; you know, always having realism is tiring. I like to mix styles, work in different genres.

LB: What do you think about your audience?

OS: I think my audience is very smart. Generally, I underestimate them. Usually, the people who come to my movies know they're tough, but they know that there is a reward, that they're going to be challenged. They're not the usual popcorn-headed numbskulls. On the other hand, I like my movies to reach out and to reach as broad a population as possible. I think that *NBK* is the riskiest movie I've done for my audience because it can really alienate people. I've always had that side; I have a side that pisses people off.

LB: Being the father of a boy, has it made you more sensitive to the issue of violence on the screen and in our society?

OS: Well, my kid was heavily into toys, war games, very young. I see in boys a tendency toward aggression. As I said in *Natural Born Killers*, the key is to acknowledge it, not to run from it. I would screen films for kids, maybe the ape scene from Kubrick's *2001: A Space Odyssey*. I'd say: This is what we are; we're animals, we were animals, this is our Darwinian chain; we have aggression in us. This is part of our nature; the next time you see it, feel this aggression, know what it is. So the next time the kid goes crazy in the schoolyard and wants to kill the other kid, gets that blind fury, hopefully, through education, the kid will be able to identify the phenomenon that he is going through. Once you identify that phenomenon, you begin the process of distancing yourself from what you are, and that is the only way to start getting a handle on violence. We have to have the philosophic understanding that we have aggression, all of us; every one of us has it in our bones. If a kid understands that, he can begin the process of identification; it's the first step of consciousness, and consciousness will ultimately lead to nonviolence. Consciousness always moves in that direction, upwards; it never moves downwards.

LB: Despite all this, are you optimistic about seeing the end of violence in our society?

OS: Yes, because, at some point, it will become unprofitable.

3

New Breed, New Blood

Quentin Tarantino

In 1992 a new film era began when a movie fanatic named Quentin Tarantino made *Reservoir Dogs*. Clearly influenced by Martin Scorsese, by Hong Kong action films, and, more specifically, by *The Killing*, Stanley Kubrick's 1956 heist movie, *Reservoir Dogs* is a striking, disturbing, and violent piece of filmmaking. It is structured in flashbacks, but to put it chronologically, the story is about one Joe Cabot (Lawrence Tierney) and his son Nice Guy Eddie (Chris Penn), who hire six men with experience to pull a heist at a Los Angeles jewelry store. The men are assigned color-themed names so that no one will know the other's identity: Mr. White (Harvey Keitel), Mr. Orange (Tim Roth), Mr. Pink (Steve Buscemi), Mr. Blonde (Michael Madsen), Mr. Brown (writer-director Quentin Tarantino), and Mr. Blue (Eddie Bunker).

The heist goes awry, and it becomes obvious that the cops have been tipped off. Two of the robbers and a couple of cops are killed, and the gang gets separated in the heat of the moment.

Quentin Tarantino has triggered a new appreciation of violence in film. (Miramax Films)

71

Mr. White brings the injured Mr. Orange to a warehouse (incidentally, a former mortuary in real life); they are joined by Mr. Pink and psycho Mr. Blonde, who shows up with a hostage, a cop. Left alone with a bleeding Mr. Orange and the cop, Mr. Blonde tortures his hostage by slicing off the man's ear with a straight razor. Ultimately, Joe Cabot and Nice Guy Eddie arrive to identify the rat. There's a shoot-out; Mr. Pink tries to flee with the loot but is caught by the police. Mr. White finds out that Mr. Orange was an undercover cop and kills him. The cops walk in and gun down Mr. White.

"I wanted *Reservoir Dogs* to feel like a book, with chapter headings for the various back-and-forth scenes," Quentin Tarantino declared. "There are separate stories as to how each character may or may not get away from the scene of the crime. As the men are previously unknown to each other and there's no clue as to who betrayed them, using different chapters was the only way to show the whole story. The men have generic code names, and they are all dressed alike, but as the chapters unfold, you gain an understanding and insight into each character." Although *Reservoir Dogs* has a structure that has been used before, it definitely gave the film a rhythm that riveted audiences. The structure itself created suspense and tension, as you quickly realized that you could not predict when violence was going to occur. The flashbacks also guaranteed Tarantino that the viewers

Warehouse of blood . . . Tarantino's *Reservoir Dogs.* (Miramax Films)

wouldn't get bored; it might have been otherwise if the story had been told chronologically. Also novel was the gritty, often offensive, racist, and sexist dialogue; these men are certainly no angels, and while they deserve what's coming to them, the audience has fun listening to their obscene patter and to their raunchy interpretation of Madonna's song "Like a Virgin." Not since Scorsese had bad language been used so stylishly. In addition to the film's roller-coaster narrative structure and its stunning dialogue, *Reservoir Dogs* has astonishing cinematography by Polish director of photography Andrzej Sekula and a startling soundtrack of banal seventies pop tunes which are used in amazing juxtaposition to the extreme violence.

If there is one scene that will be singled out as the most memorable moment, it has to be the ear-slicing scene. Although the camera pans away as Michael Madsen skillfully starts cutting off the cop's right ear, the scene remains almost unbearable to watch. Again, what you don't see is sometimes more devastating than what you do see. As the camera pulls back, you can still see Madsen's arm going up and down, which leaves no confusion as to what's happening to the cop. The aftermath of this bloody moment is, in my eyes, equally, if not more, violent. You see the cop, tied to a chair with blood pouring out of his wound. Then you see Madsen walk toward the camera, holding the poor fellow's ear. The victim is then showered with gasoline. "There's nobody who ever got a traffic ticket who's not going to enjoy that scene someplace in their mind," actor Madsen declared.

And how does Tarantino himself feel about this sequence? "I was trying to do real violence where cinema doesn't intrude. One of the things that makes the torture scene so effective is the fact that it's done in real time. Cinema isn't coming in and showing you a lot of poppy cuts. I think it's almost impossible to watch Michael [Madsen] do his dance and not enjoy his performance, and then, boom! You can't help but feel somewhat of a coconspirator for enjoying it." Tarantino also declared that he "didn't do that scene to say, 'Boy, I'm going to have a boner when this thing comes out.' If you're with the movie, you feel for these people at the end." He is not troubled by any influence such extreme scenes may have on viewers. "I'm not going to be handcuffed by what some crazy fuck might do who sees my movie. The minute you put handcuffs on artists because of stuff like that, it's not an art form anymore."

Tarantino definitely succeeds at fascinating us with scum; as repulsive as they are, it's impossible not to enjoy these guys. The reason why *Reservoir Dogs*, like Martin Scorsese's *Good-Fellas* (1990) and Brian De Palma's *Scarface*, are so effective may be that the real violence comes from the fact that we enjoy—and therefore somehow identify with—the violent characters, even if doing so is against our better judgment. "You constantly see characters do things in movies that you don't buy for two seconds, but there's a committee behind why the character does what he does," Tarantino said. "He can't do that, because if he does that, then he'll lose his half of the audience. If he says this about his wife, he'll become a sexist pig. Or if he makes these racial remarks, who the hell is going to like him? He's a racist, he's a bigot, fuck him, he deserves what he gets. I like making it very hard for you to get behind these characters, but damn it, you're going to get behind them, anyway. Maybe you don't want them to move in next door to you, but in the course of the story, you are caught up in their journey."

Quentin Tarantino worked for six years behind the counter of a Manhattan Beach, California, video store and spent most of his childhood watching films. His parents always took him to

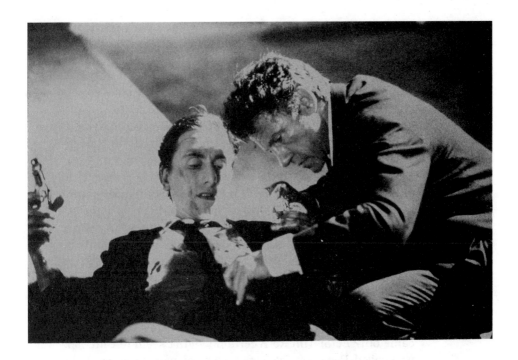

movies, even if they were not suitable for children. "The rating system meant nothing to them," the director recalled, "They figured I was smart enough to tell the difference between a movie and real life, and they were right. There was only one movie that my mom wished she hadn't taken me to, and that was *Joe* [1970], with Peter Boyle. I fell asleep. She was really happy, because she didn't want her kid to see the cops kill those hippies."

Tim Roth and Harvey Keitel in *Reservoir Dogs.* (Miramax Films)

Among Tarantino's favorite films are Martin Scorsese's *Taxi Driver*: "It's just perfect." Brian De Palma's *Blow Out* (1981): "Brian De Palma is the greatest director of his generation. This is his most purely personal and cinematic film." Sergio Leone's *Good, the Bad, and the Ugly* (1966): "Horrible brutality, hysterical humor, blood, music, icons. What more could you ask for?" De Palma's *Casualties of War* (1989): "To me the greatest war movie and the greatest indictment of rape ever captured. The Vietnamese girl's death walk has haunted me ever since." The list goes on. Tarantino also has a fascination for the work of Hong Kong action director John Woo; to him, Woo has reinvented the action movie.

In November 1990, Tarantino asked Monte Hellman of Blue Moon Entertainment to join him and his buddy Lawrence Bender (who plays a young cop in the film) as equal partners to produce *Reservoir Dogs*. Originally, Tarantino wanted to shoot the film in black and white on 16 mm, with himself as Mr. Pink and Bender as Nice Guy Eddie, since both had acting experience. (Tarantino had appeared on *The Golden Girls* and on other television series.) But with Hellman aboard, the project got bigger. Two months later, Richard Gladstein of Live Entertainment agreed to finance the film based on the value of its leading man. Both Harvey Keitel and Christopher Walken read the script, and in April, Keitel was signed on to the project (and also coproduced). In June, Tarantino went to Robert Redford's Sundance Institute to work in the director's lab, where he was able to try some of his directing ideas. With *Reservoir Dogs*, Tarantino got a chance to finally exploit all the tricks he had learned from watching his favorite films over and over. Some critics said that *Reservoir Dogs* was a rip-off of a Japanese film called *City on Fire*; others simply saw a film buff who knew how to put to good use what he had learned from his idols.

Was *Reservoir Dogs* going to be a controversial film when it came out? Actor Tim Roth certainly didn't seem to think so: "If it was called *Reservoir Bitches* and was all women, it would be controversial." Maybe the movie was not controversial, but it was completely groundbreaking. Critics recognized Tarantino's genius but seemed to think that the film's violence went a bit too far and could become an issue. "But the only thing Mr. Tarantino spells out is the violence," Julie Salamon wrote in the *Wall Street Journal.* "I have seen much movie blood spilled, yet I felt sickened by the coldness of this picture's visual cruelty. I don't think either my understanding of these particular characters or of nihilistic behavior in general was enhanced by watching one man's ear get sliced off or another man bleed endlessly from the gut." *Newsweek*'s David Ansen said: "There are buckets of blood in *Reservoir Dogs*. Some of the violence is played straight, some for black comedy. In this queasy-making torture scene, however, you may feel the director is enjoying himself a tad too much." Vincent Canby (*New York Times*) was, on the other hand, a lot more understanding: "*Reservoir Dogs* is as violent as any movie you are likely to see this year, but though it's not always easy to watch, it has a point."

True Romance (1993) was the first screenplay written by Quentin Tarantino and was brought to the screen by Tony Scott (of *Top Gun* [1986], among others). In the film, Patricia Arquette portrays Alabama Whitman, a hooker hired to seduce a geeky guy named Clarence Worley (Christian Slater), who works in a comic-book store. Clarence falls in love with Alabama and decides to bust her creepy pimp Drexl Spivey, played by Gary Oldman. Clarence kills Spivey and runs away with Alabama's possessions, not realizing that he's taken a large amount of cocaine and dropped his driver's license. The couple decides to sell the coke and heads down to California, making a stop to visit Clarence's dad, Clifford Worley (Dennis Hopper). Meanwhile, the mob, headed by Vincenzo Coccotti (Christopher Walken), wants their coke back and shows up at Clifford's after the two kids have already taken off; they shoot him. Clarence and Alabama hook up with a bunch of sleazy producers and intend to sell the cocaine but are double-crossed. Alabama is beaten to a pulp. Luckily, she finds enough strength to strike back at her attacker. There's a final shoot-out, but our heroes survive and manage to escape with enough cash to start anew.

"In one scene, there was so much fake blood flying," declared actor Bronson Pinchot, who plays a sleazy film executive, "they held riot shields over the whole crew so we wouldn't splatter them with our blood." Indeed, *True Romance* is gruesome and relentless. One of its best scenes, as in *Reservoir Dogs*, is a torture sequence involving Christopher Walken and Dennis Hopper. Since Hopper knows he's going to die, he launches into a monologue, insulting Walken's Sicilian origins. The scene is both quite funny and extremely tense; we're just waiting for Hopper's death, and we know it's not going to be pretty. The sequence with Patricia Arquette getting beaten up is also quite graphic, especially when she strikes back at her attacker with a corkscrew and finally grabs a can of hairspray, holds it against a lighter, and sets the guy's face on fire. The man collapses, and she picks up a rifle, shoots him several times, and then pummels him with it. The violence was so intense in the first cut of the film that director Tony Scott had to trim it down dramatically to receive an acceptable R rating.

True Romance, as one article pointed out, was trying to push the envelope on violence, and most critics resented the graphic scenes. *Variety*'s Leonard Klady best described the general response to the film in his review: "One of the endless variations on the couple-on-the-run subgenre, yarn provides some amazing encounters, bravura acting and gruesome carnage. But it doesn't add up to enough, as preposterous plotting and graphic violence ultimately prove an audience turnoff and will limit the film's commercial prospects." Kenneth Turan of the *Los Angeles Times* was even more outspoken on the issue of violence in Scott's movie: "The film also displays an almost religious veneration for on-screen violence, a blanket reverence for guns and blood as gee-whiz swell that is both childish and off-putting. Nothing is more irritating than a dumb film that thinks it's hip, and *True Romance* is this year's model."

"To glorify or condone violence is wrong," director Tony Scott said in answer to the attacks his film received. "But it is difficult because you have artistic feelings and ideas. Francis Bacon is one of the most violent painters in this century. My leanings have always been toward people on the edge, whether it's Francis Bacon or Gary Oldman. It is hard for me to balance public outcry against what my instincts take me to: People on the edge are people who involve themselves in violence. It has always been my subject. In painting, Bosch and Brueghel are offbeat, violently motivated painters. I'd be fighting my natural instincts." Tony Scott meant *True Romance* as a tribute to *Badlands*, the 1973 Terrence Malick film starring Sissy Spacek and Martin Sheen about the Starkweather-Fugate killing spree in the fifties, and to *The Wild Bunch*. "I am eclectic, I steal from everybody," he confessed. "As long as you can steal and make it better, then it doesn't matter. It becomes a tribute when you get caught."

Still, *True Romance*, as Christian Slater said, was a gutsy movie for a studio to make. "Violence is a tricky thing to deal with as far as publicity." In the original Tarantino script, Slater's character dies at the end of the film; now we see him and Patricia Arquette on the beach, playing with their baby boy. Without a doubt, the movie proved that crime, at least in the case of Clarence Worley, pays. The cast of *True Romance* defended the film and had a different view on the violent aspect of the story and its possible impact on the audience. "Whether it reflects the time we live in or not," Dennis Hopper said "the violence we are seeing on the screen is not what is creating the violence in our streets." For Christopher Walken, it is just a movie: "I have never confused movies with real life. I think children should be protected from traumatizing sights and sounds. But once you are grown up, you mustn't confuse a movie with day-to-day living." And Bronson Pinchot felt the film was not, as many seemed to think, amoral: "Violence and drugs are the minefield through which

Patricia and Christian tiptoe until they have a happy life. [*True Romance*] would be amoral if it showed it [violence] as something desirable."

In truth, however, the real target on the issue of the movie's graphic violence was writer Quentin Tarantino, who at that point was beginning to resent his reputation as an ultraviolent filmmaker. In his view, *True Romance* was a love story, and "the shit" that happens to the characters makes it all the more romantic. "Ultimately," Tarantino revealed, "I don't think it is a movie about violence. I think it is about romance."

Although his *Pulp Fiction* received the Palme d'Or at the Cannes Film Festival in May 1994, it did not reach the American screens until October, and by then it was by far one of the most awaited movies of the year.

Gary Oldman and Christian Slater . . . True violence in Tony Scott's *True Romance.* (TriStar Pictures)

Tarantino cowrote the Oscar-winning script with Roger Avary (who incidentally wrote and directed *Killing Zoe* [1994], for which Tarantino and Lawrence Bender were executive producers).

Pulp Fiction opens in a coffee shop where Honey Bunny (Amanda Plummer) and Pumpkin (Tim Roth) are having breakfast. They're in love and discussing a career move; they're tired of robbing liquor stores. It's time to get more ambitious and start sticking up restaurants. They kiss and stand up, holding guns and announcing to the other customers to get their wallets ready if they want to live. We then encounter Vincent Vega (John Travolta) and Jules Winnfield (Samuel L. Jackson), a pair of hit men who are under orders to recover a mysterious briefcase from a group of double-crossing amateurs.

In a segment entitled "Vincent Vega & Marcellus Wallace's Wife," we meet Marcellus (Ving Rhames), a take-no-shit mobster and Jules and Vincent's boss. Vincent is asked by Marcellus to take care of his wife, vampish Mia (Uma Thurman), while he's away. Vincent and Mia have a magical evening in a dance club, and back home, Mia searches Vincent's pockets while he is in the bathroom and finds what she thinks is cocaine. By the time Vincent returns to the living room, Mia has overdosed on his heroin. He takes her to the home of his dealer, Lance (Eric Stoltz), and with the help of Lance's wife (Rosanna Arquette), they plunge a giant hypodermic needle of adrenaline into Mia's chest and bring her back to life.

In another segment, "The Good Watch," we're introduced to prizefighter Butch Coolidge (Bruce Willis), who has been paid by Marcellus to throw a bout. He decides to double-cross the mob boss and runs away with Fabienne (Maria De Medeiros), his French girlfriend. But Butch discovers that Fabienne forgot to pack the watch that was given to him as a kid by Koons (Christopher Walken), his dead father's Vietnam platoon leader. In his apartment to retrieve it, Butch finds himself face-to-face with Vincent. Without a blink, Butch shoots him and flees. On the way back to their motel to pick up Fabienne, he (literally) runs into Marcellus Wallace; a chase ensues, and the two men end up beating each other in a pawnshop run by a southerner, who is into heavy S and M. He slams Butch (who has knocked out Marcellus) with the butt of a shotgun, ties up Butch and Marcellus, gags them, and invites his brother Zed over to join the party. While the brothers sodomize Marcellus, Butch is garded by "the Gimp," a slave dressed in full S and M gear, complete with zippered mask. Butch frees himself, kills one of the brothers, and Marcellus shoots the surviving rapist in the genitals. Marcellus and Butch are now even. Butch takes off while Marcellus says he's gonna go "medieval" on the rapist's ass.

In the last segment, "Jules, Vincent, Jimmie & the Wolf," we actually go back in time and rejoin Jules and Vincent on their assignment in the apartment of the double-crossers. They kill two men and take Marvin, Marcellus's informant, with them. A fourth emerges from the bathroom and fires at them point-blank before he is himself killed. Jules cannot believe that he and Vincent are still alive; he thinks he just witnessed a miracle and vows to give up his life of crime. But right now the pair must deliver the briefcase and Marvin, whom Vincent accidentally shoots in the car, splattering the inside of it with blood in broad daylight. They stop at the home of Jimmie (Quentin Tarantino), Jules's friend, and get the mess cleaned up under expert supervision and help from the Wolf (Harvey Keitel).

The film comes full circle as Vincent and Jules are having breakfast at the same coffee shop which Pumpkin and Honey Bunny are holding up. After a convincing speech about his newfound spirituality, Jules and Vincent walk away with the mysterious briefcase and return it to Marcellus.

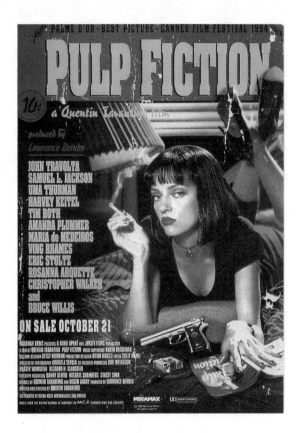

As the title implies, *Pulp Fiction* takes its inspiration from the popular, and often grisly, cheaply printed—and illustrated—crime fiction of the thirties and forties. After the success of *Reservoir Dogs*, Tarantino decided to return to an old idea he'd had about writing three different stories, using the same characters, moving them in and out of these stories, and to have it all work together in one movie. "The idea behind *Pulp Fiction*," said Tarantino, "was to take the oldest situations in the book, the one's you've seen a zillion times—the boxer who's supposed to throw a fight and doesn't, the mob guy who's supposed to take the boss's wife out for the evening. The third story, 'The Wolf,' is basically the first five minutes of every Joel Silver movie. Two hit men come and kill these guys, and then cut to Arnold Schwarzenegger a hundred miles away, and eventually the other stories converge."

As in *Reservoir Dogs*, there is a sort of timelessness about

Shoot to kill
. . . John
Travolta and
Samuel L.
Jackson in
Tarantino's
violent mas-
terpiece *Pulp
Fiction.*
(Miramax
Films)

the look and feel of the film; putting aside contemporary refer-
ences, the story could have easily taken place in any era. It's that
peculiar style—as well as the narrative structure, the offbeat dialogue, and the dark humor—that makes *Pulp Fiction* enjoyable
despite the nonstop violence. The scene in the car during which
Vincent accidentally shoots a black kid who is sitting in the
backseat presented a problem for John Travolta. "That scene to
me was the hardest part of saying yes to the project. In the original script, I shoot the guy once in the throat and he's still alive,
so I have to shoot him in the head to put him out of his misery.
Then we worry about the mess. It was the scene most like the
torture scene in *Reservoir Dogs,* and I didn't think it was going to
be funny." In the film, Vincent shoots the kid only once and kills
him instantly. Another most-talked-about scene precedes the
sequence in the car and has Travolta jamming Uma Thurman in
the chest with a giant hypodermic needle. "That's actually my
favorite sequence as far as the reaction I've had so far, because
you have half the theater giggling like hell and the other half div-
ing under their seats," Tarantino said. "That's really cool."

The challenge with *Pulp Fiction* was to top *Reservoir Dogs*
but also not to disappoint the audience's expectation. Tarantino
was in the same position as Martin Scorsese after *Taxi Driver.*

Also of concern was the level of violence in the film, which, by the time it was released, had become a publicist's play for getting everyone to see the film. For Tarantino, the dilemma was "Do I relish it [the violence] and want to go even further in that direction? Or do I say, I'm gonna show you what I can do with a bedroom comedy—same kind of dialogue, same basic movie, but without the violence? Well, I think you're kind of a fool going with either of those things." Tarantino apparently is not yet ready to do his *Age of Innocence*.

Pulp Fiction was very well received, even by critics who had felt uncomfortable with *Reservoir Dogs*. "When he offsets violent events with unexpected laughter," Janet Maslin wrote in the *New York Times*, "the contrast of moods becomes liberating, calling attention to the real choices the characters make. Far from amoral or cavalier, these tactics force the viewer to abandon all preconceptions while under the film's spell." David Ansen of *Newsweek* agreed that *Pulp Fiction* not only was a visual masterpiece but also had great depth of character: "It's not just the plot twists that surprise, or the startling outbursts of violence, or the deft way that the most grisly scene can explode into black humor. This is one crime movie that revels in the quotidian details of character."

Quentin Tarantino once pointed out that if you look at his films the violence in them almost follows the rules of the old Hays Code. "Violence was never a major issue in the old days of Hollywood. You could have as much violence as you wanted as long as the bad guy dies in the end or denounces his sins. The thing those films specialized in is what I specialize in when it comes to violence. It's not so much about graphic violence, but there's a brutality to it. When Raoul Walsh or Howard Hawks shot violence, it was brutal, man."

Violent Effects—An Interview With Greg Nicotero

"I wouldn't slaughter a character in one of my pictures without 'em," said *Evil Dead* director Sam Raimi of the three musketeers of special effects—Bob Kurztman, Greg Nicotero, and Howard Berger. Together they formed a company called KNB EFX Group, Inc., and have concocted some of the movies' most violent images, images one would be afraid to even try to conjure up.

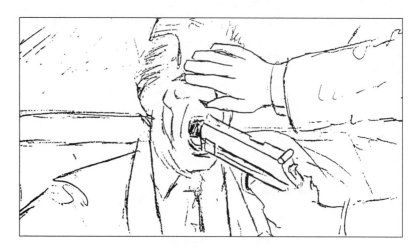

Greg
Nicotero's
storyboards
for *Pulp
Fiction*'s most
violent
scenes.

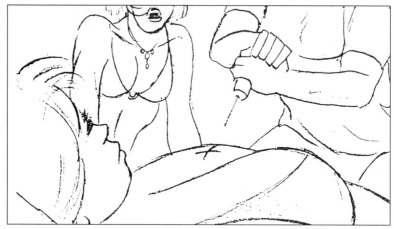

But it's their job and they're good at it. Actually, the first thing people probably remember about *Reservoir Dogs* is the ear-slicing scene, and if you mention *Pulp Fiction*, they'll say, "The scene when Uma Thurman ODs and Travolta stabs her with a needle, wasn't that cool?" At the same time, what we saw on the screen—as well as what had to be cut out to obtain an R rating—came from KNB. Of course, it's all make-believe, and yet KNB's contribution to these movies has had an incredible impact on audiences, causing some people to rush out of the multiplexes. In fact, their effects have made these movies ultraviolent.

Laurent Bouzereau: Could you describe how you designed the violence in *Reservoir Dogs*?

Greg Nicotero: Our association with Quentin Tarantino was actually very interesting; my partner Bob Kurtzman wanted to have a script written, and a mutual friend introduced us to Tarantino. A script entitled *From Dusk Till Dawn* was eventually written. It almost was a kind of a gag when Quentin said to Bob, "Well, fine, I'll write the script for you for *X* amount of dollars, but when my movie *Reservoir Dogs* gets going, you'll have to do the effects for free." It was sort of a tradeoff. We were in the middle of doing *Army of Darkness* [1993] when Quentin called and said, "*Reservoir Dogs* is going, and you guys have to come and do it." Of course the [*Dogs*] producer was saying, "You're going to do it for free; Quentin said you'd do it for free." Ultimately, we made a deal that we were all happy with and sat down with Quentin and went through the script. There were several "gags" that they had asked us to do. One of them was the girl getting shot in the car by Tim Roth; they wanted her to get shot in the throat. We made an appliance to actually spread the blood out of her neck. The main thing I like about Quentin, who is very much like John Carpenter and Martin Scorsese, is that he wants flexibility built within his effects. You read the script, and you prepare the effect, but once you get on the set, you're at the whim of the director. . . . So on *Reservoir Dogs* we learned that Quentin Tarantino needed flexibility. Anyway, we built this throat appliance; subsequently, I don't think you really see anything in the film. Then we gave them a couple of dummies for the scene when one of the characters shoots two cops in a car; they just squibbed the shit out of them. The main effect was the torture scene with Michael Madsen. I went down when they were rehearsing the film. I met the actors, including the guy who got his ear cut off by Madsen, and I watched them "block" the scene. I remember thinking how horrifying that scene was. We made a two-piece appliance; one of them was glued over the real actor's ear, and we would blend it with a hairpiece. The second piece was an ear that could be easily sliced up from the other part. Quentin said he wouldn't show the actual cutting of the ear, but we built it that way so that he would have the flexibility to show it or not. Quentin and I also discussed another gag and the possibility of a shot between Michael Madsen's legs looking at Tim Roth and squibbing his feet. You know, like in Peckinpah's *Straw Dogs* [1971]. Ultimately, he didn't need that shot. With *Reservoir Dogs*, it was very much cut-and-dry, no pun intended. I just remember them calling from the set, saying: "We need more blood!" And we would say: "But we just gave you five gallons yesterday. . . ." They'd reply: "We need more!"

LB: What is the blood made of?

GN: The blood is made of red and yellow powdered food coloring and Karo syrup. But the way that Quentin had scripted it, we had real-time blood and flashback blood. He actually wanted the real-time blood to have a different color than the flashback blood. It's something that doesn't really come out in the film, but when we were shooting, there was a real important difference. He wanted to have a "cartoony" quality for the flashbacks; we put more white in it. What's amazing is that the two little pieces of rubber we used in the ear-cutting scene sent people out of the theater. The impact is incredible, and it shows how powerful people's imagination is, because you don't really see Michael Madsen slicing up the ear. The effective part is that Madsen walks into the frame holding the ear.

LB: You said people were shocked by the violence in that scene. What kind of effect did it have on you?

GN: It doesn't affect me that way because my trained eye notices things that other people may not see. Too often, being in the film industry has ruined going to the movies for me. On the other hand, there are times when screen violence really upsets me, like the opening of *GoodFellas* [1990], when they stab the guy in the trunk and shoot him. I didn't expect it; also, the sound of the knife was what really shocked me. I felt I had just witnessed a real murder. Of course, with shows like *Cops* on TV, we're getting

to see real dead bodies, so when we go to the movies, it doesn't seem as disturbing.

LB: Tell me how you designed the scene in *Pulp Fiction* when Uma Thurman ODs and John Travolta stabs her in the chest with a syringe.

GN: In our meeting, I said we should do a reverse shot where you take the syringe without the needle and you put it on Uma's chest and you yell, "Action!" and you pull it away. Then you reverse the film and you get this incredible blow and impact. But that was never shot. If that shot had been in the film, it would have been cut out, anyway, to get an R rating. I "storyboarded" all the scenes we were going to work on to find out from Quentin what he intented to see and what we needed to build. With the needle scene, we could have done it in different ways; we could have done it with a retractable needle; we could have done it with a dummy torso or with a reverse shot. Basically, for that scene, we designed a bunch of torsos that we could stab and an appliance that Uma wore on her chest. What's interesting is that when we got on the film we were told to be prepared that none of our work would end up on the screen. A lot of it was shot specifically so that they would have stuff to cut out to give to the ratings board. It happens a lot; that's why most of the time we shoot a bloody version and a nonbloody version. The ratings board has problems with blood. If it was blue blood, it wouldn't be a problem, like with *Evil Dead 2* [1987]; we had black blood, green blood, orange blood, etc. . . . . Also, if you're dealing with an alien or a monster, you can kill it all you want. In *Interview With the Vampire* [1994], Tom Cruise gets his throat slashed and lies in a pool of blood, but it doesn't matter because he is a vampire. If he had been a human character, that scene would have never made it to the screen. If you see blood gushing out as opposed to blood on a character's shirt, for instance, then that's also a big issue in terms of the ratings board.

LB: What other scenes did you work on in *Pulp Fiction*?

GN: There was the rape scene that in itself was one of the most hideous scenes in the movie. We had initially talked about doing a couple of things; we were going to have Butch slice the rapist's chest and then stab him. Ultimately, that stuff didn't end up in the film. I found out that, for Quentin, the physical violence is not as important as the actors' performances, anyway. Certain directors would want to show everything, but not him. Still, that scene is quite violent because the way that effects work is that less is always more. What was driving the film was the characters' reactions to the violence, not violence itself.

LB: Tell me about the scene in the car during which John Travolta accidentally shoots a kid who is sitting in the back.

GN: That's one of my favorite scenes in the movie. Originally, in the script, Travolta shot him, but the guy wasn't dead. Finally Travolta decided to put him out of his misery, put the gun in his mouth, and shot him a second time. We were going to show the head explode for the ratings board. I liked that scene because they don't shoot him once like in the film; they shoot him twice. When we were on the set, Quentin decided to only shoot him once. We blew up the head with an air mortar. An air mortar is like a scuba tank placed in the dummy head with a big funnel;

we would fill the funnel with fake blood, oatmeal, chunks of latex, etc. . . . and you push a button, it opens up a valve and blows all the stuff out. So what you get is an instantaneous blood splat on the back window of the car. We did it three times! But you see, they had shot the scene with the actors first, and they had used a lot more blood. So we used another head and this time filled it up completely with nasty stuff; we squibbed it and blew the hell out of it. Then we made a full body dummy of the guy who got shot that was used in the trunk of the car and which you see for a split second. I think it was actually an old dummy we had used in another film that we repainted for that shot.

LB: Do you do any kind of medical research when you have to design your effects?

GN: My background was premed college. My dad is a physician. I remember on the set of *Day of the Dead* [1985], which was my first movie, George Romero came to me and said, "We're gonna cut that actor's arm off, and we're going to cauterize it with a torch." I suggested, for instance, that we put a tourniquet on him first. I also created sixteen cadavers for the film *Gross Anatomy* [1989], which is about medical school. We did a film for HBO called *Citizen X* [1994] about a Russian serial killer, and the director wanted a year-decomposed body. So we did sketches and sent them off to my dad and to some medical advisers.

LB: Have you noticed any changes between the violence in the movies you grew up on in the seventies and the violence in films like *Pulp Fiction*?

GN: Basically, and I'm talking very generally, the people who get killed deserve it in today's movies. In *Pulp Fiction*, none of those people are good; they're all assholes. In the seventies, in slasher movies, for instance, innocent people were murdered. Today the villains get killed, and in a way, the violence that's done to them is justified.

LB: In 1996, *From Dusk Till Dawn* came out. KNB designed and created all the special makeup effects on the film; it was written by Tarantino, based on a story by your partner Bob Kurtzman and directed by Robert Rodriguez. The film stars George Clooney, Quentin Tarantino, Harvey Keitel, and Juliette Lewis. How do you feel about the film?

GN: I think that one of the most interesting things about *From Dusk Till Dawn* is that that the tone changes literally 180 degrees midway through the film. The first half of the film is a very intense horrific portrayal of two bloodthirsty killers on the run from the law. Their acts of violence are very real. . . . The second half of the movie makes a complete left turn, and when you have men and women morphing into these hideous vampire creatures the tone of the violence is completely different—it's more of a slapstick, Sam Raimi–inspired type of film. Many people feel that the first half is more standard Tarantino, whereas the second half is more like *Night of the Living Dead* [1968]. And that's true.

LB: Robert Rodriguez, who directed *El Mariachi* in 1992 and *Desperado* in 1995, shoots gunfights as if they were dance numbers. Do you think that his style in a sense makes the violence accessible and not really threatening? Would you compare him to Peckinpah, for instance?

GN: At the end of *The Wild Bunch*, when Ernest Borgnine and William Holden are being shot, Peckinpah used slow motion; their deaths are very dramatic. Robert's style is the exact opposite; it's fast editing and quick cuts and flashy shots and moody lighting. It's much more composed, much more choreographed in that respect than films like *The Wild Bunch* or any other films of Peckinpah. Robert loves editing. . . . He cuts his own movies.

LB: I think that the most violent scene in *From Dusk Till Dawn* is when we see this poor woman who was kidnapped by Tarantino and Clooney, dead, soaked in her own blood after the character played by Tarantino raped her and murdered her.

GN: I read a very interesting review in the *L.A. Weekly* where they felt that that was a flaw in the film; they thought that making Quentin's character a sex offender flawed the movie, but I disagree with that. To me, showing that side of Quentin's character allowed you to gather some sympathy for his brother played by George Clooney. It separated the two. George's reaction to the murder of the woman made him more sympathetic. That was actually not in the original script; it was added when Quentin started doing his rewrite.

LB: Do you find it objectionable that Clooney sort of becomes a hero at the end of the film?

GN: That's the way the world is. The world is not set up where the good guys always win and the bad guys always get punished. That's not the way things necessarily happen. George Clooney at the end is not really a hero; you want him to survive because everyone else, except for Juliette Lewis, has literally been slaughtered. And at the end of the movie, he even tells her, I may be a bastard but I'm not a fucking bastard, and he tries to redeem himself when he says to her, I can't take you with me, go off and start your life over again. Things are not always fair; sometimes good people get killed and the bad guys get away . . . Our society has always been that way. . . . Movies didn't create it.

John Woo

"After I saw [John Woo's] A Better Tomorrow *[1986], I went out and bought a long coat, and I got sunglasses, and I walked around for about a week dressing like [actor] Chow Yun-Fat. And to me that's the ultimate compliment for an action hero—when you want to dress like the guy."*

—QUENTIN TARANTINO

Although he's been making movies since 1973, Hong Kong director John Woo's reputation only began to grow in the United States in the last five years. Today he is regarded by many directors, such as Quentin Tarantino and Martin Scorsese, as the man who reinvented the action genre and redefined screen violence. In a Woo film bullets fly, people don't get shot at once or twice but hundreds of times, and all of it is shown in slow motion, from as many angles as possible. Woo, in many ways, takes over where Peckinpah left off. In his film *Hard Boiled* (1992), starring Chow Yun-Fat, who is to Woo what De Niro is to Scorsese, babies in a maternity ward are caught in a crossfire, and the hero shoots back with a gun in one hand and an infant in the other; that's a scene that you wouldn't find even in a *Rambo* movie. With a strong and ever-growing cult following and with the release of *Hard Target* (1992), Woo's first American movie, starring Jean-Claude Van Damme, some of the director's early pictures have surfaced in this country, including *The Killer* (1989) and *Bullet in the Head* (1990.) While the violence in

John Woo on the set of his first American movie, *Hard Target*, starring Jean-Claude Van Damme. (Universal Pictures)

his films is over the top and seems to have been inspired by comic books rather than by reality, Woo's movies always have heart and most often concern honor, friendship, loyalty, redemption, and love. The violent scenes are filmed like ballets, with the actors moving between bullets like dancers. For that reason, the violence seems surreal, almost cartoonish at times, and although Woo declares that he actually hates violence, the seed of his fascination with it goes back to his childhood. "When I was a kid, I saw a lot of it. My family was poor, and we lived in the slums. There were drug killings every day, and I remember two big riots where people died in front of our door, killed by the police. I want to use the violence in my films to send a message. I do not chase violence for its own sake but for the beauty of the idea. I also think we need some kind of hero. The hero is ourselves, not just someone who kills all the bad guys but someone who emphasizes how we might build up dignity."

It was inevitable that Woo sooner or later would come to America. Producer Jim Jacks decided to talk Universal Pictures into hiring Woo to direct *Hard Target*, a film about a man (Lance

Henricksen) who arranges an extra-special hunting expedition in which the prey is a human being. When a man is killed, his best buddy (Jean-Claude Van Damme) decides to avenge him. The studio at first was reluctant. In the action scenes of a John Woo movie, there are probably more people killed than in all the *Rambo* films combined. *The Killer* had had trouble with the MPAA. Even Woo's first movie *Young Dragon* (1973) had proved to be too much for Hong Kong's censorship board. "So the studio had to be convinced that I would take full responsibility for this [the amount of violence in *Hard Target*] and make sure John doesn't go too far," Jacks said. After Universal Pictures chairman Tom Pollock saw *The Killer*, he agreed to give Woo a "shot." But telling Woo to tone down the amount of violence—and the body count—in his film was like asking Woody Allen not to be funny. For one scene in *Hard Target*, Woo wanted more and more killers; Jim Jacks had to tell him: "John, we're in the middle of the bayou. Where are these people coming from? And we'll have to spend time killing them." Woo's style was definitely in the way. "Chinese heroes can be as ruthless as the villains," he explained. "Here [in the United States] the hero and the villain confront each other, and if the villain runs out of bullets, the hero can't shoot him. He has to wait for the villain to pick up a knife or a club."

When *Hard Target* was shown to a test audience, people laughed; they didn't seem to understand Woo's style, either, which turned out to be too sophisticated and too complicated for such a film. To add insult to injury, when it was first submitted to the MPAA, it received an NC-17, which made it commercially unreleasable in the United States. "This poor man has never dealt with anything like this before, and with this ratings-board problem he's a bit bewildered by the whole thing," Jim Jacks told *Daily Variety*. "He's made a set of cuts, but the board felt that wasn't enough yet, and he's making another set of cuts right now. I don't think it's the amount of blood but, rather, the number of deaths."

John Woo was frustrated with the whole process; in Hong Kong, the censorship board always explains where the problem is. Woo feels that over there they respect his style, his work, and never want to destroy his vision. But on *Hard Target*, the MPAA would not explain anything to the director; the feedback was at best vague. "So we did it [the cutting] by guessing," Woo said. "The sixth time, [one of them] told me, 'I don't like violence! I don't like it!' I was mad. You don't like it, don't go to the movie! They don't care about your purpose, what your real idea is for the action. My kind of action is like a ballet, like a dance scene. They didn't care. I really learned a lesson from that."

In 1996, Woo's action film *Broken Arrow*, starring John Travolta and Christian Slater, was a smash at the box office . . . but did not deliver much punch on the screen. In fact, the violence in the film is so tame that one wonders *who* really directed the picture: Woo or the studio? Could it be that after getting his wrist slapped on *Hard Target*, Woo has decided to compromise his vision? It certainly seems like it . . . or maybe Woo is just waiting for a better tomorrow.

Luc Besson

Like John Woo, French director Luc Besson has been a household name in his country for many years but has only recently reached a mainstream American audience with *The Professional* (1994). His earlier film *La Femme Nikita* (1990) was a mild success in the United States and was remade by John Badham as *Point of No Return* (1993), starring Bridget Fonda.

La Femme Nikita is about a junkie (Anne Parillaud) who is sentenced to death after a bloody shoot-out. Although she is officially "dead," she is, in fact, being brainwashed and trained by a secret government agency to become a political assassin. "*Nikita* explores a hard, dirty world," explains Luc Besson. "In our world, man can do good, but he invariably chooses to be evil. *Nikita* is the story of someone who commits an extreme and irreversible act and is trying to move on to redeem herself and start over. But life is never that simple or clear-cut—we never stop paying for the things we do. We can never wipe the slate clean and turn the dial back to zero." And Nikita does pay a high price for her freedom. But at the same time, by becoming an assassin, she finds a way to exorcise the senseless violence she committed in the past through violence put to good use, or so she thinks. When she falls in love with Marco (Jean-Hugues Anglade) and discovers that violence is not the only form of communication, she realizes that she is trapped by the organization that has transformed her into a perfect killing machine. Her only way out is to disappear. "I definitely wanted the first twenty minutes to be very violent in order to prove that the only answer, the only way to escape violence, is love," Besson claimed. "I know that seems simplistic. To me it is the best answer."

Hong Kong director John Woo is regarded by many as the man who reinvented the action genre. . .

. . .and redefined screen violence.

A similar message prevails in *The Professional.* Stansfield (Gary Oldman) is a corrupt Drug Enforcement Administration boss whose thugs slaughter a young girl's entire family in a drug deal gone awry. Her trashy mother is shot in her bath, the slutty older daughter is shot in the hallway, the abusive dad is riddled

Whoever said the French couldn't kick ass? Director Luc Besson has proved they can in *La Femme Nikita* and *The Professional.* (Gaumont)

with bullets as he crawls on the floor, trying to escape, and the innocent baby brother is also killed—but we're spared the sight of his murder. The girl, Matilda (Natalie Portman), finds refuge with her next-door neighbor, Leon (Jean Reno), who happens to be a "cleaner," a paid assassin.

Leon and Matilda develop a father-daughter relationship; Matilda opens Leon's eyes to the world—he is a loner who lives completely removed from society, and she hopes to learn his killing skills in order to avenge the murder of her baby brother. (She doesn't seem to care about the rest of her family.) In the end, Leon takes matters into his own hands and only half succeeds when he is killed, along with Stansfield.

The violence in *The Professional* is almost relentless: "It [violence] is an undeniable part of life," Besson declared. "I am the type who won't harm a fly, and I'm very forgiving. But if somebody in the street tries to knock down my daughter, I would kill the guy in five seconds. I try to be a normal human being, but I'm a beast on this part. And in that way, of course, everyone is like me. We can't forget that the genetic things inside us are much, much older than the Ten Commandments. I wanted to explore a story that has this dark beast in it, but that is very much about becoming more human, less beastly." With *The Professional*, Besson wanted to make the violence extremely graphic and visually stylistic so that the innocence and beauty of the relationship between Leon and Matilda would be magnified. Using the example of *Gone With the Wind* and saying that if you removed the Civil War (more to the point, if you removed the violence) from the picture, the love story would seem rather dull, Besson also feels that screen violence loses its purpose when it isn't linked to a powerful story. "*Romeo and Juliet* is very violent, with two families who kill each other. It [the violence] gives more power to the love story."

Another critical issue in *The Professional* is the reaction of the young girl in the face of violence; she believes until the end that violence is the only answer to violence. One of the most intriguing moments in the film is when Matilda is doing target practice with Leon; she holds a rifle and shoots a man —with blank ammunition. Like Matilda, I felt completely excited when she hit her target. While some may conclude that *The Professional* sends a dangerous message, Besson argues that "a movie is a story, an invention. I think what you see on television is a lot worse in that sense because a lot of that violence is real. That's what's dangerous. Anyway, it's only adults who worry so much about all this—kids know there's a difference between movies and reality."

4

Mafia and Gangs

Scarface(s)

"Mr. Hays.
Dear Sir,
You are responsible for the morality of our films. Such pictures as Little Caesar and other gang pictures are more destructive to the morality of the people and the civilization of our country than any other single force today. The public expects you to censor these movies as well as the characters of stars."

This letter was sent anonymously to Will Hays, who was then head of the ratings board, on February 17, 1931. So when producer Howard Hughes and director Howard Hawks proceeded to make *Scarface* (1932), their gangster epic loosely based on the life and times of Al Capone, starring Paul Muni as Tony Camonte, the censors were extremely worried about the movie's repercussions. It appeared that the film was the glorification of a villain and of his violent actions. It was also coming out at a time when movies such as *Little Caesar*

99

(1930) and *The Public Enemy* (1931) had been extremely controversial. As a consequence, there was a public outcry against violent movies, especially gangster pictures.

The Hays office asked Howard Hughes to remove many scenes and insert an antigun message in the picture and even suggested a whole new denouement which would have Muni being put on trial and hanged. When Hughes told Hays that Muni was doing a play and was unavailable for reshoots, Hays replied: "Get a double!"—and that's exactly what Hughes did. He complied with the story change.

The title also presented a problem: At one point the film was called *Yellow*. (Without his guns, our villain turns yellow, a cringing, pleading rat.) Finally, the film was released as *Scarface, the Shame of a Nation,* with the ending showing Tony going "yellow" and getting killed by the police while attempting to escape. But the film ran a disclaimer after the opening credits:

> This picture is an indictment of gang rule in America and of the callous indifference of the government to this constantly increasing menace to our safety and our liberty. Every incident in this picture is the reproduction of an actual occurrence, and the purpose of this picture is to demand of the government: "What are you going to do about it?" The government is your government. What are *you* going to do about it?

When the film came out, Howard Hughes fought and threatened to bring to trial anyone who had the power to impose local censorship on the film. Released in the midst of great controversy, *Scarface* reached cult status as the best screen portrayal of the gangster era. It had a high body count and shocked audiences with its realistic depiction of crime and violence.

If there had not been Howard Hawks's *Scarface*, we would have been deprived of the De Palma 1983 version, written by Oliver Stone, which, like the original, became the center of controversy. Only this time the controversy was not riddled with bullets; it was drenched in blood.

May 1980: Fidel Castro releases 125,000 prisoners and sends them to Miami. They are all welcomed as survivors of communism, and the state provides them with money and homes. Tony Montana (Al Pacino) is among the refugees, and he quickly understands that drug dealing might offer a way for him to rise above his meager existence. After Montana's first successful but

dangerous mission, Frank Lopez (Robert Loggia), the king of
cocaine, takes him and his best friend, Manny (Steven Bauer),
under his wing. Tony has only one wish, and that is to have "the
world and everything in it," including Elvira (Michelle Pfeiffer),
Lopez's gorgeous girlfriend. Lopez finds out that Montana wants
to take over his kingdom and tries to eliminate him. He fails, and
Tony shoots Lopez in return. Alejandro Sosa (Paul Shenar), a
rich dealer, assigns Tony the mission of killing a delegate at the
United Nations who is determined to expose the drug connection.
But Tony refuses to carry out his mission when he realizes that
he will also have to murder the man's wife and children. Tony's
empire falls to pieces. He shoots Manny, who has secretly married Tony's sister, Gina (Mary Elizabeth Mastrantonio), for whom
he has always had incestuous feelings. Tony and Gina are savagely murdered by Sosa's elite killers, and thus ends the man
best known as Scarface.

"Look, you guys are going to have to fire me, and you can
finish the process yourselves. I think we are affecting the effectiveness of the film, and I won't work, and I don't care anymore,"
director Brian De Palma told Universal Pictures when his film
Scarface, which had been submitted four times to the MPAA, still
got an X rating. "For those who remember the original Howard
Hawks–Howard Hughes *Scarface* with Paul Muni," reporter Todd
McCarthy pointed out in an article for *Variety*, "a small irony
stems from the fact that each murder in that film was signified
with an X fashioned out of lightings and sets." He also pointed
out that the original classic was the subject of intense pressure
for deletions and was banned or cut in many cities and states.
Fifty years later, history was repeating itself, and the X marking
that was imposed on the film by the MPAA also meant murder for
the filmmakers.

It had taken producer Martin Bregman three years to bring
Scarface to the screen. In his career he has produced *Carlito's
Way* (1993), also directed by De Palma, *Serpico* (1973), *Dog Day
Afternoon* (1975), and *Sea of Love* (1989), all starring Al Pacino.
The production was plagued by protests from Miami's Cuban
community, who claimed that the film portrayed Hispanics in an
unfavorable light. "Making a movie is like mounting a military
campaign. You want nothing coming suddenly from left field,"
Bregman later declared. "Demonstrations, that's what worried
me. How do you shoot a movie in a street with a demonstration
in progress? It's hard enough to do it with everybody's coopera-

tion. It angered me that nobody asked to see the script before they made judgments. When they did ask, I told them to go to hell." To avoid production delays and media circus, the filmmakers decided to shoot *Scarface* in Los Angeles. The first *Scarface* was also deemed ethnically offensive. The filmmakers and the board of censors received pressure from the Italian community.

When the 1983 film was finally finished, Brian De Palma reportedly received death threats from real-life mobsters. Then the MPAA refused to give the $23.5 million gangster movie an R rating. The board claimed the film was both excessively violent and filled with offensive language. "It is not excessive," De Palma insisted, referring to the violence in his film. "We previewed it, and no one walked out because of any violence—in fact, nobody walked out!" De Palma told the *New York Times* that *Scarface* was at best a middle-range R picture. Bregman said that the film's content wasn't even a hard R. What was the problem, then? This was not De Palma's first run-in with the censors. In 1980, *Dressed to Kill* had initially been slapped with an X rating. In order to get the commercially acceptable R, De Palma had had to tone down dramatically the sex and violence in the film.

The ratings board felt that the shoot-out at a club was too violent. De Palma was shocked by the verdict of the MPAA. He thought he had been extremely careful to avoid the use of explicit violence. But he had to keep cutting to satisfy the board. "We would fix one part, and then they would suddenly raise questions about another part that they'd never mentioned before. After the fourth submission, I said to Universal, This is crazy. It's hurting the movie aesthetically and commercially. I'm not doing any more cutting."

De Palma also accused Classification and Rating Administration chairman Richard Heffner of having a vendetta against him. "When *Dressed to Kill* came out, I gave an interview calling Heffner a censor, which he is. Since then he has had a personal vendetta against me." Heffner denied the accusation, saying that he didn't know De Palma enough to be angry at him or to have a vendetta against his work. "Nothing could be further from the truth," Heffner said in regard to the director's accusation. "I appreciate the publicity value of attacks on the mean old censor. But we rate films, not filmmakers. On the invisible scale that we carry in our heads, we felt *Scarface* deserved something stronger than an R. The accumulation of violence and language was just too much. We consider ourselves responsible to parents, and we

didn't think many parents would cheer us for giving this film an R rating." De Palma thought Heffner just wanted him to bend down; the director even received support from critic Roger Ebert, who said that Heffner had a personal ax to grind against the filmmaker.

Producer Martin Bregman pointed out that the MPAA also objected strongly to the word "fuck" and other harsh, sexually charged expletives. There were more than 180, the MPAA claimed. "You go to a playground in New York City and listen to the nine-year-olds," Bregman told Julie Salamon (*Wall Street Journal*). "You'll hear some words. A kid going to this movie isn't going to go out and contact his local cocaine dealer. We painted that world as bad as it is." Curiously, Jack Valenti, president of the MPAA and chairman of the appeals board, told *Newsweek* at the time that he'd want his fifteen-year-old daughter to see *Scarface* because it was an antidrug film.

Robert Rehme, who was then president of Universal's theatrical motion-picture division, declared that under no circumstances would the studio release *Scarface* with an X. Alan Friedberg, the president of the Sack Theaters chain in Boston, said that the situation with *Scarface* proved the need for an "M for Mature" or "A for Adults" rating. Friedberg agreed that the film was violent and strong but argued that there was no reason to put it in the same category as a porno movie.

With the film scheduled to open on December 9, 1983, in approximately one thousand theaters, the situation had to be sorted out quickly. An appeal was scheduled for November 8, after both De Palma and Bregman said that there would be no further cutting. Actually, Bregman had been so certain that *Scarface* would receive an X despite the changes De Palma had already made that he had arranged for the appeal before the final verdict reached him. De Palma was thrilled. If they won the appeal, the moviegoers would see what the MPAA considered an X, and the filmmaker was convinced that everyone would agree that the film didn't deserve one. On the other hand, if the film-maker lost the appeal, Universal would either have to accept the X or recut the film, against De Palma's wish.

The appeal was heard by a board consisting of about twenty theater owners, studio executives, and independent distributors. The version the board watched was the second of the different versions edited by the filmmakers, which, De Palma claimed, was hardly different at all from the first cut. *Time* magazine film critic Jay Cocks read to the board a letter he had written to Brian De Palma which argued that *Scarface* did not deserve an X rating. He was followed by Maj. Nick Novarro of Broward County, Florida, who stated that the situations depicted in *Scarface* were true to life. Martin Bregman later declared that there was not one scene in *Scarface* that hadn't been pulled out of police files. The chain-saw scene, for example, not only really happened, but there were even more victims involved. Novarro said that there was a need for movies like *Scarface* and insisted that young people should see it because "it shows the ugliness behind the drug trade."

This time, however, the appeals board said that Heffner and the CARA members were wrong; seventeen out of twenty board members voted in favor of overturning the X rating. De Palma was ecstatic and claimed that if he had lost the appeal on *Scarface*, he would have taken a lawsuit all the way to the Supreme Court. He argued that an X rating prohibited parents from taking their own child to see a movie. "That seems to me illegal. I spoke to a lawyer who suggested that if I were to bring a lawsuit against the rating system I might win. It's restraint of trade." Despite the victory, Bregman was still angry, saying that the ordeal had cost the studio a lot of money and that prints hadn't gone out because of the delays in getting the proper rating for the film. At the same time, some outsiders said that the decision to give *Scarface* an R rating was purely for economic reasons; the verdict had been given by the appeals board, which, unlike CARA, was composed of industry people. "I'm not naive about the composition of the appeals board," Richard Heffner told the New York *Daily News.* "But since I took over the rating board in 1974, we've rated 3,500 films. The studios have had an economic interest in all of those films, and yet our ratings have only been overturned a few times."

In any case, what audiences saw was basically the first cut of the film. Did the controversy over cutting or not cutting *Scarface* help the film? Did it give the filmmakers more publicity? According to Martin Bregman, there were still people who wouldn't go see the film because the MPAA had initially classified it X and they feared it would be too violent. For the most part, critics mentioned the battle over the rating of *Scarface* in reviewing the film and tried to decide whether or not it had been worthy of the dispute.

Richard Heffner, who believed that the filmmakers promoted their movie by attacking the rating systems, clarified a few points in an article for the *Wall Street Journal* by arguing that he and his "civilian" colleagues, as Heffner himself called them, did not classify movies in terms of what they found distasteful. "We are not moralists, critics, or cops." He also insisted that just because a film was true to life, parents weren't required to expose their children to these realities. "And thanks to the industry's self-imposed rating system," the *Journal* article concluded, "they don't have to. Which is, I firmly believe, just why we don't have censorship in this country!"

Some critics found the movie over the top and too long; others found it entertaining *because* it was over the top. *Scarface* had created a lot of brouhaha because of the fights with the MPAA over the violence; when the smoke cleared, many critics acknowledged the intensity of the film but didn't think that it was more violent than your average gross-out horror flick. "Is *Scarface* as violent as its reputation?" David Ansen wrote in *Newsweek.* "Yes and no. The violence is constant (as are the four-letter words), the body count is astronomical, the infamous chain-saw scene unnerving. But De Palma doesn't linger on gore. Any recent horror film is more graphically grisly. If *Scarface* makes you shudder, it's from what you think you see and from the accumulated tension of this feral landscape."

Indeed, how many of us think we actually saw the chain

saw slicing up the victim in the bathroom of the motel? The combination of the sound and the close-up of the blood splattering in Tony's face as he is forced to watch his companion being tortured and killed led us to believe we saw more than we actually did. There were many other violent moments in the film; beatings, hangings, shootings, you name it. At the same time, this was *Scarface*, a gangster movie, and it required that much violence to convey a vivid and arresting portrayal of that world. But as producer Martin Bregman put it, the film was ahead of its time, and *Scarface* did not become a blockbuster, although today it has reached cult status. Its chain-saw sequence has become almost as notorious as the shower scene in *Psycho*.

Seven years after *Scarface*, De Palma directed a film version of *The Untouchables* (1991); aimed at a mainstream audience, the film was not as violent as it could—or should—have been, and neither was De Palma's *Carlito's Way* (1993), which reunited him with producer Martin Bregman and Al Pacino. However, there is in *The Untouchables* a scene worth mentioning for its extreme brutality. It shows Al Capone (Robert De Niro) at a banquet, standing up and giving a speech to his fellow mafiosos about team spirit. As the speech goes on, we understand that one of the guests has not been a good team player. Capone grabs a baseball bat and cracks the skull of the traitor; blood spurts out on the other guests, and in De Palma's grand style, the camera rises from above the table as the victim's blood pours out across the white tablecloth.

The Corleone Saga

To some, *The Godfather* (1972) can be considered that day's answer to *Gone With the Wind*. While this might overstate its status, Francis Coppola's film version of Mario Puzo's bestselling novel certainly marked an important moment in film history and in the acceptance of on-screen violence.

The Godfather follows the saga of the Mafia's Corleone family, headed by Don Vito Corleone, played by Marlon Brando. The story begins in 1945 with the wedding of Corleone's daughter Connie (Talia Shire). There we meet his sons, Michael (Al Pacino),

Sonny (James Caan), and Fredo (John Cazale), and his legal adviser and adopted son, Tom Hagen (Robert Duvall). Corleone is approached by a rival family, the Tattaglias, to join them in the sale of narcotics to America. Corleone refuses and is later shot by a gunman. He survives, but his son Michael avenges his father and kills the two men responsible for the shooting. With his life now at risk, Michael is sent to Italy, where he meets and marries a beautiful young woman. Unfortunately, he is betrayed, and his wife is killed by a car bomb intended for him. After a rival family war takes the life of Sonny Corleone, a peace is negotiated by the five Mafia families. Michael returns to America to serve at the right hand of his father. After Vito dies, Michael brutally attacks the heads of the other families and consolidates his empire in an orgy of bloodletting.

The most violent moment in *The Godfather* is, without a doubt, Sonny's assassination. He dies à la Bonnie and Clyde when he is ambushed at a highway tollbooth and is riddled with machine-gun bullets. This scene was shot in one take. About

Bulleted . . .
James Caan
in Coppola's
Godfather.
(Paramount)

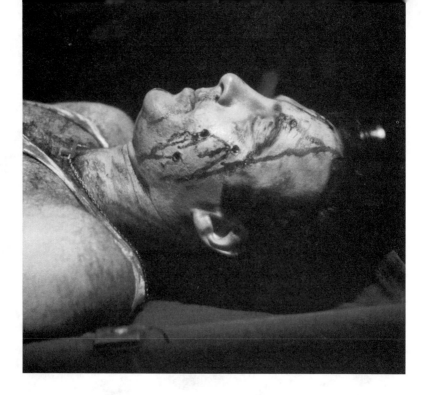

110 brass casings containing gunpowder squibs, and packets of blood were rigged on actor James Caan's body, face, and hair. His car had about two hundred predrilled holes filled with squibs that detonated during the attack. Other scenes of extreme violence in *The Godfather* showed actor Lenny Montana's hand impaled by a knife and his eyes popping out as he is being garroted and Michael Corleone shooting a police officer right between the eyes. In another, "Mo" Green is shot in the eye right through his glasses. Ironically, Don Corleone gets to die peacefully while playing with his grandson amid tomato plants. (Two truckloads of plants were provided for this poignant scene!)

Another memorable shock occurs when Hollywood producer Woltz (John Marley) wakes up one morning and discovers the head of his beloved horse in his bed. Initially, makeup artist Dick Smith was going to use a fake head for the scene, but the result looked phony. A real head was obtained from a slaughterhouse in New Jersey; after it was used for the scene, it was packed and sent to the SPCA. Apparently that scene had people more outraged than any other violent moments in the film; after all, many characters are shot, garroted, and blown up in the course of the movie, but still the audience was most revolted by the horse's cruel death. "People are more upset by the death of animals than they are about the death of human beings," Coppola complained.

Most critics loved the movie; it was instantly perceived as a masterpiece despite the fact that it was an extremely violent film whose central characters are Mafia murderers. Vincent Canby wrote in the *New York Times* that *The Godfather* was "one of the most brutal and moving chronicles of American life ever designed within the limits of popular entertainment." Judith Crist, on the other hand, found the movie reprehensible: "*The Godfather* is as 'good' as the novel—and as essentially immoral—and therefore . . . far more dangerous. . . . The whole function of the film is to show us that Hitler is a grand sort of family man, gentle with children." So, even though the film set box office records and became an instant classic, it is still seen as an ethnic slur by some members of the Italian-American community.

The Godfather received ten Oscar nominations and won for Best Picture, Best Actor (Marlon Brando), and Best Screenplay (adaptation by Mario Puzo and Coppola). Despite this amazing success, Coppola initially had no interest in directing a sequel and even suggested to Paramount Pictures that Martin Scorsese replace him. Then the studio made him an offer he couldn't refuse; $1 million—which, in 1974, was a substantial figure. With *The Godfather, Part II*, Coppola did the impossible and made a film more successful than the original. The continuing saga focused on the life of Michael Corleone but also looked back at Don Vito Corleone's early days (with Robert De Niro in the role). The film received Oscars for Best Picture, Best Director, Best Supporting Actor (Robert De Niro), Best Screenplay (Puzo and Coppola), Best Score (Nino Rota and Carmine Coppola), and Best Art and Set Decoration (Dean Tavoularis, Angelo Graham, and George R. Nelson). It was followed sixteen years later by *The Godfather, Part III* (1990) in which an aging Michael Corleone tries to remove himself from the world of crime but is inevitably sucked back in. Although not as well received as the two previous films, it did get some unusual attention when, in Valley Stream, New York, two groups of teenagers shot at one another on opening night. The fight killed one teenager caught in the crossfire, while one other and two adults were wounded. And in Manhattan a man was slashed in the face during the showing of the film after an altercation with several other men.

For those interested in numbers—and for the record, twenty-three characters died (virtually all violently) in *The Godfather*, sixteen died in *The Godfather, Part II*, and more than twenty-one died in *The Godfather, Part III.*

In *The Godfather Companion* author Peter Biskind pointed out a strange "life imitating art" event which took place at the same time *Part III* was being completed: Marlon Brando's thirty-two-year-old son Christian shot to death his pregnant sister's boyfriend. He declared at the time that she had confessed to him that her boyfriend abused her physically. In *The Godfather*, a fistfight between Sonny Corleone and sister Connie's boyfriend occurs under similar circumstances. Marlon Brando was quoted as saying that, like the character of Sonny Corleone, his son Christian "always had a very bad temper and could be explosively violent when angry."

GoodFellas and Casino

"**W**hen you see the violence, it should be shocking," said Nicholas Pileggi, cowriter of *Good-Fellas*, with Martin Scorsese, and author of the book *Wiseguys*, which inspired the film. "Some books and movies have made violence an acceptable form of behavior. It is not in my book or in this movie." *GoodFellas* is the true story of Brooklyn hood Henry Hill as he told it to Pileggi while in the Witness Protection Program. We follow Henry (Ray Liotta) from his early days in Brooklyn in the mid-1950s, when he is taken under the wings of Mafia leader Cicero (Paul Sorvino) and meets other mafiosos, including his hero James (Jimmy) Conway (Robert De Niro) and psychopath Tommy DeVito (Joe Pesci), through the 1980s, when Hill is incarcerated. The film is often brutal, especially in its beginning, with De Niro and Pesci "whacking" (murdering, in gangster parlance) someone in the trunk of a car who they thought was already dead; Pesci stabs him with a huge kitchen knife, and De Niro shoots him. The scene is shown twice in the course of the film, the second time in slow motion. There's also a scene when Pesci (who received an Oscar for Best Supporting Actor) goes ballistic and shoots a kid in cold blood. There are many beatings and deaths and lots of blood. The smell of violence hangs throughout the film, but Scorsese explores this sordid real-life

Mafia family saga with both irony and humor, which make *GoodFellas* fascinating. Although the film was generally well received, it greatly upset the Italian-American community. It felt that the film was cruel, ruthless, and inaccurate and demanded that Warner Bros., the distributor of *GoodFellas*, ban the movie altogether. That idea was, of course, "whacked."

In 1995 Martin Scorsese again teamed with Nicholas Pileggi to write a film entitled *Casino*, loosely based on Frank "Lefty" Rosenthal, a casino manager who was banned from gaming after a series of public hearings. The film is about the rise of gambler Sam "Ace" Rothstein (Robert De Niro) in 1970s glittering and decadent Las Vegas. The story focuses on his romance with Ginger Mc-Kenna (Sharon Stone), and on his friendship with partner Nicky Santoro (Joe Pesci).

"*Casino*, in a nutshell, is about mob connections in Vegas; it's *GoodFellas* in Vegas," makeup artist Greg Nicotero said. "We did a scene where a guy's head is crushed in a vice. We made an appliance that the actor wore on his face with an air bladder underneath so that the eye could bulge out. We also did a fake head so that you could actually see it crush. Evidently, this sequence was quite controversial, and it was trimmed considerably because of ratings. We worked on a scene where Joe Pesci stabs a guy with a pen . . . we used a fake head for this particular shot. There's also a scene where they're torturing a guy and hold his arm down and smash it with a hammer. We put a hole in the table; the actor put his arm through the hole and we replaced it with a fake arm. Then there is the baseball-bat scene [during which Joe Pesci gets beaten up and thrown half-dead into a grave]."

Robert De Niro portrays gambler "Ace" Rothstein, whose romance with the alluring Ginger (Sharon Stone) ignites Martin Scorsese's *Casino*, a tale of greed and betrayal set in 1970s Las Vegas. (Universal Pictures)

How does Scorsese react to violence? Does he hold back, or is he concerned? "Not at all!" Nicotero said. "He kept saying: 'What can you do? Show me what we could do.' He was very enthusiastic about the effects we could create. For example, the dummy body we built of Joe Pesci, which is thrown in the grave, had arm movement, head movement, jaw movement. It had a bladder in the chest to fake breathing, and also there was a tube in the mouth so when they shovel dirt on the face, the tubes could blow dirt out of the mouth. I don't think Marty had ever worked with something so elaborate. He really went for broke. The way Scorsese shoots is that he pushes it as far as he can humanly push it. He wants it as intense as possible. I think his goal is to shock people into the brutality of it all, hoping that it will have a cathartic effect. If it's so horrible to watch, you'll never want to do it. All I know is that when they threw the two dummies in the grave and they started burying them and we were blowing into the tubes to make them breathe and move, I kept thinking to myself, this would be the most horrible way to die. . . ."

The Warriors

Beyond the somewhat glamorized world of gangsters and organized crime, there are gangs. More than any other ultraviolent movies, gang movies are a mirror of our society. The violence depicted in these films can be viewed every night on the six o'clock news. Some of these movies have even been accused of generating and inspiring gang violence on our streets . . . And *The Warriors* (1979), in a sense, started it all.

"These are the armies of the night. They are 10,000 strong. They outnumber the cops five to one. They could run New York City. Tonight they're all out to get The Warriors." Thus was promoted Walter Hill's study of gang violence in New York, which spawned more violence on the streets than any other film. In fact, the real-life events that it supposedly generated were more bloody than what was actually shown on-screen. The opening of the

"These are the armies of the night. They are ten thousand strong. They outnumber the cops five to one. They could run New York City. Tonight they're all out to get The Warriors." (Paramount)

113

movie introduces us to the nine leather-vested members of a Coney Island gang called the Warriors on their way to a gang convention in the Bronx. Hundreds have come to listen to a leader named Cyrus, who has declared a truce for the purpose of the

meeting. Cyrus wants all the gangs to march as one against the city; everyone seems to agree until Luther, a psycho who heads a gang named the Rogues, shoots Cyrus, creating a complete debacle. The Warriors are blamed for the shooting, and as they try to get back to Coney Island, they have to fight rival gangs who want to avenge Cyrus's death. The gangs communicate with each other through a call-in disc jockey and announce their plans to wipe out the Warriors with the song "Nowhere to Run." As the battle begins, our "heroes" fight against each individual gang on their turf and even have a close call with a gang of girls—the Lizzies. Most of the Warriors make it back to Coney Island. At that point, they have a final confrontation

Michael Beck and Deborah Van Valkenburgh . . . Warriors. (Paramount)

with the Rogues, and the truth about Luther having murdered Cyrus is revealed. He is killed, and the other gangs acknowledge that they were wrong to blame the Warriors. A rival gang leader declares, "You Warriors are good. Real good."

To maintain authenticity, the film was shot on location in Manhattan, Brooklyn, Queens, and Coney Island, and featured a cast of unknown actors. Scripted by Walter Hill and David Shater, it was based on a 1965 novel by Sol Yurich. The book was an update of Xenophon's account of how ten thousand Greek mercenaries fought their way across Persia in a long retreat to the sea in 401 B.C. The film followed the same theme and felt very much like an odyssey through gangland. It's almost as if the Warriors are being tested by the gods through a series of could-be-deadly tests. If they succeed, they'll achieve immortality.

Unavoidably, the production ran into some real gang-related problems. Hill, producer Larry Gordon, and executive producer Frank Marshall agreed at the outset not to use real gang members as extras. When the word about the film spread, real gangs got upset and put the filmmakers on the spot. Very quickly, Hill and company learned to basically remain calm and not confront the gangs.

Although actors were used, the movie looks authentic; at the same time, its Peckinpah-like style (the use of slow motion and quick editing in the fight sequences) presents its grim subject in a highly stylized fashion which makes the film fun to watch. In *The Warriors*, the violence operates at different levels. As *Time* critic David Denby pointed out, the violence depicted in the film "represents moral rather than physical strength."

Some reviews predicted that the movie would do well despite its nature. "As the first upcoming 'gang' pictures cycle, *The Warriors* offers audiences a taste of what's to come," *Variety* wrote, "bonecracking violence, dialogue consisting mostly of expletives, and an emphasis on the more degrading aspects of human nature. Under Walter Hill's forceful direction, the Paramount release should do well with the bare-knuckle crowd, along with those anxious about this subculture." The *Hollywood Reporter* was more sensitive to the message the film had about youth: "Hill maintains a taut feeling of violence to break through at any moment, but he also indicates the despair and frustration that restricts these young people." Inevitably, the violence was the issue: "Does the movie glorify violence?" Stephen Farber asked in his review of the movie in *New West*. "Of course, it does, but at least it doesn't try to deny this, as the sanctimonious gang movies of the fifties often did." But few could have predicted the violence that *The Warriors* would generate within a few days of its nationwide release.

It opened on February 9, 1979, in 670 theaters; by the middle of March, three young men had been killed by *Warriors*-inspired fights, and several other brawls had broken out at movie theaters showing the film across the country. The first killing took place on February 12 at a Palm Springs drive-in. There, a white girl attracted the attention of black gang members called the Blue Coats. When a white gang, the Family, came to her rescue, a shooting ensued, and a Family member was killed by a .22-caliber bullet. In Oxnard, California, an interracial fight involving more than twenty participants resulted in the stabbing death of a black teenager.

A third killing took place in Boston on February 15. On their way back from seeing the movie, several members of a white Dorchester gang apparently got into an altercation. At one point, someone yelled, "I want you!"—quoting the film—and one of the teens was attacked with a knife. He died six hours later. In the New York City area, rest-room plumbing was ripped out by vandals and seats were slashed in a movie theater showing *The Warriors.* A South Central Los Angeles citizens group demanded the recall of the film, claiming that it incited violence between black and white youths. The protest against the film took a larger scope when church and local citizen groups joined Dr. Ernest H. Smith, an L.A. pediatrician, and claimed that the film was dangerous to all Americans regardless of race or creed. A group of New York anticrime crusaders picketed a Times Square theater showing of the film. But box-office wise *The Warriors* was doing well, having grossed $4.7 million in six days.

After the first two incidents, Paramount Pictures offered to pay the security tab at any theaters in need of it, and *The Warriors* was pulled off the screen where crimes had occurred. "We just didn't anticipate this," said studio executive Gordon Weaver. "God knows we're sorry about what happened. We'll try to make sure to the best of our ability, and the ability of the theaters playing our film, that this won't happen again." One exhibitor had this to say about *The Warriors*: "This film is attracting a different kind of crowd, not your usual moviegoers. They're a little rougher and nastier than usual. Let's just say these aren't the people who go to see *The Goodbye Girl.*"

Within two weeks of the film's release, however, Paramount announced it was canceling its $100,000 *Warriors* ad campaign, which showed all the different gangs featured in the film posing together as one big "nasty" family, and told exhibitors they could halt their showing of the film if they feared it might generate violence. The studio was criticized at the time for banning its advertising of the film; some feared that a precedent was now established to block the distribution of certain movies. What was worse was that the precedent was being established by the distributor of the film itself! It was suggested that the problems had to be handled by the exhibitors, who, knowing their turf, had to make a judgment on whether or not to show certain movies in their theaters. "Why should I sacrifice this picture just because a few kids might rip up my seats?" one exhibitor said. "They do that any-ways on films that don't even make money. I can pay for my maintenance repairs out of the popcorn sales for this picture."

A new campaign was created that only carried the title of the film in the spray-can style followed by a line: "*The Warriors* can be seen in these theaters at these times." According to Paramount's Gordon Weaver, "the original ads gave the wrong identification to the movie." So the studio decided it was best to just give information, as opposed to hyping the film with a campaign. Paramount did not want to seem that it was in any way exploiting the situation; keeping a low profile became its policy.

Following the events in Boston, National Association of Theatre Owners (NATO) president A. Alan Friedberg and attorney Joseph Hurley, representing Paramount, defended *The Warriors* at a public hearing. "There is no causal relationship between movies and real life. Motion pictures are a mirror, a reflection of the real world in which we live. To change that is to change behavior of citizens. To pin it [the violence] on a movie or a TV show is begging the question. We're talking about demented people who would have done what they did, anyway." But views differed during the hearing, and Hurley came to the defense of the film, claiming that any action against the film would be a violation of the First Amendment. "If it was my boy who had been killed," Hurley said, "I'm sure I'd be here trying to blame something for it. That's understandable. It's human nature." Testifying at the hearing was one victim who was tortured and beaten for two hours by three men who had offered him a ride and who blamed it all on *The Warriors*.

Subsequently, Paramount was sued by the family of the Boston boy who was killed. After watching the film, the court rejected the family's argument that *The Warriors* was an incitement to violence and ruled that Paramount was not responsible for the death. "Although the film is rife with violent scenes," Justice Francis O'Connor said, "it does not at any point exhort, urge, entreat, solicit, or overtly advocate or encourage unlawful or violent activity on the part of the viewer. It does not create the likelihood of inciting or producing 'imminent lawless action' that would strip the film of First Amendment protection."

In March the U.S. Catholic Conference had given *The Warriors* a "Condemned" rating, meaning that the film was objectionable to Roman Catholics. In the fall of 1980, director Walter Hill had to fight another unexpected battle against the French distributor of the movie. Following a screening at the Deauville Film Festival in France, the distributor decided to abridge the early scenes depicting the gathering of the street gangs in the Bronx and their call to rise up and take over the city. Some of the battles were also edited. As a result, Walter Hill wrote a letter published in *L'Express*, the French equivalent of *Time* magazine:

Filmgoers of France:

The cuts made by the censor on *The Warriors* force me to reject all authorship of the version currently shown in Paris.

I don't wish to make a special plea for my motion picture. I simply wish to add my name to the long list that believes what can happen to one film can happen to all films: that believes when one freedom is abridged all freedoms are endangered: that believes censorship is an insult to the dignity of the individual and an insult to the idea of democracy. Walter Hill.

Boulevard Nights (1979), directed by Michael Pressman, took a look at Chicano teens in East Los Angeles and opened a month after *The Warriors* to similar incidents of violence. Executive producer (and onetime actor) Tony Bill said at the time that gang violence in Los Angeles happens all the time regardless of what movie is playing at the local theater. *Boulevard Nights* star Richard Yñiguez agreed and felt that the film had not been designed to incite violence, although there were unfortunately always people waiting to pick a fight, anyway.

Putting the 'Hood in Your Face

Dennis Hopper's *Colors* (1988) is about two cops (Sean Penn and Robert Duvall), members of the L.A.P.D.'s special unit CRASH (Community Resources Against Street Hoodlums), who are partnered against the mounting violence in Los Angeles. Producer Robert Solo conceived

Colors after making the film *Bad Boys* (1983) with Sean Penn. The actor became involved with developing *Colors*, which was initially written by Richard DiLello, who set the story in Chicago. When Dennis Hopper got involved, the script was rewritten by Michael Schiffer, and the setting was changed to Los Angeles. Robert Solo's goal with *Colors* was "social realism" in the tradition of *Blackboard Jungle* (1955). But the L.A.P.D. saw red when they heard of *Colors*. The police were upset by the idea of the film's being released, since they knew it depicted vivid scenes of gang violence and dealt with the rivalry between the Crip and Blood street gangs. In 1987

there had been 387 gang-related killings in Los Angeles County, and therefore the police had good reason to fear violent outbreaks between the different gangs at theaters showing *Colors*.

Colors . . . Director Dennis Hopper is surrounded by members of the "Crips" (real and extras) who display their gang sign language. (Orion Pictures, photo by Merrick Morton)

The film provoked two distinct reactions: Some felt it glorified violence, while others said it showed the stupidity of killing over a color (or gang insignia). In fact, there was nothing in *Colors* that gang members did not already know. Still, local officials tried to discourage exhibitors from showing *Colors*. Of course, Robert Solo was outraged: "The film is not a film that is going to stir someone to violence. More violence, perhaps, over the years has been stirred by horror movies and chop-shockery movies and ax-murder movies than anything like this."

Was Dennis Hopper worried? "Yeah, a little bit," the director declared at the time the film was about to be released. "The L.A.P.D. didn't want me using the real names of the gangs. But the gangs were happy we used their names. They felt it was authentic. If people come out of the theater saying, 'Hey, this isn't going on,' they're full of it." Meanwhile, the movie provoked protests from groups as divergent as the NAACP, the Los Angeles

County Sheriff's Department, and the Guardian Angels, who even demonstrated in front of Sean Penn's house. When the film finally opened, one theater owner put up a warning sign that said: If You Are Wearing Gang-Related Clothing, You Will Not Be Admitted. Yet, on opening weekend, *Colors* pulled in crowds, without heavy violence, despite one brief fistfight involving rival gang members in Culver City, California. Unfortunately, the peace was short-lived when, in late April 1988, a nineteen-year-old was killed in a gang-related shooting outside a theater showing *Colors* in Stockton, California.

Mario Van Peebles's *New Jack City* (with Judd Nelson and Ice-T) triggered many violent incidents across the country . . . (Warner Bros.)

The expression "New Jack" is used to describe a new mood and tone that dominates modern urban street life. Mario Van Peebles's *New Jack City* (1991) is about the rise and fall of American mobster and New Jack drug lord Nino Brown (Wesley Snipes). The film follows his life of crime and shows how drugs can help the underprivileged form a powerful criminal organization and a culture spawned by crack cocaine in the inner cities. The story was inspired by true stories of black gangsters, such as Oakland, California's Felix Mitchell, who organized a lucrative drug empire. Coscreenwriter Thomas Lee Wright was actually inspired to write the tale of a drug lord at the time he was hired to put together a draft of *The Godfather, Part III* and heard of drug kingpin Nicky Barnes, who ruled Harlem's heroin trade in the 1970s. Producers George Jackson and Doug McHenry then hired journalist-screenwriter Barry Michael Cooper, whose coverage of the New Jack phenomenon had caught their attention, to work on the story.

The film was well received: *Variety* wrote: "[The] picture's powerful antidrug sentiment will pack a punch with urban audiences fed up with violence and decay." But it also triggered a series of violent events and riots around the United States, including what was described as a "two-hour rampage" in Los

120

Angeles and the fatal shooting of a nineteen-year-old Brooklyn moviegoer.

When the media and some theater owners denounced the film for provoking violence in real life, *New Jack City*'s producers counterattacked: "Our film . . . is the latest example of the news media's tendency to deal with complex issues via headlines rather than analysis. In their reporting on the violence surrounding *New Jack City*, some elements of the news media have neglected to put each episode in context." According to the producers, the shooting of the nineteen-year-old stemmed from a housing-project rivalry, and the riots in Los Angeles, Las Vegas, Chicago, and Sayreville, New Jersey, erupted after the theaters' managers denied access to ticket holders. "Those who argue, as many have, that our film encourages viewers to imitate the violence they've seen on-screen are wrong," producers McHenry and Jackson stated. "The real cause of violence at the theaters is not cinematic images of drug culture but decades of poverty in our communities. Chronic unemployment, inadequate education, dilapidated housing, poor health care, a lack of public services, and an apathetic bureaucracy do not breed civility."

On the other hand, Mark Crispin Miller, a professor of media studies at Johns Hopkins University, told the *New York Times*, in connection with the events surrounding *New Jack City*, that "we've finally reached the point where screen violence is so graphic and extreme that spontaneous imitations like these are inevitable. The need to outdo competitors constantly has necessi-

. . . as did *Boyz N the Hood*, John Singleton's film about black youth and gangs in South Central Los Angeles. (Columbia Pictures)

tated a level of violence that certainly would have amazed people even as recently as ten years ago, but now has become routine for viewers." Whichever way we look at the problem, and as director Bill Duke (*A Rage in Harlem*, 1991) put it, "You won't find a black filmmaker in this country today who could honestly say he's confident this violence won't have any impact on the future of black filmmaking."

The title *Boyz N the Hood* (1991) was taken from a cut written by Ice Cube on the first album of rap group N.W.A. Written and directed by John Singleton, who grew up in South Central Los Angeles, *Boyz N the Hood* was shot there and is a realistic depiction of life in that neighborhood. The film focuses on three friends: Tre Styles (Cuba Gooding Jr.) and the two Baker brothers, Doughboy (Ice Cube) and Ricky (Morris Chestnut.) Tre tries desperately to escape a world of crime, decadence, and violence, while Doughboy is unable to pull himself away from gang life. On the set, three members of a South Central gang were hired as consultants. Among them was one young man confined to a wheelchair as a result of a shooting incident.

Although the film had an antiviolence message, *Boyz* triggered a spree of violence that left at least one person dead (a man was fatally shot after a midnight showing of the movie at a drive-in) and more than thirty wounded. Five people were shot in or near a theater complex in Universal City, California, and a crowd dispersing after a gunshot was fired in a theater in Minneapolis was then victimized by a drive-by shooting. Yet it didn't slow down business, and Columbia Pictures, the distributor of the film, agreed to pay for added security at theaters showing *Boyz*.

Excellent reviews acknowledged the talent of the filmmaker as well as the importance of the film's antiviolence message. "One in 21 black American males will be murdered at the hands of fellow black American males," *Hollywood Reporter* film critic Duane Byrge wrote. "That's the grim social frame of this turf-tough depiction of young black male survival in South Central Los Angeles. Written and directed by 23-year-old, first-time filmmaker John Singleton, *Boyz N the Hood* is a booming, heart slam of a film." And Roger Ebert (*Chicago Sun Times*) wrote: "It's not a gang film or action film but a tremendously life affirming story . . . not simply a brilliant directorial debut, but a film of enormous relevance and importance."

John Singleton was naturally upset about the violence that surrounded the release of his film, but he told the press that he was not responsible for any of it: "I didn't create the conditions in which people just shoot each other." According to him and to Steve Nicolaides, his producer, the violence was more an indication of the degradation of American society than a reflection on the film itself. "It is a society that breeds illiteracy, economic depravity, and doesn't educate its kids," Singleton declared, "and then puts them in jail. My film is about family, love, and friendship." In another interview, he pointed out that "the day we stop letting people make films about social issues is the day we'll have the Holocaust again."

Shortly after the (stormy) releases of both *New Jack City* and *Boyz N the Hood*, controversy surrounded the Paramount Pictures ad campaign for *Juice* (1992), a film directed by Ernest R. Dickerson, who received the highest acclaim as a cinematographer on such films as Spike Lee's *Malcolm X* (1992), *Jungle Fever* (1991), *Mo' Better Blues* (1990), and *Do the Right Thing* (1989). The movie is about four young hoods growing up in Harlem whose lives are shattered by crime and violence, and the original poster showed a picture of four expressionless black men, one of them holding a gun. The gun was airbrushed from the later poster. Accused of creating an irresponsible campaign for the film, Paramount declared that the decision to remove the gun was purely a creative decision and had not been done in fear that the weapon might incite violence.

Yet a *Hollywood Reporter* story quoted Jay St. John, an L.A.P.D. detective, as saying that the ads for *Juice* were "like waving a red flag in front of a bull." Charles V. Richardson, president of Tri-Ad Communications Group, a company that advises film companies on African-American marketing strategies, declared: "It [the ad] suggests to me a characterization of black male youths that in New York's current racial climate is of questionable value." Indeed, many felt that the poster, if placed on bus shelters and subway platforms, might convey the wrong message regardless of what the film was really about. But Barry Reardon, president of Paramount's Motion Picture Group/Worldwide Distribution, disagreed with this attitude and felt that the ad campaign did not communicate the wrong message: "If you don't market the picture in a way that's faithful to the finished product, you are going to attract an audience that is totally unprepared for this movie. This [*Juice*] is a tough, gritty film, and we have to represent it in an accurate and honest way." While the gun was airbrushed from the poster, the trailer for the film still showed killings, gunshots, and intense chase scenes.

In 1993 the U.S. Department of Justice published the following statistic: "Black youth make up 42 percent of the number of juveniles held in custody . . . while they represent only 16 percent of the U.S. population under age eighteen. A black youth between the ages of ten and seventeen is six times more likely to be charged with a violent crime than is his white counterpart—he is eight times more likely to be arrested for murder." With those numbers in mind, watching *Menace II Society* takes on a whole new meaning; in the film, young Caine (Tyrin Turner) is raised by his grandparents in a Watts housing project—his father was killed over a drug deal, and his mom died of an overdose. He finds himself implicated in the murder of a local grocer and sinks into a life of crime, as if doomed by his heritage. There seems to be a glimmer of hope that he might be able to escape his fate, but unfortunately, even with the best intentions, Caine's future will inevitably be soaked in blood.

Twin brothers Allen and Albert Hughes were raised in inner-city Detroit, and their mother tried to keep them away from gangs by buying them a video camera. Thus began their filmmaking careers. With *Menace II Society* (1993), the Hughes brothers wanted to make a movie that would shock audiences and force them to confront the reality of life in inner cities. This was not *Rambo,* where the public is charged by the violence and cheers at the screen. On the contrary, the Hughes brothers wanted the violence to force the audience to turn their faces away from the screen. Tyger Williams wrote the script, based on a story by him and the Hughes brothers. Although the film was shot on a shoestring budget, it was critically acclaimed. "Fierce, violent and searing in its observation, the film makes prior excursions seem like a stroll through the park," wrote Leonard Klady in *Variety.* "*Menace II Society*," David Hunter said in the *Hollywood Reporter,* "is the most brutal and affecting film yet to deal with the dead-end existence in the ghetto." The film is indeed violent and even had to be toned down in order to avoid an NC-17 rating; the MPAA deemed it too brutal and bloody and asked that three scenes showing bullet entry and exit wounds be either trimmed or completely cut out. The most violent incident surrounding the release of *Menace* involved the murder of a motorist by two teenagers who had supposedly been "hyped up" by watching the movie. They were arrested and sent to jail.

Twin brothers Albert and Allen Hughes, directors of *Menace II Society*. (New Line Cinema)

Films about gang and street violence in general generate good box office despite the fact that they do not always have stars and are made rather cheaply. Are these movies dangerous? Should they be censored? Dr. George Gerbner, dean of the Annenberg School of Communications at the University of Pennsylvania, pointed out, at the time *The Warriors* came out, that this type of film tends to scare people who see themselves as potential victims and think that censorship is their protection. In fact, however, crazies who choose to watch violent movies are already inclined to think of themselves as the type depicted on the screen. Therefore, censorship is hardly the solution; the function of these movies is to remind us that violence surrounds us and should not be ignored.

5

Revenge

Straw Dogs

"I intend it to have a cathartic effect. Someone may feel a sick exultation at the violence, but he should then ask himself, What is going on in my heart? I want to achieve a catharsis through pity and fear."

—SAM PECKINPAH ON HIS FILM *STRAW DOGS* (1971)

During the sixties and seventies, with war in Vietnam, political assassinations, and the rise of urban crime, violence became part of our everyday life. Inevitably, the movie screen became bloodier, and while movies about bad guys and antiheroes were still popular, vigilante films became equally successful.

The title *Straw Dogs* was suggested to Sam Peckinpah by a quotation from the *Tao Te Ching* by philosopher Laotsu: "Heaven and earth are ruthless and treat the myriad creatures as straw dogs. The sage is ruthless and treats people like straw dogs." This title was much better than *The Square Root of Fear*, which

Susan George, assaulted in Peckinpah's *Straw Dogs*. (ABC Pictures Corp.)

had been suggested by ABC, the producers of the film, or *The Siege at Trencher's Farm*, the British potboiler by Gordon Michaels on which the movie was based.

Straw Dogs, the movie, has a wimpish, bespectacled American teacher (English in the book), David Sumner (Dustin Hoffman), on sabbatical, who moves with his wife, Amy (Susan George), to her native Cornish village in an attempt to escape his country's violence. Involved with his research, he soon begins neglecting his wife. The neighborhood toughs who are working on the couple's house feel David is an intruder in their community, and they constantly challenge him, proving him to be spineless in the face of violence. They even go as far as to kill David and Amy's cat and hang it in their bedroom closet. Instead of confronting his tormentors, David agrees to go out hunting with them. While David is gone, Amy is visited by a man she used to date (Del Henney). He tries to seduce her, and when she refuses, he forces himself on her. Another one of the workmen (Ken Hutchison) walks in and gleefully rapes Amy as well, but she doesn't tell David what happened. Meanwhile, a local retarded boy (David Warner) accidentally kills a young girl, and David rescues him. When the locals come to get him, David decides to strike back and kills all of the attackers.

During production, Sam Peckinpah asked British playwright Harold Pinter for some input on the script, which Peckinpah had written with David Zelag Goodman. Pinter's reaction to the material was, to say the least, not encouraging:

Dear Sam Peckinpah:

I enjoyed our meeting a while ago, but I'm sorry you've asked for my comments on the script. I have to tell you I detest it with unqualified detestation. It seems to me totally unreal, obscene not only in its unequivocal delighted rape and violence but in its absolute lack of connection with anything that is recognizable or true in human beings and in its pathetic assumption that it is saying something "important" about human beings. How you can associate yourself with it is beyond me. I can only consider it an abomination.

At the same time, Pinter was in a sense describing exactly what Peckinpah was trying to accomplish with *Straw Dogs*, and

According to Peckinpah, *Straw Dogs* reflects the violence that exists within us all. (ABC Pictures Corp.)

if nothing else, the author's extreme reaction might have encouraged the director to pursue the project. Pinter's attitude might have been part of what Peckinpah felt was happening to the world; we, as human beings, tend to deny that we are violent, and to him, this denial is more dangerous than violence itself. "If we don't recognize that we're violent people, we're dead," Peckinpah declared. "We're going to drop bombs on each other. I would like to understand the nature of violence. Is there a way to channel it, to use it positively? Churches, laws, everybody, seems to think that man is a noble savage. But he's only an animal, a man-eating, talking animal. Recognize it. He also has grace and love and beauty. But don't say to me that we're not violent. It's one of the greatest brainwashes of all time."

Production on *Straw Dogs* in late 1970 did not run smoothly. Peckinpah appeared on the set drunk most of the time, yelling, screaming, infuriating his colleagues and the producers. In other words, Peckinpah was up to his usual routine. At one point, he was even hospitalized with walking pneumonia. The rage that slowly builds inside the character of David in the film seemed to inhabit Peckinpah himself. The rape sequence with Susan George was the most difficult to shoot. The actress was uncomfortable, mainly with the fact that Peckinpah wanted her to be completely naked, and threatened to walk off the movie. She confronted Peckinpah and asked him to shoot it without showing her nude. Eventually, the directed relented but added that if the result was not satisfying, they would have to shoot it his way.

"For a week, we shot the rape scene," Susan George recalled. "On the first day, I arrived absolutely petrified. Sam came in to work and sat with his legs crossed, in a little ball on the floor in front of the couch where I was raped, and he never moved, and he never said a word to me for five days. He did talk to Del Henney and gave him a terrible time. He started saying things like what a dreadful lover he was. He provoked Del terribly, but he never said a word to me. When Del was on top of me, he would be saying things like 'Christ almighty! Is this it?' It was really unbelievable. I used to try not to listen to that, but he never said one word to me, just smiled at me from time to time. And he did what I begged him to do, which was focus my eyes and upper body and let me tell the story. Sam was so volatile and lethal on the one hand and so quiet and kind and loving on the other—that's what's fascinating about him."

The final gruesome scene in *Straw Dogs* in which David kills his attackers shows how his character has changed from one who intellectualizes everything and believes that true pacificism is the answer to violence to one who has discovered the animal instinct in him. "I'm not saying that violence is what makes a man a man," Peckinpah declared. "I'm saying when violence comes you can't run away from it. You have to recognize its true nature in yourself as well as in others and stand up to it. If you run, you're dead, or you ought to be." With *Straw Dogs*, Peckinpah said he wanted to explore the degree of violence that exists in a man and to make us realize that basically we're just a few steps up from apes in the evolutionary scale. In the film, David uses every means he knows to kill his attackers; he even becomes ingenious and clever. As in the final scene in *The Wild Bunch*, the bloodbath in *Straw Dogs* is relentless, proving one more time that Peckinpah's instinct for realism has led him to graphic displays of violence. "It was a phony Hollywood fallacy to have people get shot and not seem to be dead. I don't mind saying that I myself was sickened by my own film [*Straw Dogs*]. But somewhere in it there is a mirror for everybody. If I'm so bloody that I drive people out of the theater, then I've failed."

The MPAA initially gave *Straw Dogs* an X rating (the scene of the second rapist sodomizing Amy proved to be a real problem

Dustin Hoffman, fighting fire with fire in the film's brutal climax. (ABC Pictures Corp.)

131

with the censors), and the film had to be considerably trimmed down to get an R. Peckinpah said that the cuts struck out "thirty-five percent of the effectiveness" of one of the most violent sequences in the film. Aaron Stern, then the code's administrator, admitted that a movie of the quality of *Straw Dogs* should not be given a label that usually defined pornographic films; on the other hand, the extreme violence was too intense for an R rating. In order to release the film widely, ABC decided it was best to make cuts in it.

"Sam said he was making a film about violence and the senselessness of it," declared producer Dan Melnick, "and how we can all be moved to it. As far as I was concerned, we were making a film about the violence inherent in all of us and how accessible it was to us, [that] we were all capable of rage that could lead us to kill." At an early screening of the film in San Francisco, audiences were reacting wildly. Melnick felt that the public would be devastated, shocked, and horrified, especially during the siege at the end of the film. Instead, he heard six hundred people shouting, "Kill him! Get him!" He thought at that point: My God, what have we unleashed? Right after the show, the producers, Peckinpah, and his editors were discussing the movie in the lobby when an angry man who had sat through the picture came up to them screaming and saying: "That's the most disgusting thing I've ever seen. I'm a pacifist, and I'll kill you for making it."

When Peckinpah's brother Denny went to the opening of *Straw Dogs* in Fresno, he heard an old lady screaming: "Hit him! Hit him again!" when Dustin Hoffman kills one of the attackers. The film was obviously getting two kinds of extreme reactions: Audiences either loved it and cheered at the violence or were outraged by it and found the experience sickening. "You can't make violence real to audiences today without rubbing their noses in it," Peckinpah said. "We watch our wars and see men die, really die, every day on television, but it doesn't seem real. We don't believe those are real people dying on that screen. We've been anesthetized by the media. What I do is show people what it's like. When people complain about the way I handle violence, what they're really saying is 'Please don't show me; I don't want to know.' "

Like the public, critics were also split about the film. Paul D. Zimmerman of *Newsweek*, for instance, thought *Straw Dogs* was brilliant and wrote that it was doubtful Peckinpah could ever make a better film and that the rape sequence was "a masterful piece of erotic cinema, a flawless acting out of the female fantasy of absolute violation." In her *Wall Street Journal* review entitled "Breaking the Gore Barrier," Joy Gould Boyum found: "For while bloodshed and pain are necessary to the development of plot and theme, such explicitly ghastly images of mutilation as the film offers distract from them. Who cares what Mr. Peckinpah has tried to tell us about human nature when all we can remember (aside from our intense involvement in the victory of our out-numbered and puny hero) is the sight of steel jaws closing on a man's head?"

But two reviews, one from Richard Schickel in *Life* and the other from Pauline Kael in the *New Yorker*, sent Peckinpah to the doghouse. "Even though Peckinpah is on record as saying his aim is 'to rub their noses in the violence of it,' some critical objections to *Straw Dogs* will undoubtedly begin and end with the judgment that he has exceeded his aim here," Schickel wrote. "And God knows the squeamish deserve fair warning about this picture. In honesty, however, I'd have to say that it was bearable to me, perhaps because a regular movie reviewer these days must develop a surgeon's impersonality to blood and death and suffering."

Pauline Kael addressed, among other issues, the fact that *Straw Dogs* asked the question "What would you do if someone tried to invade your house to kill an innocent person?" The answer to that is obvious. Most of us would do whatever we can to defend justice, even if it meant to use violence, although it might disgust us even if we won. As Ms. Kael points out, by using violence, we would feel robbed of our humanity. "And here is where we can part company with Peckinpah, for the movie intends to demonstrate not merely that there is a point at which a man will fight but that he is a better man for it—a real man at last. The goal of the movie is to demonstrate that David enjoys the killing and achieves his manhood in that self-recognition."

To those who admired the film, Peckinpah's *Straw Dogs* was a masterpiece; to its critics, the movie promoted authoritarian attitudes. "I'm not a fascist," Peckinpah once declared, "but I am something of a totalitarian." Naturally, *Straw Dogs* became successful. People were attracted to the controversy that surrounded the picture. Audiences might also have been intrigued by the special notice that accompanied the newspaper ads for the film: "*Straw Dogs* unleashes such dramatic intensity that this theater is scheduling a five-minute interval between all performances."

Peckinpah said he never meant *Straw Dogs* to be entertaining; he wanted to show violence as it is so that people could recognize it. Instead, the director discovered that audiences were thrilled by the violence in the movie. "I don't put violence on the screen so that people can enjoy it. I want them to understand what it is, but unfortunately most people come to see [*Straw Dogs*] because they dig it, which is a study of human nature and which makes me a little sick." The audience reaction might have made Peckinpah a little sick, but at the same time, it didn't go unnoticed, and many producers decided to exploit the public's thirst for vigilante movies.

Marathon Man

In John Schlesinger's *Marathon Man* (1976), Dustin Hoffman plays Babe Levy, a marathon-runner wannabe and a history student at Columbia University who's writing a thesis on the McCarthy era. In the 1950s his father shot himself after he was accused of being a Communist; Levy kept his father's gun and wants to prove him innocent. Babe has no idea that his brother, Doc (Roy Scheider), who he believes is in the oil business, is in fact a spy, known as Scylla. Scylla smuggles diamonds out to South America to pay off Szell (Laurence Olivier), a notorious Nazi dentist also known as *Der Weisse Engel* (the White Angel), who rats on his former colleagues for a price. But Szell's brother, who keeps the diamonds in a safe-deposit box in New York, has a fatal car accident which forces the former Nazi to come out of hiding. Szell wants to go to the bank, but he's afraid he's being double-crossed by Scylla, and he murders him. Szell thinks that Scylla might have told his brother something before he died; he captures Babe and tortures him, only to find out that Babe knows nothing. It turns out that Scylla's partner, Janeway (William Devane), and Babe's girlfriend, Elsa (Marthe Keller), were working together. There's a shoot-out, and Elsa, Janeway, and Szell's henchmen are killed. Babe catches the Nazi coming out of the midtown Manhattan bank with the

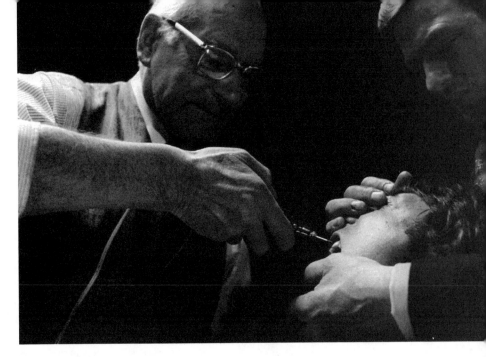

What's the drill? . . . Laurence Olivier as a former Nazi dentist intends to get information from his victim, played by Dustin Hoffman. (Paramount)

diamonds, and they have a final confrontation. As Szell is about to kill Babe, he trips while attempting to retrieve the gems and accidentally stabs himself with a large, retractable switchblade worn around his wrist. Babe throws his father's gun away and takes off.

Many critics found the violence in Schlesinger's film repulsive and thought it even spoiled the initial potential of the story; others (including myself) found the violence entirely necessary not only to the story but also to Dustin Hoffman's character. "*Marathon Man* wins an R for violence and a V for vertebrae snapping loudly," Charles Champlin wrote in the *Los Angeles Times*. "It is graphic in its violence and the dying so gray-green as in real terminating life. The sensitive are forewarned and forgiven for being able to take bloodletting or leave it alone."

There is extreme violence throughout *Marathon Man*, which is faithful to the novel and the screenplay by William Goldman. At one point, Scylla is attacked in his hotel room by a man who tries to strangle him with a nunchaku (two hard wooden sticks connected by a wire). Scylla defends himself; the wire is wrapped around his hand, and blood pours. Ultimately, Scylla knocks down his attacker and snaps his neck. Ouch! Scylla is eventually murdered by Szell. With his switchblade, the Nazi cuts Scylla open from his belly button up. Szell uses the weapon later on

135

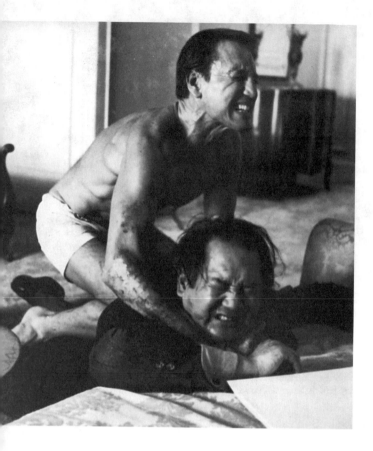

when a Jewish jeweler and concentration-camp survivor recognizes his onetime jailer; Szell slashes the poor man's throat and escapes.

The most famous sequence of the film is probably when Szell tortures Babe with a dentist's drill to find out if "it's safe"; in other words, if he can go to the bank to get his diamonds. Adding to the sound effects of the drill and Hoffman's screams is Laurence Olivier's laconic—and brilliantly delivered—speech of warning to his victim: "Life can be that simple. Relief, discomfort. Which of these I next apply— that decision is in your hands. So take your time and tell me. Is it safe?"

The interesting psychological aspect of *Marathon Man* lies in the fact that Babe

Roy Scheider in a neck-snapping moment from John Schlesinger's *Marathon Man.* (Paramount)

is a character who refuses to believe that his father was a Communist traitor. His father died because he refused to defend himself; he refused to fight back. Babe uses the weapon with which his father killed himself to shoot Janeway—a real traitor— at the end. When Szell stabs himself with the knife he used to murder Scylla, it's as if Babe's revenge has come full circle in some kind of weird ritual. The last image of Babe throwing the gun away shows that now that justice has been done, he has no further need for a weapon. But violence was the only way for him to accomplish his revenge; it was his only chance to survive. He also knew when to stop; others don't.

136

Death Wish

In the winter of 1971, musician turned author Brian Garfield had gone to a party with his wife, actress Shan Willson, thrown by a publisher on New York's Upper West Side. Garfield noticed that something was strange with his ten-year-old convertible which he had parked on the street. Indeed, the back window had been slashed; it wasn't a case of vandalism. The author had left a coat in the backseat which was visible through the plastic rear window. There was no real damage; the author had planned on changing the window, anyway, and the coat was old and filled with cigarette burns.

However, Garfield had an instinctive and very specific thought: If he had seen the S.O.B. do it, he would have killed him. "Of course, I wouldn't have really killed him because I don't carry a gun and I'm not an expert on armed combat, and even if I had been an expert and armed, I'm sure I wouldn't have killed somebody for the crime of putting a knife through an old window of a ten-year-old car. But what interested me was that automatic fantasy response—that I would have killed him if I'd seen him. If I could react that strongly to something that trivial, which hadn't even taken place in my presence, how would a character who was a little bit haywire react if something more powerful happened to affect him?"

This thought was reinforced by another event that had happened to Garfield's wife not too long before; while she was in a subway station, a couple of kids had snatched her purse. When she ran after them, they eventually dropped the purse, and she got it back. Garfield asked himself what would have happened if the kids had been armed. From these two events, Brian Garfield began concocting a story for a novel. The first working title was *Jones*, with the central character, Mr. Jones, an archetypal city dweller, a New York Everyman. Quickly, the author realized that his protagonist had no dramatic conflict, so a new character named Paul Benjamin emerged in his place. Benjamin was an accountant—middle-aged, middle-class, liberal. Dissatisfied with "Jones" as a title, Garfield tried to find a new one: "My editor's wife came up with it during a drunken evening when we were all sitting around trying to figure out what to call the book. She

The disturbing double-rape sequence in *Death Wish*. Notice Jeff Goldblum in his first role as one of the rapists. (Paramount)

actually didn't propose it as a title. We were discussing the story itself—this was before I'd written it—and she said, 'My God, this character sounds like he has a death wish.' And I said, 'That's the title!' " Hence *Death Wish*, the novel, was born. The story is about a liberal New Yorker who goes ballistic after his wife has been murdered and his daughter raped, leaving her in a catatonic state. In his search for revenge, he eventually gets his hands on a gun and becomes a notorious vigilante whose mission is to wipe out the city's bad guys. In the last chapter of the novel Paul becomes aware that a policeman has seen him and has recognized him as the vigilante killer. But instead of arresting him, the cop turns away, pretending he hasn't spotted Paul and allowing him to escape. "The novel is about a man who puts the fantasy of taking the law into his own hands into practice and finds out it's become a nightmare," Brian Garfield said. "He's become a psychopath, and the more he kills, the more he goes haywire. By the end of the story he's shooting down unarmed children just because they look suspicious to him. He's become corrupted by violence. That's the point of the book."

Death Wish, the novel, was written quickly, so fast that Garfield regretted not having spent longer elaborating his plot and developing the characters. However, he spent enough time on it for the story to affect him personally: "I got inside the character. In fact, I got so paranoid that it was very difficult for me to simply go across the street to the grocery store. I didn't want to leave the apartment. I felt that muggers were lurking everywhere." When the book was finally published, Garfield was surprised by the good reviews; "We felt that the book might be interpreted as a kind of white-backlash statement," the author said, "which it isn't supposed to be."

Death Wish, along with another novel written by Garfield entitled *Relentless,* were bought by the production team of Hal Landers and Bobby Roberts. Given the option of writing the screen adaptation for either book, Garfield decided to work on *Relentless.* Landers and Roberts hired Wendell Mayes to adapt *Death Wish* to the screen. "I saw his [Wendell Mayes] original draft of *Death Wish,* which was essentially what you saw in the film, except a lot of complication and idiocy in it were deleted before it hit the screen. That was my last connection with the film until I saw it at a screening a week before release." In his original draft, Mayes kills off Paul at the end of the story. The cop who has been tracking him all along finds him dead, murdered by the same hoods who did in Paul's wife and raped his daughter. The cop picks up Paul's gun and takes over as the vigilante. This ending was changed again for the final version of the film.

Death Wish, the movie, is about a man named Paul Kersey (Charles Bronson) who works in an architectural firm and whose wife, as in the book, is killed and daughter raped by three hoods (one of them played by Jeff Goldblum!) pretending to be delivering groceries. The daughter is catatonic and is sent to a clinic. Distressed, Kersey buys twenty dollars' worth of quarters at the bank and fills a sock with them. Criminals appear on every street corner, and his weapon does splendid work on the assailants. Kersey is sent out of town on business to work in Tucson on a housing project. When he returns to Manhattan with a gift-wrapped gun, he carries out his mission to rid the city of scum. Eventually, Kersey gets shot, but not before reducing the number of muggings in New York by half. To take credit for this drop in crime, the police offer to dispose of the evidence against him if he'll leave town. Aware that publicizing Paul's capture would cause the crime rate to skyrocket again, the cops let him depart quietly. Kersey moves to Chicago, and at the airport he sees a gang of youngsters dancing around after knocking down a girl. Kersey cocks his hand at them as if it were a gun; he is about to get back into action.

"The essential difference, to me, between the book and the

movie," Garfield said, "is that the book suggests that this kind of thing could happen and that it's a dangerous possibility. The movie suggests not only that it could happen but that it ought to happen." Garfield found the whole police conspiracy ridiculous. In the book, it was just one cop, one individual, who made a personal decision to turn his back on Paul. "The movie makes it a matter of police policy. It's a very dangerous recommendation, I think."

In terms of the casting of his leading character, Brian Garfield had had in mind Henry Fonda or Gregory Peck. Fonda reportedly said the script was "repulsive" and turned it down. By then, producers Landers and Roberts had sold the property to Italian movie tycoon Dino de Laurentiis, who, in turn, hired British director Michael Winner to helm the movie. Winner had worked with Charles Bronson a number of times and offered him the role. Garfield found the choice wrong for the movie: "Bronson does not project sensitivity. The worst effect his casting had on the film was to make the transition from ordinary citizen to killer almost invisible, and the transition really is the story. That's all the story has—the exploration of the change that takes place in the man. I'm told that Bronson's reaction when he was asked if he wanted the part, before he had read the screenplay, was 'I get to shoot muggers? Good!' I can't testify to the truth of that. I wasn't there. But . . ."

"Its message, simply put, is: KILL. TRY IT. YOU'LL LIKE IT," wrote Vincent Canby in his *New York Times* review under the headline "*Death Wish* Exploits Fear Irresponsibly." *Variety* agreed and called the film a "poisonous incitement to do-it-yourself law enforcement." So did critic Penelope Gilliatt of the *New Yorker*, who declared that the film was "enough to make thugs of us all." Richard Schickel of *Time* wrote "*Death Wish* is a meretricious film—in its curious lack of feeling even for innocent victims of crime, in its hysterical exaggerations of an undeniable problem, and especially in its brazen endorsement of violence as a solution to violence."

After the film was released, Brian Garfield complained about receiving hate mail from strangers who believed he had created a recommendation for fascism. "They probably haven't read the book," the author said. "The book is not the film." According to Garfield, the movie took his idea and turned it viciously inside out. "In the novel, Paul was psychotic. In the movie, he becomes a hero. In the movie Charles Bronson doesn't shoot

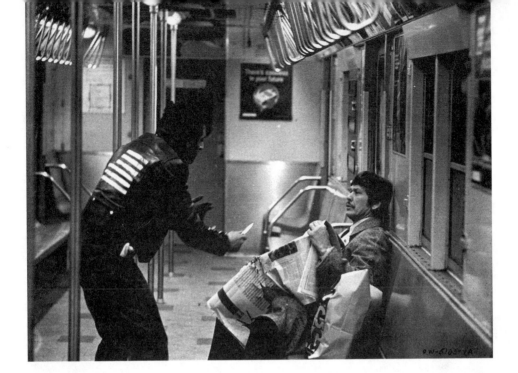

Michael Winner's film made a killing at the box office and started a wave of vigilante movies. (Paramount)

anybody who doesn't draw first. He might as well be a cowboy hero on a white horse. It's a dangerous distortion of the original story."

Death Wish was also criticized because it painted an unreal portrait of Manhattan. A number of reviewers pointed out that the film had been written by a Los Angeles screenwriter, produced by someone who seldom left Rome, and directed by a British director. What did they know about New York City? "Violence is not typical of New York alone," responded de Laurentiis. "Singapore, Amsterdam, Tokyo, Detroit, London, Chicago, Paris, and Rome are all plagued by the same problem. All big cities are jungles. New York is the symbol of all the metropolitan areas of our planet." For him, *Death Wish* addressed all law enforcement agencies and lawmakers and slapped them in the face with the reality of violence in the streets. At the same time, he insisted that the film was in no way an invitation to take to the streets with a gun. "But it is an invitation—an open invitation—to the authorities to come up with remedies to the problem of urban violence, and fast. I do not want people to become Paul Kerseys. I want the proper authorities to take care of the problem." Charles Bronson—who was fifty-three at the time the film was made—confirmed that he felt no personal identification with Paul Kersey and that he believed in the law. At the same time, he

Charles
Bronson in
Death Wish
. . . victim
or killer?
(Paramount)

also declared that if someone in his family was mugged, he "would probably start out looking for the one directly responsible myself."

Death Wish became an instant box-office smash. When the film came out, *New York Times* reporter Judy Klemesrud became intrigued by the *Death Wish* phenomenon and took to the streets to interview people who had seen the film. Most of the thirty people she talked to seemed to have enjoyed the film:

One older woman called *Death Wish* a "lovely and very comfortable picture." Although she didn't approve of killing, at least Charles Bronson's victims were all bad guys. She concluded by saying she was glad the police let him go at the end. A forty-three-year-old advertising salesman declared that if we had more people like Charles Bronson, there would be less crime; the man added that he would like to do something like Bronson but he couldn't see how he could get away with it. A twenty-six-year-old dancer who had been mugged four times in Manhattan said she could certainly go along with the Bronson character's reaction to violence. A thirty-year-old pregnant woman from Brooklyn thought what Bronson did was the right thing; "No one else is doing anything," she claimed. "Our system isn't working today. So you've got to protect yourself." A film student, on the other hand, found the film "technically tacky" and decided that aside from the fact that it exploited people's fear of mugging, it was just short of being a B movie. Another man found *Death Wish* completely racist, although Charles Bronson's character doesn't discriminate among black, white, and Puerto Rican muggers.

"This kind of movie plays out the fantasy of getting even," said Dr. Harvey Schlossberg, director of psychological services for the New York City Police department. "It's not dangerous; it's the kind of thing people cheer when the bad guy gets his comeuppance. It's a fantasy release, something we all want to do. For most people, it's the equivalent of a very satisfying dream." Schlossberg did add, however, that the movie might give bad ideas to really disturbed people. "No, I don't think there's anything to worry about," said Dr. Edwin H. Church, a Manhattan psychiatrist. "But if you had a mind that's in a delicate balance, *Death Wish* could tip it a bit." Dr. James A. Brussel, another Manhattan psychiatrist, agreed with his colleagues that it was very unlikely that *Death Wish* might arouse any psychotic drives or obsessions to kill. Interestingly enough, Brussel admitted that he himself carried a licensed .32 revolver even when he went to the bathroom.

To support his thesis against the film, Garfield pointed out in an interview with the *Los Angeles Times* the case of a Chicago bus driver who shot and killed a man—later discovered to be unarmed—who was trying to rob him. The driver later told the police he decided to carry a gun after he saw *Death Wish*. "My point is that vigilantism doesn't solve problems—it only creates new ones," said Garfield. "It increases the level of violence instead of reducing it. We've had vigilantes throughout history, and they always produce the same inevitable result—chaos and violence and injustice." Director Michael Winner subsequently thought there was absolutely no link between movies and violence. "It's a lot of hearsay. A lot of witch-hunting. A lot of finger-pointing. . . . Throughout history dramatists have simply recorded what's going on in society. The violence in society was far greater before the advent of film and television than it is now. There were the most bloodthirsty wars, the most dreadful mass murders. It was far less safe to walk the streets in Victorian England than it is today. People were regularly garroted in St. James's Park. I cannot believe if six blows are moved from a cer-

tain film that a mugger will wake up one morning and say, 'I'm
not going to mug and rob today. I'm going to join the youth hos-
tel and help young people.' "

Inevitably, *Death Wish* was followed by *Death Wish II*
(1982), *Death Wish 3* (1985), *Death Wish 4: The Crackdown*
(1987), and *Death Wish V: The Face of Death* (1994). All of them
bombed.

Casualties of War

When the subject of violence
against women in film is raised, Brian De Palma's name, it
seems, naturally follows. His horror thrillers and the way women
get killed in them have earned him the unfair reputation of being
a misogynist. So when De Palma decided to make *Casualties of
War* (1989), which deals with the brutal rape and murder of a
Vietnamese girl by a squad of GIs, one might have thought that
the director was challenging those who never miss a chance to
criticize him. Indeed, *Casualties of War* is extremely violent not
only in its subject matter—like *The Deer Hunter* (1978), *Platoon*
(1986), and *Full Metal Jacket* (1987), it brings home the issue of
the Vietnam War and violence and depicts what happened in
Vietnam in a simple, dramatic story.

Michael J. Fox portrays Erikson, the "cherry" of the squad.
He's just arrived in Vietnam, and during a night firefight he
becomes trapped in a caved-in Vietcong tunnel. As he is trying to
free himself, an enemy soldier is closing in on him from underground. Luckily, Meserve (Sean Penn), Erikson's hard-nosed
sergeant, pulls him out and saves his life. Later, the squad's
radio man is killed by a sniper, which fuels his buddies' anger,
and when the squad is ordered on a dangerous, long-range
reconnaissance mission, Meserve tells his men that they'll be
taking along some "portable R and R"—a young woman whom
they will kidnap and rape while they're in the jungle. Erikson
can't believe that his sergeant is serious until he unwillingly
finds himself part of the abduction of Oahn (Thuy Thu Le), a
young Vietnamese villager. All the men, except for Eriksson, take
their turn with the girl; one of them has to put a knife to her

throat to achieve an erection. Another just participates to avoid
being scoffed at by his buddies. Now Meserve is afraid that the
man he once saved is going to rat on him. Later, the victim is
brutally murdered. Although he was unable to save her, Erikson
avenges her memory by bringing his squad to trial.

Michael J.
Fox, Thuy
Thu Le, and
Sean Penn in
De Palma's
*Casualties
of War*.
(Columbia
Pictures)

Casualties of War was based on a short nonfiction piece
written by Daniel Lang and published in the *New Yorker* in 1969.
The piece later turned up in a book under the title "Casualties of
War." The screenplay, written by David Rabe, downplays the fact
that the real Erikkson (all the names in the book except for the
victim's are pseudonyms) acted on religious principles. "The
crime was so heinous, it doesn't need a religious point of view to
be condemned," De Palma said. Indeed, the crime is heinous.
While the execution of the young Vietnamese girl was filmed from
all possible angles, making the scene almost unbearable to
watch, De Palma shot the rape itself from a distance. We, as the

audience, do not experience her terror at that point; what we experience, on the other hand, is Erikson's perception of the event. "I'm interested in what Erikson saw," De Palma declared. "How do you shoot a rape? Well, there are twenty thousand ways to shoot a rape—like shooting a love scene." Inevitably, De Palma expected to be attacked by the critics for making yet another film with a woman as a victim; "Violence toward women is completely politically taboo. You get backlash from the media and from the audience. It's out of fashion. Still, I've always felt that suspense movies work better when you have a woman in peril and not a man. Because women are just physically more vulnerable and more interesting to watch."

On numerous occasions, De Palma has commented on his attraction to violence and the presence of so much of it in his work: "When people talk about violence in cinema, it's like talking about cheese on pasta; it sort of comes with the dish. And that's what makes the dish good." And: "Violence is extremely beautiful. Violence is cinematic. Film is a medium in which you can explore very strong, violent emotions." Also: "It [Violence] can be misused and done clumsily, but I'm very good at it." De Palma was also tired of being accused of showing gratuitous violence. Because *Casualties of War* was based on a true story, the director hoped that this time the critics would acknowledge that he was using violence for two reasons: to make a cinematic point and to provoke a strong reaction that's appropriate to the story. "In *Casualties*, I wanted a violence that made people feel the agony of the fighting, not something that numbed them." De Palma wanted people who saw *Casualties* "to feel what violence can do to human lives—that a killing creates a situation that can't be gone back from. That it changes the persons who do the killing."

Art Linson, who produced the film, acknowledged that it was a very disturbing piece of material; "If a disturbing movie like this can do well, it will encourage Hollywood to try to make other movies that aren't so pat and that challenge audiences." In a strange twist of fate, the critics did not hate the film and did not hate De Palma for it; it was, however, not a success at the box office. At the same time, *Casualties of War* marked an important step not only in De Palma's career but also in terms of its message: "When atrocities are committed," he said, "one usually likes to dismiss them by saying they were done by psychopaths, crazy people, people we have no connection to, in particular, isolated incidents. I thought it was important to try to understand what

146

drove these men to do what they did, and in many ways it serves as a metaphor for a whole involvement in this particular irrational and brutal war."

Deliverance

"In Deliverance, *for once, man is rape victim as well as rapist; this assault brings into the open sexual fantasies and fears that the characters cannot tolerate. They will go to any lengths to avenge the sodomy, and audiences, equally anxious to exorcise the image of male humiliation, want to accept their vengeance as a necessary tribal ritual."*

—STEPHEN FARBER, *NEW YORK TIMES*

In John Boorman's *Deliverance* (1972), Lewis (Burt Reynolds) has convinced three of his friends, Ed (Jon Voight), Bobby (Ned Beatty), and Drew (Ronny Cox), to join him for a canoeing weekend down the uncharted and dangerous rapids of a river before the entire valley disappears as the result of a new dam project. On the second day of the trip, Ed and Bobby find themselves held at gunpoint by two backwoods men, one of whom sodomizes Bobby; the other is about to rape Ed when Lewis comes to his friends' rescue by shooting one rapist with an arrow. The second escapes. The body of the dead man is buried. The four friends continue their dangerous descent of the rapids; Drew disappears overboard, and the two canoes capsize.

After Lewis breaks his legs, Ed takes over the leadership of the group. They are convinced that Drew was shot by the rapist who managed to run away, and Ed kills a man he finds lurking on a cliff without even being certain he is the one who raped Bobby. They dispose of the body and, later on, find Drew's body wedged between rocks. Unable to determine how he died, they sink his body and concoct a story designed to conceal what really happened. The men go through one final set of rapids and reach their destination. Lewis is hospitalized, and although suspicious, the sheriff is unable to shake their story and allows the men to go home. At night, Ed is haunted by the nightmare of the hand of one of the dead men rising from the waters. He awakens in a cold sweat next to his pregnant wife, who is in her own way awaiting her deliverance. But Ed, now a killer, will probably never get his. *Deliverance*, based on a novel by James Dickey (who appears in the film in the role of a cop), is about a group of men who must unite in order to survive in a savage backwoods environment. The four friends are presented as rather fastidious straight arrows, at first, but ultimately are forced to confront not only the violence of nature but also the violence in themselves. *Deliverance* has one of the nastiest and most upsetting rape

Burt Reynolds and Ronny Cox in John Boorman's savage and controversial *Deliverance*. (Warner Bros.)

scenes ever put on film: Ned Beatty is sodomized and forced to squeal like a pig.

At the beginning of the film, Lewis, the character played by Burt Reynolds, tells his friends that by building the dam "they're going to rape this whole country." This sentence is an awful premonition of what is yet to happen to the four buddies and establishes that they are the victims of nature's violent revenge. "But what the film most eloquently denounces," French critic Michel Ciment wrote in his biography of director John Boorman, "is the

notion of violence as an initiation, as the acquisition of a techni-
cal skill. Unlike certain of Sam Peckinpah's heroes, Ed [Jon
Voight] does not regard himself as more of a 'man' after the
slaughter. The myth of regeneration through violence, a myth
fundamental to American civilization, is portrayed as a pathetic
delusion."

Ciment argues that Boorman's depiction of violence in
Deliverance "belongs to a classic American tradition. Where some
filmmakers—most notably, Peckinpah—have had recourse to
staccato editing or slow motion to render palatable a series of
complacent shock effects, the unbearable tension of Boorman's
mise-en-scène is generated, rather, through the impression of
continuity (e.g., the rape scene filmed mostly in long shot, the
second murder encompassed within a vertiginious circular movement)." John Boorman said: "What I wanted was not to show violence in itself—you don't see too much blood in the film—but to
confront both characters and spectators with the reality of violence. It's very important for me, for example, that the victim
takes a long time to die: it was intended as an antidote to the
kind of death one normally sees on the screen, happening so
quickly, so banal as to be hypocritical."

Deliverance
dealt with
four friends
faced with the
reality of rape
and murder.
(Warner
Bros.)

Cape Fear

Cape Fear (1962), which was remade by Martin Scorsese in 1991, is another film that shows a peaceful man who has to turn to violence in order to survive. The original *Cape Fear* directed by J. Lee Thompson three decades earlier, caused quite an uproar before its release. Based on the novel *The Executioners* by John D. MacDonald, it concerns a vicious psychopath named Max Cady (Robert Mitchum) who has returned to a small town after spending eight years, four months, and fourteen days in prison. Attorney Sam Bowden (Gregory Peck) witnessed Cady beating up a woman, and it was his testimony that sent the defendant to jail. Cady vows that Bowden will at last learn something about loss and starts harassing the attorney's wife (Polly Bergen) and his fourteen-year-old daughter (Lori Martin). When Cady poisons the family's dog, Sam turns to his friend, Chief of Police Dutton (Martin Balsam), who in turn tries to discourage Cady from staying in town. But Cady brings in his own lawyer, and Dutton has to back off. As a result, Sam hires a private detective (Telly Savalas), who, after tailing Cady, finds out that he has battered a young woman (Barrie Chase). But the victim refuses to testify. When Cady terrorizes Sam's daughter, causing her to run out into the street and to have a near fatal accident, Sam wants to shoot the man himself, but his wife stops him. Instead, Sam hires three thugs to go after Cady. But all this does is build a case against Sam. This time, using his wife and daughter as bait, Sam lures Cady to a houseboat up the Cape Fear river. Cady almost succeeds in his design to rape the daughter, but Sam finds the strength to deal with him at his level and beats him. Instead of shooting Cady, Sam has him arrested and put behind bars for the rest of his life.

Cape Fear had problems with the Production Code before a scene was shot. After reading James R. Webb's script for *The Executioners*, the Code's Geoffrey M. Shurlock wrote to Universal explaining that because of the script's "sadistic brutality" and "extreme sex suggestiveness" it was unapprovable.

The story contained many brutal moments, more so than in average crime pictures of its time. The scenes in question showed Cady brutalizing a young woman he picked up in a bar; Cady be-

ing beaten up by several men, with one of them using a bicycle chain; Cady drowning a detective in charge of protecting Sam and his family at the houseboat; Cady threatening Sam's wife and spreading raw egg on her chest; Cady and Sam fighting. In March 1961 the producers again discussed the issue of *Cape Fear* with the board of censors, which still wouldn't budge. The censors still strongly disapproved of the protracted, graphic depiction of the hired men who set upon Cady with a bicycle chain, and they were not at all pleased with the final, climactic struggle between Sam and Cady in which both men go at each other with table legs and pokers. (In the film version, Sam strikes Cady with a stone.) Citing a "storm of protest" against film violence, the censors implored Universal to tone down *Cape Fear.*

After showing the finished film to the board, producer Cy Bartlett and director Jack Lee Thompson, who had toned down the violence from what had originally been written in the script, still had to take out several feet of film from the two drowning sequences (the first one being fatal to the cop guarding the Bowdens' houseboat, the second involving Sam himself). The controversy spread to Europe, and it was reported that *Cape Fear* was released in England with 161 cuts from the U.S. version. In protest, Polly Bergen canceled her British promotional appearance.

The violence inflicted by De Niro on Nick Nolte and his family (Juliette Lewis and Jessica Lange) was judged over the top by certain critics, who said *Cape Fear* was *Friday the 13th* taking itself seriously. (Amblin Entertainment/Universal Pictures, photos by Phil Caruso)

Gregory Peck and Robert Mitchum, who both appeared in the original *Cape Fear*, made cameo appearances in Scorsese's remake. (Amblin Entertainment/Universal Pictures, photo by Phil Caruso)

Critics at large found the movie too violent; *Variety* called *Cape Fear* "an amoral entertainment" and wrote: "It [the film] will arrest those who dote on the genre, or repel others who will peg it as a horror tale for its own sake and without any other point to make. It is definitely not for the impressionable young." Bosley Crowther (*New York Times*) felt that *Cape Fear* was a "pitiless shocker . . ." More to the point, Crowther said: "And the word on it [the film] is: don't take the children. If you want to be horrified, that's your business. But don't expose the youngsters to the ordeal of watching the film." He finally concluded: "But this is really one of those shockers that provoke disgust and regret. There seems to be no reason for it but to agitate anguish and a violent, vengeful urge that is offered some animal satisfaction by that murderous fight at the end." One wonders what the same critics would think of Martin Scorsese's take on the same story, which, quite frankly, made the original film seem tame.

"We're dealing with the characters more on the level of a psychological thriller as opposed to the sexual threat," screenwriter Wesley Strick explained about his own adaptation of *The Executioners*. Scorsese's *Cape Fear* is definitely more violent and more shocking than the original. To begin with, his visual style exploits more the suspense angle of the story; the camera never

stops moving, the sounds are constantly magnified and reso-
nant, and the use of the original Bernard Herrmann score (reorchestrated by Elmer Bernstein, which also features cues from
Herrmann's unused score for Hitchcock's *Torn Curtain* [1966])
enhances the escalating terror.

By far the most graphically violent moment in the film is
when Cady (Robert De Niro) is in bed with a woman, played by
Illeana Douglas. He puts handcuffs on her and then breaks her
arm, bites off a large chunk of her right cheek, spits it out, and
proceeds to punch her several times. The Swedish censors board
actually tried to cut that one "bit" from the film (a total of eleven
seconds), claiming that that particular sequence was "an induce-
ment to violence." Scorsese and the studio's foreign-distribution
branch appealed the case, and in the end, his *Cape Fear* was
released in that country uncut.

Another of the film's violent moments shows Cady stran-
gling a cop (Joe Don Baker) with a piano wire. As for the scene
during which Cady gets beaten up by three men, Scorsese was
able to show what J. Lee Thompson wasn't allowed to film, and
this time around, we see all the punches and get a good look at
the bicycle chain and what happens if you're whacked with one.
There are many other disturbing moments, especially toward the
end of the film, when Cady has the whole family at his mercy;
the idea of what he could, or might, do to them is almost as
frightening as any violent action on his part.

As in the original film, the initially nonviolent protagonist,
Sam Bowden (Nick Nolte), has to compromise his own values in
order to save himself and his family. In the remake, however,
Martin Scorsese created a more multidimensional family (Jessica
Lange as the wife and Juliette Lewis as the daughter.) The Bowden family is actually quite dysfunctional. Sam flirts with other
women, and his daughter, is a provocative teenage brat, who
goes as far as to let Cady kiss her—before she finds what he's
really capable of. Cady, as played by De Niro, is also a lot sleazier
than the character played by Mitchum. (Robert Mitchum, Gregory Peck, and Martin Balsam, who appeared in the original *Cape
Fear*, all have cameo appearances in Scorsese's version.) Most
critics pointed out that De Niro's sadistic Cady was similar to his
Travis Bickle of *Taxi Driver*. De Niro said that to him Cady was
like "Alien or the Terminator. Cady is the bogeyman. . . ." It's
interesting that many people thought that Cady did not die at the
end of the film; "I tried to show that he died," Scorsese declared

after he kept being asked if he was planning a sequel to the film. "I don't know why everybody doesn't think he died." Screenwriter Wesley Strick said he "tried to create a psychopath who is more interesting, who has a real sense about himself being on a religious quest. The vengeance that he's seeking is pure and just and cleansing. Not only for him but for Sam, too. I mean, he absolutely believes that he's Sam's doom, but he's also Sam's redemption."

"I don't find Sam's reaction to violence that difficult," Nick Nolte said of his character. "It's not what we usually portray emotionally in movies as far as heroes are concerned, but it is heroic in a certain way; he recognizes every weakness. He's absolutely forced to. In fact, he is covered with blood and is horrified by it and is horrified to acknowledge the savagery to which he has descended." Nolte's Sam was representing Cady in a case of physical abuse; Cady raped a woman who was promiscuous. Outraged by his client's cruelty, Sam did not pursue his defense zealously, and Cady was sent to jail for fourteen years. At the end, Sam has Cady in his power, and as he is about to smash his head with a large rock, the madman is carried away by the current and drowns. It is fate that prevents Sam from killing a man—something he thought he could never do; it is not a choice like in the original *Cape Fear*. Scorsese appears to be telling us that in the nineties killing a man who deserves to die has become a lot easier than it used to be. Still, as Nolte pointed out, Sam is disgusted with the thought of violence, and after Cady dies, Sam looks at his hands and washes the blood off them.

"I didn't like the vigilante implications of the story," Scorsese said. "I certainly didn't want to promote the idea that guns ultimately solve problems. You know, there comes a point when a man's gotta be a man and shoot this guy down. If you could tell the story with another kind of sensibility, it would just be more ironic and full of dread, more a fable of the thin veneer of civilization. This perfectly decent guy has committed an ethical transgression, but in a sense it was the decent thing to do. But now, of course, this is all coming back to haunt him, and it escalates into this really grotesque life-and-death confrontation." Scorsese's *Cape Fear* was influenced by horror classics, such as Mark Robson's *Isle of the Dead* (1945) and Jacques Tourneur's *Cat People* (1942), and the result is a study that is both scary and violent and done for a mass movie audience. The film was quite successful; it tapped into today's fascination with real life and fictional psychopaths and killers. Critics were also a lot nicer toward Scorsese than they had been thirty years earlier toward. J. Lee Thompson, although John Powers of the *L.A. Weekly*, for example, thought *Cape Fear* was *Friday the 13th* taking itself seriously. In fact *Cape Fear* is a topnotch thriller, an essential movie in Scorsese's body of work that revealed the director's perfect understanding of yet another genre. Yes, *Cape Fear* is violent, bloody, and nasty . . . and filmmaking at its best.

The Rambo Series

In the summer of 1969 author David Morrell was twenty-six. A graduate student of Penn State University, he wanted to become a novelist and found inspiration watching the news on TV. A firefight in Vietnam he saw on the CBS Evening News and the riots that were erupting in American cities that summer gave him an idea, and Morrell was moved to write a book in which the war in Vietnam literally came home to America. He decided that his central character would be a Vietnam veteran, a former Green Beret Congressional Medal of Honor winner, suffering from post-traumatic stress syndrome. But this man needed a name. "One of my graduate-school languages was French," Morrell said, "and on an autumn afternoon, as I read a course assignment, I was struck by the difference between the look and the pronunciation of the name of the author I was reading, Rimbaud. An hour later, my wife came home from buying groceries. She mentioned she'd bought some apples of a type she'd never heard about before, Rambo. A French author's name and the name of an apple collided, and I recognized the sound of force." Thus was born one of America's most famous screen heroes—Rambo.

At the same time, Morrell read a newspaper account of a group of hitchhiking hippies who had been arrested by the police in a southwestern town, stripped, and completely shaved. This story triggered another question in Morrell's mind: What if his hero, having become a loner traveling the road, was arrested under similar circumstances? How would he react? Morrell imagined that Rambo would escape.

In Morrell's novel, entitled *First Blood*, the police chief, named Wilfred Teasle, is a Korean War hero. When he is hunting Rambo, he uses some of the tactics he learned in Korea, but they can in no way compete with the guerrilla methods his opponent acquired in Vietnam. "Almost killed," Morrell explained, "Teasle struggles down the mountain, accepts the help of Rambo's Special Forces instructor, and hunts Rambo yet again, with the result that Teasle's town is virtually destroyed, Teasle is killed, and

A French writer named Rimbaud . . . a type of apple called Rambo . . . and bingo! American hero Rambo was born. (TriStar Pictures)

Rambo is executed by his former instructor, who takes the top of his head off with a shotgun."

The novel was finished in 1970, and Morrell submitted it to his literary agent along with a dissertation on John Barth. Within three weeks, *First Blood* was sold to a publisher. One of the most memorable book reviews, which appeared in *Time* magazine, claimed that the novel represented a new kind of fiction, "carnography," violence's answer to pornography. Shortly after that, *First Blood* was sold to the movies, and it took about ten years before the film reached the screen. There were about eighteen different scripts written, and such directors as Richard Brooks, Martin

Ritt, Sydney Pollack, John Frankenheimer, and Stanley Kramer were all linked at one point or another to the project. Paul Newman, Al Pacino, Steve McQueen, Robert De Niro, Clint Eastwood, Nick Nolte, Brad Davis, Michael Douglas, and Powers Boothe were all possible choices to play Rambo. Eventually, two distributors, Andrew Vajna and Mario Kassar, stepped in and got the film under way, with Canadian director Ted Kotcheff behind the camera. Sylvester Stallone was chosen to play Rambo, and Kirk Douglas was to portray Colonel Trautman. (In the book he was just a major.) Douglas was replaced later on by Richard Crenna. Brian Dennehy was cast as Teasle. Credited as screenwriters were Michael Kozoll and William Sackheim and Sylvester Stallone, who, in his revisions, made sure that Rambo was perceived as reluctant to use force and that each time he did, it seemed justified; Stallone wanted Rambo to be portrayed as a sympathetic victim, not a killing machine.

Few remember that *First Blood* was not a violent movie. "On the screen," Morrell pointed out, "he kills one man by accident. (A rock thrown at a pursuing helicopter causes a vicious deputy to lose his balance and fall to his death in a gorge.) Later, Rambo bumps a stolen truck against a pursuing car filled with gun-blazing deputies. They veer off the road and fail to avoid a car parked along the road." And that's it. In Morrell's novel, the body count was much, much higher. "My intent was to transpose the Vietnam War to America," the author said, "whereas the film's intent was to make the audience cheer the underdog."

Three endings were conceived for the movie: In the first, a wounded Rambo is carried out of the police station. That version was never filmed. In ending number two, Rambo walks to Trautman, grabs Trautman's gun, and shoots himself. Ending number three has Rambo breaking down and walking out, with Trautman at his side. The film was tested with both of these endings, and when asked if they wanted Rambo to live or die, audiences were evenly split. The producers had to make the final decision, and Rambo lived.

"Vietnam is to *First Blood* as rape was to *Death Wish*," critic Janet Maslin wrote in the *New York Times*. "It's the excuse for a rampage of destruction." Peter Rainer of the *Los Angeles Herald-Examiner* declared: "*First Blood* is a sado-masochistic revenge fantasy that might have been cooked up by the *Soldier of Fortune* crowd." Whether the critics liked it or not, *First Blood* was a huge success upon its release in 1982. Stallone's Rambo immediately became a cult hero not only in America but around the world, and the first film was followed by *Rambo: First Blood Part II* (1985) and by *Rambo III* (1988).

The sequel begins with John Rambo in a hard-labor penitentiary. He is offered a mission: return to Vietnam to find out if MIAs are still held prisoners. When he comes back to the States, he'll be granted pardon. But the mission has been sabotaged from the beginning. In his attempt to save several MIAs, Rambo is captured and tortured on an electrified rack under the supervision of a Russian named Podovsky (Steven Berkoff). Rambo is also dipped in leech-infested water and threatened to have his eye carved out with a red-hot knife. Luckily, he is saved by Co (Julia Nickson), his sidekick, and strikes back with a vengeance not only against those who tortured him but against those who betrayed him as well.

Rambo: First Blood II, written by Sylvester Stallone and James Cameron (!) and directed by George P. Cosmatos, was a lot more controversial than its predecessor. For one thing, Rambo had become a phenomenon; suddenly, there were Rambo toys and even a Rambo animated TV series. Parents complained; they felt the movie was putting a stamp of approval on violence. In their minds, Rambo glorified violence, and kids, who are constantly looking for role models, were bound to want to follow his radical ways of dealing with rage, frustration, and injustice. As a result, angry parents organized protests against Rambo toys in Connecticut. The film also irked Vietnam vets, who found it to be inaccurate and unrealistic. In England the case of twenty-seven-year-old mass murderer Michael Ryan (who one day showed up dressed "à la Rambo" and gunned down a bunch of innocent people and then killed himself) was blamed on the film. Charles Champlin wrote in the *Los Angeles Times*: "I tried a body count the other afternoon, but gave up after two dozens because there was no reliable way even to estimate how many fell to the bombs, rockets, and perpetual load automatic weapons. The deaths by knife and steel arrow were easier to assess. I can't believe the full toll is less than 100." But who cared? The public kept coming back for more.

David Morrell had been hired to write a novelization of *Rambo II* based on the Stallone-Cameron script and later also turned out a novel inspired by *Rambo III*, this time based on the screenplay Stallone had cowritten with Sheldon Lettich. "The truth is, Rambo hates war," Morrell claimed in his hero's defense.

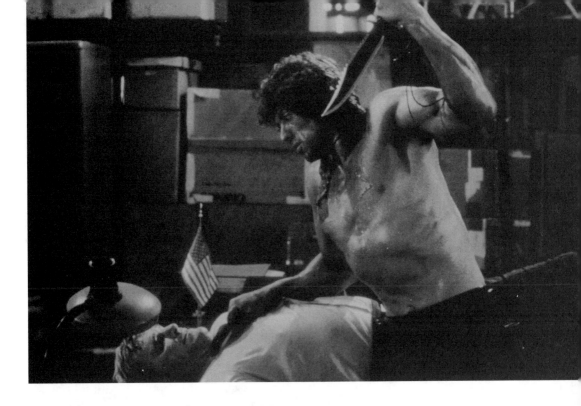

"He loathes what he is and what he has been trained to do. He reacts with justified rage only when pushed to the wall. On the set of *Rambo III*, Stallone and I talked at length about that issue. Anger's a last-resort emotion, we agreed. People shove you around, and most of the time you acquiesce. Why retaliate unless it's a critical issue? If your family's threatened, you have to respond. Or your life. Or your country. But it has to be a genuine threat. Otherwise, it's better to back away. Because if it's necessary to retaliate you have to go all the way, and you have to accept the consequences. That's the secret to Rambo. Fate pits him against relentless bullies, and like the gunslinger determined to retire, he reluctantly straps his gun back onto his waist."

Morrell had initially been hired to write the script of *Rambo III* and came up with the concept that ultimately stayed in the film; in his version, Trautman (Richard Crenna) is a military adviser in Central America. His wife and daughter come to visit him and are kidnapped by enemies from a neighboring country. Rambo, who since his last battle has been living removed from the world with Buddhist priests, finds out what's happened to his former superior and goes on a one-man rescue mission. Stallone and Lettich, using the initial concept, got rid of the wife and kid, changed the story to

Rambo . . . carnography, violence's answer to pornography.

159

fit the war in Afghanistan, and decided to have Trautman be kidnapped by the Soviets.

In England the British Board of Film Classification made twenty-four cuts to *Rambo III*, amounting to over one minute of deleted violence. In Germany, on the other hand, people protested against the rating of the film, which they felt was far too soft considering the amount of violence it depicted. In America, *Rambo III*—which was directed by Peter Macdonald —was considered one of the most violent films ever made, and the National Coalition of TV Violence listed 245 separate acts of violence in the movie. The coalition claimed that *Rambo III* had twice as much violence as the other two Rambo movies, depicted 123 deaths, and was anti-Russian. "This film glorifies violence and will promote violent ways of thinking and behaving in the millions of children, adolescents, and young adults who see it," National Coalition psychiatrist Thomas Redecki claimed. In their statement against the film, the members of the coalition listed all the acts of violence committed in *Rambo III*. Among them: Rambo slams Russian head into wall; Rambo pulls an extremely large knife; Rambo blows away Russians with machine gun; Rambo detonator explodes Russian guards graphically, etc. Wheelchair-bound Ron Kovic of the Disabled War Veterans (he was portrayed by Tom Cruise in Oliver Stone's *Born on the Fourth of July* [1989]) was among the protesters.

Antiwar activist Jerry Rubin, director of the Los Angeles chapter of the Alliance for Survival, decided to ingest only organic juice and amino acid pills for sixty-three days—one day for each million spent on the $63 million film. At the end of his hunger strike, Rubin delivered a giant peace-symbol pizza to Stallone, but the actor wasn't home that day.

"Then there's the Rambo backlash. Politics," David Morrell declared. "In October 1987, Nicaragua's president Daniel Ortega made a speech at the United Nations. 'Let president Reagan recall,' Ortega said, 'that Rambo exists only in the movies. The people of the world do not want Rambos. The people want men of peace.' The U.S. delegation walked out in protest, justifiably, as far as I'm concerned, because Ortega was wrong on several counts. Rambo exists in print as well as in movies. And Rambo, like the people of the world, wants peace." Now the word "Rambo" is used in connection with sports, politics, wars—in short, macho stuff. At the time *Rambo III* was released, however, TriStar Pictures tried to downplay the macho image of the film and released a newspaper ad showing an older woman from Queens, New York, wearing a Rambo T-shirt. The ad read: "You don't have to be macho to love Rambo." The following week, the film's distributor brought forth another ad. In it a career woman says: "I believe in self-reliance, being aggressive and expressing anger openly. Kind of like Rambo."

David Morrell never tried to deny that Rambo was a violent character, but only as a last resort. "If your idea of entertainment is *The Sound of Music*, the *Rambo* movies aren't for you. They're action pictures. You could say that their action's excessive. But the *Star Wars* movies have far more violence. Of course, *Star Wars* happens a long time ago in a galaxy far away, whereas Rambo addresses controversial contemporary issues. It's true that most Vietnam vets didn't suffer post-traumatic syndrome. But then, most of them didn't belong to the Special Forces, Rangers, Recon, or Seals. The soldiers in those cadres learned skills no one should ever have to learn, let alone put into practice. Their missions were nightmares with long-lasting psychological consequences." As for Stallone, he declared that he made *Rambo III* because of the pain that the Afghan people have suffered as a result of the brutal war of the Soviets, who forced 6 million of them to leave their homes and exterminated another million of them. "So I don't think the question is whether *Rambo III* commits a few violent acts," Stallone said. "The millions of atrocities and brutal acts against a helpless people . . . are the ones that should be counted."

David Morrell recalled that one day, on the set of *Rambo III* in Israel, kids were crowding around Stallone, screaming, "Rambo! Rambo!" The star turned to Morrell and said: "See, it isn't me they're hugging. It's Rambo. The children don't know about the politics and the controversies. They see him as a hero. A protector. He's violent, sure, but reluctantly, and they know he's on their side. Against the bullies. In defense of the helpless."

6

To Protect
and to Serve

Dirty Harry

"I know what you're thinking; did he fire six shots or only five? Well, to tell you the truth, I forgot myself in all this excitement. But being that this is a .44 magnum, the most powerful handgun in the world, and it could blow your head clean off, you have to ask yourself one question: Do I feel lucky? Well, do you, punk?"

—CLINT EASTWOOD AS DIRTY HARRY

"Go ahead, make my day!" Eastwood in *Sudden Impact.* (Warner Bros.)

Although he didn't get credit on the film, this famous line from *Dirty Harry* (1971) was written by John Milius, himself a gun collector as well as screenwriter and director extraordinaire. " 'Are you lucky, punk?' Yea. That's all vintage Milius, I suppose," John Milius told *Playboy.* "I got a little tingle. I guess I just thought it was me at the time. It was a good line and *Dirty Harry* was highly regarded—mostly by nuts—when it came out. It didn't have the kind of legendary gloss that it does now. The speech 'This is a .44 magnum, the

163

Clint
Eastwood
as Harry
Callahan with
his .44 mag-
num in Don
Siegel's *Dirty
Harry.* Notice
the marquee
is showing
Eastwood's
*Play Misty for
Me.* (Warner
Bros.)

most powerful handgun in the world,' the cops loved that." By
today's standard, *Dirty Harry* seems tame; but back in 1971 it
received a lot of heat because the hero, played by Clint Eastwood, was a cop with his own rules who cured violence with violence and was perceived by many as not that much different
from the criminals.

Dead Right, as it was initially entitled, was going to star
Frank Sinatra, with either Irvin Kershner or Sidney Pollack behind the camera. Universal Pictures owned the script, and at
some point, Paul Newman, who wouldn't star in the film, was
going to produce it. Eventually, the script got to Warner Bros.
and fell into the hands of Clint Eastwood, who then hired his
friend Don Siegel to direct the film.

Dirty Harry begins with a sniper (Andrew Robinson) shooting an innocent young woman while she's taking a swim in her
sundeck pool. The killer signs himself Scorpio and demands
$100,000 from the police, threatening other deaths. Harry Calla-
han (Clint Eastwood), of the San Francisco Police Department, is
advised by his boss, Lt. Bressler (Harry Guardino), and the may-
or (John Vernon) that they have decided to pay off the killer. We
then follow Harry in action as he stops a robbery. Later on,
against his will, he is assigned a partner named Chico (Reni
Santoni). The sniper shoots another innocent victim. Based on a
hunch that the killer will come back to the same district, Harry

and Chico stake out a rooftop. They spot the killer, but he escapes.

The sniper advises the police that he has kidnapped a fourteen-year-old girl and that she'll die unless he's paid $200,000. Harry delivers the money and is viciously attacked by the sniper. Chico, who's been following the action from a distance, emerges and is wounded in the gun battle that follows. Harry manages to drive a switchblade into the killer's thigh. Harry tracks down the killer through the doctor who stitched up the knife wound. The sniper lives in the keeper's quarters at a football stadium, and that's where Harry catches him and tortures him in the middle of the deserted playing field. Although the girl's body is found, the killer is released, and the district attorney accuses Harry of torturing a suspect. Harry begins harassing the sniper, who eventually pays a big brute to beat him up and then blames it all on Callahan.

As Harry predicted, the killer strikes again; this time, he has hijacked a school bus filled with children. Disregarding his orders, Harry comes after the psycho and kills him. As police sirens approach, Harry tosses his badge away.

"As a human being, I have really had very little contact with violence," Don Siegel declared, "and no contact with the kind of

Do you feel
lucky, punk?
(Warner Bros.)

hopeless psychopathic killers and cops I have developed in my pictures. As a human being, I constantly tease people, have fun with them, make them laugh." *Dirty Harry* was anything but funny; the film is dark, almost depressing. Comparatively, the character of Harry Callahan is very similar to that of James Bond, as conceived by author Ian Fleming. In the novels, Bond is a grim, dark character, and the plots, while cartoonish when they reached the screen, were extremely bleak. In *Dirty Harry*, many innocent people are killed, and Callahan is not the superhero that he became in the subsequent Dirty Harry movies. Critics were not gentle toward the film; *Variety* offered a checklist of all the acts of violence committed in the film and suggested that it was a disgrace that parents were allowed to take their children to see *Dirty Harry* (the film was rated R) but couldn't take them to Stanley Kubrick's *Clockwork Orange*, which had received an X rating. Garrett Epps of the *New York Times* was outraged by *Dirty Harry*, calling it "a film without mercy" and saying that it was relentless and graphic in its depiction of violence. "Is it too much to ask that these films not be made? We do not need any more laws governing what can be shown and what cannot; but we can all place some pressure on producers

Critic Pauline Kael said *Dirty Harry* condoned fascism and encouraged vigilante spirit and reactionary behavior. (Warner Bros.)

and distributors to stop offering us Fascist propaganda and sadomasochistic wet dreams. If we do not, we may soon find our screens completely filled with screaming faces, broken teeth, and rivers of red, red blood."

The most talked about review at the time, however, was Pauline Kael's in the *New Yorker*. She basically said that *Dirty Harry* condoned fascism and police brutality and accused the film of encouraging a vigilante spirit and reactionary behavior.

166

"I'd say she's crazy," Clint Eastwood declared at the time. "It's not about a man who stands for violence; it's about a man who can't understand society tolerating violence. When *Dirty Harry* came out, it was at a time when an awful lot of films had been done concerning the rights of the accused, and all of a sudden this film came along where somebody was concerned with the rights and the comfort of the victim. So somebody called that Fascist. Well, I don't think it's Fascist. He was just a man who didn't understand. . . . He says to the district attorney, 'Well, if that's the law, if a man can be sent out on the streets on a technicality like that, then the law's wrong,' and that's the way he believed. Now, whether that's right or wrong, that just happened

to be one character I play. I've played other characters which are purely [the] opposite."

When asked if he felt any responsibility toward the amount of violence in the film, Don Siegel replied: "I dimly remember that at the end of *Hamlet* there are five bodies lying around, so that's balderdash. This constantly plainted ditty against violence—if people didn't want it, they wouldn't go to the movies. I loathe gratuitous violence. I fight very hard against it. My violence is very sharp and abrupt. I infer violence—it's lying there, waiting for you—but I don't really have that much violence in my pictures, and certainly in *Dirty Harry* there wasn't." One cannot completely agree with Siegel on that particular point. The film is extremely

"A man's got to know his limitations."
Hal Holbrook and Clint Eastwood in *Magnum Force.*

167

violent, although it is true that it is not depicted in a graphic fashion. Still, the random killings are upsetting. Watching the naked dead body of a young woman being dragged out of a pit is haunting. Then there are the scenes of the killer beating up Harry and of Harry torturing the killer. At the same time, in these scenes the violence is never gratuitous; to the contrary and as they should, they advance the story and help us understand the character's motivations. "I thought *Dirty Harry* had something to say, and I felt we said it," Siegel declared in his defense, "even though Pauline Kael couldn't understand it." Clint Eastwood agreed with his director that the film's violence could not have any effect on the susceptible. "If a weak or unhinged person mirrored Dirty Harry, he'd be on the side of the right because he's on the side of good as opposed to evil. *Dirty Harry* is not a story about a sicky. If you do a story like *Taxi Driver*, it's a story about a sick man who's ready to go out and shoot people. Now if you mirrored that character, then that would be something, but the Dirty Harry character is a man on the side of the public and on the side of tranquillity for the public."

Dirty Harry became a phenomenon, and the film made Clint Eastwood a legend and a hero, maybe not in the eyes of the critics—that came later—but at least in the eyes of the public. In 1974, after the police began searching for the notorious Zebra killer, the graffito Dirty Harry, Where Are You When We Need You? appeared on a wall in San Francisco. Only Clint Eastwood could do something about this; he had heard the call.

Credited for the *Dirty Harry* screenplay are Harry Julian Fink and R. M. Fink, and Dean Riesner. As stated earlier, some of the most famous lines from the film were written by John Milius. In fact, for all his deals at the time, Milius received money—not a lot according to him—and a gun. "I had to have an object to remember the movie by," Milius recalled. "The gun cost two thousand dollars, and I wanted it and my money, which at the time wasn't much—thirty-five thousand dollars. I had to do the script in three and a half weeks. I said, 'Well, I know where the gun is, and I can't start until I have it.' They said, 'Why don't you go get the gun?' I said, 'Okay. I can go get it.' They said, 'Well, then you could start today?' and I said, 'No, I'd have to look at the gun for a whole day. I'd get it today, and I'd probably have to look at it tomorrow, and I could start the day after.' They said, 'We'll get the gun.' So they sent a limousine to get the gun. I started that night." Without doubt, John Milius was the man to write the sequel to *Dirty Harry*. Milius paired up with Michael Cimino (*The Deer Hunter*), and together they brought back Dirty Harry in *Magnum Force* (1973).

Dirty Harry's competition . . . Mel Gibson and Danny Glover in Richard Donner's *Lethal Weapon*. (Warner Bros.)

Magnum begins with union leader Carmine Ricca (Richard Devon), accused of murdering a labor reformer and his family, leaving court a free man for lack of evidence. His freedom is short-lived when his limousine is stopped by a cop, who pulls out his gun and shoots down Ricca and his entourage. Harry Callahan, who has been demoted from homicide to a stakeout squad by Det. Lt. Neil Briggs (Hal Holbrook), shows up at the scene of the crime with Early Smith (Felton Perry), his partner. Later, Callahan runs into a colleague, Charlie McCoy (Mitch Ryan), who seems to be on the verge of a nervous breakdown, and then checks into target practice, where he meets a group of new rookies: Ben Davis (David Soul), John Grimes (Robert Urich), Phil Sweet (Tim Matheson), and Red Astrachan (Kip Niven).

Within weeks, the city is strangely inundated by a wave of killings, with the victims all being connected to gambling, prostitution, and narcotics. Briggs thinks that a notorious Mafia boss is behind the killings, but Harry, because of a ballistics check, believes that his buddy McCoy has snapped and is responsible. Harry's theory is proved wrong when, during an investigation, McCoy is shot by one of the rookie cops. Harry puts the pieces together and is now certain that Davis, Grimes, Sweet, and Astrachan are behind the murders. He confronts them, and they admit their guilt; their vigilante committee was formed to show their resentment against judges who constantly free criminals. They ask Callahan to join them, but he refuses. Harry tells Briggs of his discovery, but it turns out that Briggs is the head of the vigilantes. During a final confrontation in a shipyard, Callahan eliminates the rookie cops and Briggs.

169

Magnum Force, which Ted Post directed, is by a long shot (no pun intended) the best of all the *Dirty Harry* sequels. As in the original film, it has some memorable lines, such as: "There's nothing wrong with shooting as long as the right people get shot" and "A man's got to know his limitations." "Mike Cimino came up with it [the latter] when we were dealing with the first scene in New York," Clint Eastwood recalled. "I always liked a recurring kind of theme. We decided the Hal Holbrook character was to become the antagonist in the film, and Harry feels the other guy should know his own limitations." The story of the rookie cops as death squad was inspired by a real-life Brazilian death squad—a Fascist subgroup within the police force was acting as judge and killing criminals. Again, Pauline Kael deplored the violence in the film: "A violent movie that intensifies our experience of violence is very different from a movie in which acts of violence are perfunctory. I'm only guessing, and maybe this emotionless business means little, but, if I can trust my instincts at all, there's something deeply wrong about anyone's taking for granted the dissociation that this carnage without emotion represents."

Magnum Force was a hit and was followed by three more sequels. In *The Enforcer* (1976), written by Stirling Silliphant and Dean Riesner and directed by James Fargo, Callahan is paired with a female partner, Kate Moore (played by Tyne Daly), to battle an underground group of terrorists; the criminals kidnap the mayor (John Crawford) and hold him hostage in the abandoned prison of Alcatraz. Callahan successfully stops the villains, but his partner is killed (a fate befalling most of his assorted partners) during the shoot-out. Unfortunately, *The Enforcer* was not completely convincing. Perhaps the emotional link between Harry and Kate got in the way; having been criticized for being emotionless and only driven by violence by many reviewers, this attempt at making Harry more "human" only managed to take away the edge that made Harry "dirty."

Sudden Impact (1983), written by Joseph C. Stinson, was directed by Eastwood himself. After following Callahan on his usual and now-familiar cleaning up of the city's scum, the screen's favorite San Francisco detective is again in trouble with the brass and is assigned a seemingly inconsequential murder of a local hood. Harry discovers that other, similar murders have been committed, and they all lead him to Jennifer Spencer (Sondra Locke), an artist who has come back to town to avenge a brutal gang rape that took place ten years earlier and ruined her and her younger sister's lives. To make matters worse, one of the rapists is the son of Callahan's chief of police. The kid could not live with the guilt of what he did, tried to kill himself, missed, and has been wheelchair-bound ever since. Jennifer continues her vigilante ways until the group's leader gets to her after he shot the chief of police and his son. Callahan rescues her, shoots the madman, and makes it look as if he were the one responsible for all the prior killings. *Los Angeles Times* reviewer Kevin Thomas wrote in his article "Orgy of Violence in *Sudden Impact*": "As one violent deed leads to another, Locke emerges as a Dirty Harriet to match Eastwood, amid lots of tough deadpan repartee that isn't the least bit funny, considering the increasingly lawless, blood-soaked circumstances. 'Everyone wants results, but nobody wants to do what has to be done,' says Harry by way of self-justification—an attitude that eventually absolves Locke too. It's this kind of thinking that makes Harry as dangerous as the criminals he pursues with such zeal." *Sudden Impact*, however, gets thumbs up for the memorable line "Go ahead, make my day!" and for the "cinematically correct" staging of the violent set pieces, with the best one taking place in a deserted amusement park.

The Dead Pool (1988) was directed by Buddy Van Horn. In Steve Sharon's script, a sleazy producer named Peter Swan (Liam Neeson) has made a list of celebrities whom he believes will die soon; each person on it gets killed in sequence, and Harry Callahan takes over the case. In fact, however, Swan is just a red herring, and Callahan, this time paired up with a newswoman named Samantha Walker (Patricia Clarkson), ultimately cracks the case—and apprehends the real psychopath responsible for the killings. With *The Dead Pool* (seventeen years after the original), the series took a nosedive. While still entertaining, the film lacked the edge that had made the Dirty Harry movies famous.

By now, an aging Dirty Harry has much to compete with. *Die Hard* (1988), *Lethal Weapon* (1987), and their sequels, the Steven Seagal, Sylvester Stallone, and Jean-Claude Van Damme movies make Dirty Harry seem like Prince Charming. Yet it seems that those films, with the exception of the *Die Hard* and *Lethal Weapon* series, have more to do with pyrotechnics than characters and story. In any case, regardless of all the criticism, *Dirty Harry* and *Magnum Force* are responsible for setting the seventies and eighties trend in action films and new standards in screen violence that to this day are still unsurpassed, though they have been consistently imitated and copied.

Walking Tall

On the heels of *Dirty Harry* came director Phil Karlson's *Walking Tall* (1973), based on the real-life story of a bat-wielding sheriff, Buford Pusser, and his one-man war against local corruption. It was released amid great controversy. After his wrestling career has ended, Pusser (Joe Don Baker), moves back home to sixties Selmer, Tennessee, with his wife, Pauline (Elizabeth Hartman), and their two kids, where he plans to start farming. Pusser doesn't recognize his hometown, which is now run by a corrupt sheriff who supports illegal gambling and prostitution. During a fight in one of the most popular saloons, the Lucky Spot, owned by a bunch of vicious rednecks, Pusser is nearly beaten to death. He survives and goes back to beat up his attackers with a bat. He's put on trial but wins the sympathy of the jury. The whole town, he finds, is on his side,

Bat man . . . Joe Don Baker in Phil Karlson's *Walking Tall.* (Cinerama Releasing)

172

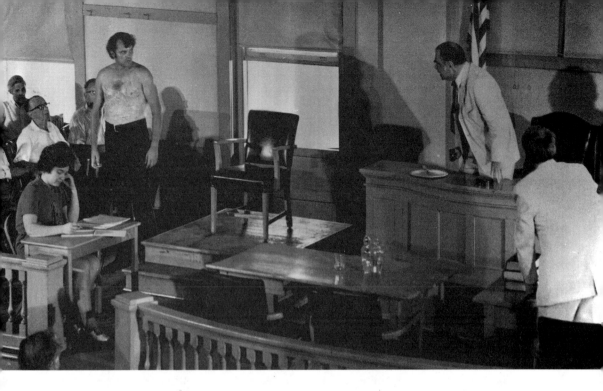

and he decides to run for sheriff. His opponent tries to kill him but crashes his own car into the river instead.

As local sheriff, Pusser intends to clean up the town. He and his family turn out to be in constant danger, but he always seems to stand tall. After killing the local madam, Callie Hacker (Rosemary Murphy) in self-defense, Pusser and his wife are ambushed. She dies, and he is practically disfigured. Later, Pusser strides out of the hospital, drives his car into the Lucky Spot, and kills the two men responsible for his wife's murder. Police arrive and take Pusser outside as outraged citizens start demolishing the gambling club. Law and order has finally returned to Selmer, Tennessee.

To W. R. Morris, his biographer, Pusser was a "living monument to justice," a folk hero, a modern-day Wyatt Earp. The somewhat romanticized film, written by producer Mort Briskin, was voted one of the best films of 1973 by *Rolling Stone*. But when Buford Pusser died in a car crash the following year on his way to Memphis to announce his starring role in the sequel to *Walking Tall*, few tears were shed in the real town of Selmer, Tennessee. It appears the film had little relation to the real-life Pusser: since he had retired, Buford had become a public nuisance and embarrassment. Between 1970 and the time of his death, the man was

Bufford Pusser (Joe Don Baker) shows his scars to the court to prove his right to take revenge on the gang that beat him up. (Cinerama Releasing)

173

Walking Tall was loosely based on the real-life story of Sheriff Buford Pusser (*left*). (Cinerama Releasing)

arrested on charges of larceny, official oppression, assault with a deadly weapon, and destruction of property. When he wasn't autographing pickax handles, Pusser spent his time slapping people around.

True or not, *Walking Tall* was a box-office loser when it was first released by American International Pictures and promoted as a violent movie. Originally, it had received an X rating for violence and was condemned by the U.S. Catholic Conference. The distributor decided to rerelease the film with a new tag line, "When was the last time you stood up and applauded a movie?" and promoted the movie as a love story. The new poster showed Buford and his wife (although today the home-video release shows the hero carrying his stick). Almost overnight the "new" *Walking Tall* became a runaway hit, and its success baffled everyone; "I just don't understand why a violent film that advertises itself as a violent film," said Gordon Stulberg, then president of Twentieth Century-Fox, "suddenly starts doing business when it starts advertising itself as a love story."

Critics, however, saw the film for what it really was: "The blood-pounding excitement that most of the street westerns aim for is simply box-office excitement," Pauline Kael wrote in the *New Yorker*, "but in *Walking Tall* it is integral to the fundamentalist politics that probably all of us carry inside us at some primitive level—even those of us who watch this picture appalled. . . ." The film was followed by a couple of sequels, *Part 2, Walking Tall*

(1975) and *Final Chapter—Walking Tall* (1977), both starring Bo
Svenson as Pusser, a television movie entitled *A Real American
Hero* (1978) with Brian Dennehy, and a 1981 *Walking Tall* TV
series, also with Svenson.

Mad Max

Max Rockatansky (Mel
Gibson), the hero of *Mad Max* (1979), Mad Max 2 (1981; retitled
The Road Warrior in the United States), and *Mad Max Beyond
Thunderdome* (1985), has often been compared to a futuristic
Dirty Harry. In Australian-made *Mad Max*, our society is in
decay, and the inner-city highways have become the arena for
death games between nomad bikers and a handful of dedicated
cops like Max. A road chase between Max and crazed biker
known as the Knightrider (Vince Gil) results in the death of the
latter, whose buddies, headed by a psycho named Toecutter

George
Miller's Mad
Max, the
Dirty Harry of
the future.
(Warner
Bros.)

(Hugh Keays-Byrne), come to town to seek revenge. Max and his partner, Jim Goose (Steve Broley), arrest the drug-crazed Johnny the Boy, a member of Toecutter's gang, after he and his buddies rape a young couple. Johnny is released on a legal technicality and Goose is hunted and burned alive in his car by the Toecutter gang. Horrified, Max quits the force and takes his wife, Jessie (Joanne Samuel), and their baby, Sprog, on a vacation. But the biker gang catches up with them, murders the baby, and leaves Jessie a vegetable for life. In a state of complete madness, vengeful Max returns to the force and hunts down and kills the nomad bikers one by one in an orgy of nonstop violence.

Today there are at least four different versions of *Mad Max*. (The U.S. distributor even found it necessary to dub in American voices on the original soundtrack out of fear that audiences might not understand the actors' Australian accent.) The film, which made an international star of Mel Gibson, was banned in New Zealand because of fear that its violence and antisocial behavior might be emulated. In France it was also perceived as excessively violent and received an X rating, carrying with it a 33 percent surtax, which eventually forced the European distributor to postpone its release. It took two years before *Mad Max* could be shown in France. Were these reactions justified? Though not as graphic as *Walking Tall*, the film has such energy from beginning to end that it seems a lot rougher than it really is. In fact, we only see the beginning and the aftermath of violence, never the actual act. Even the most violent moment in the film, the killing of baby Sprog, is well handled; all we see are the baby's little shoes flying and falling on the road. I lived in France at the time of the film's release, and I remember people talking about the death of the baby, saying that they actually saw the infant being ripped apart by the bikers. Of course, none of this was shown in the released prints, but the power of the film and the horrifying situations depicted in it led the audience to believe they saw more than they did. "I don't want to see blood and guts on the screen," director and coscreenwriter George Miller said. "A good horror flick will often keep the monster just out of the screen. I tried to do this, too. What is out of the frame is always more effective than what is in the frame. But violence is a part of us, and I don't think that we understand it very well. There is an ugly side to each of us, and I have tried to communicate it. I know sometimes people don't like to hear that. But if you make

Ultraviolence, bloodshed, and nastiness . . . Miller's *Mad Max 2: The Road Warrior*. (Warner Bros.)

concessions to the audience, you'll get lost along the way."

"*The Road Warrior* is rated R for a very good reason," Jimmy Summers wrote in the industry trade magazine *Box Office*. "Its violence is quick and occasionally off-camera, but its impact will leave audiences weakened. It's not for everyone." Ron Goulard of *Twilight Zone* magazine concurred: "The movie is full of violence, bloodshed, and nastiness, but it moves at such an exhilarating pace and does all the tricks so well that you get caught up in the whole dippy story." Like *Mad Max*, the sequel didn't have much of a plot. Director George Miller's intention was to re-create another brutal and violent futuristic action film. In this new episode, civilization has broken down completely, and gangs are roaring through the wasteland for the most precious commodity, fuel. Max has become a solitary figure who joins a communal group, the life-support system of which is a refinery. The commune is constantly under threat and attacks from marauders, led by a man named Humungus (not a misnomer), until Max becomes involved and violently destroys the enemy in a dangerous but ultimately successful chase.

"People say, 'You must be very interested in violence.' " George Miller declared. "And in a way I am, but in relationship to death, in confronting death. I worked as a doctor for two years; six months were in big-city emergency wards, where you see peo-

This particularly gruesome shooting scene from Paul Verhoeven's *RoboCop* was trimmed down to avoid an X rating. (Orion Pictures)

ple die in a fairly extreme state. People die; babies are born. I know this is reflected in the two *Mad Max* films, which are fairly preoccupied with extreme situations. In that sense I see them as having a lot of elements of horror movies." *The Road Warrior* is a lot more graphic than its prequel; at one point, a kid's boomerang goes right through the skull of one of the bikers. Later, the boomerang, which is made of metal, slices up all the fingers of a man who is trying to catch it. Women are raped and killed and men are tortured—and this time, we get to see it all. Perceived generally by the critics as B movies and as plotless, the first two *Mad Max* films do have an unusual visual style and memorable action sequences which made them quite popular with the general public. *Mad Max* and *The Road Warrior* were followed by *Mad Max Beyond Thunderdome* (1985), which George Miller codirected with George Ogilvie. In their attempt to reach a broader audience, the filmmakers softened up the story and turned their hero into a comic-book character when they paired Mel Gibson, as Max, with Tina Turner, the evil Auntie Entity. In the film, Max comes upon the city of Bartertown and survives a battle to death in the Thunderdome arena. He is exiled to the desert and is rescued by a tribe of wild children. Together they team up to destroy Auntie Entity. *Thunderdome* is at best rough around the edges, a bit sadistic, but it has no real graphic violence in it, and deprived of an original style, the Mad Max series sadly came to an end.

RoboCop

Dutch director Paul Verhoeven's vision of the future of law enforcement in *RoboCop* (1987) is as bleak as that of the *Mad Max* movies; the central character is as ruthless as Max and Dirty Harry put together. A cop, played by Peter Weller, is killed in the line of duty, and he is reconstructed as a machine, a RoboCop, who still has human feelings and memories of his violent death. RoboCop seeks revenge and hunts down and kills the creeps who murdered him.

The version that was shown in theaters was not the director's cut; originally, the film was a lot more violent and received an X rating. Director Verhoeven had to recut *RoboCop* seven times in order to get an acceptable R rating. "On *RoboCop*, I feel the original cut was better. The original was more violent, and I think that worked better. It was funnier. The scene, for example, when the young executive is killed [by the robot ED 209] in the boardroom was much more violent. We did not shoot the inserts until later; we rebuilt part of the set, and we did more stuff which was all in the first cut of the film. There were fountains of blood. The robot ED 209 went on and on and on. [The robot had machine guns built into its unit.] The guy was already dead, but the robot was still shooting, and all that blood was spurting out. It was extremely, absolutely fascinating, I thought. After that, when the robot finally stops, one of the actors says. 'Somebody call the paramedics.' I have seen that version with a test audience, you know, and people were exploding with laughter after this tension.

"The whole thing was so interesting, so artistic, I would say. It was ultraviolence and then ultrahumor. Of course, by toning that down, people are still laughing, but they never laugh on the first line; they laugh on the second line, when somebody says, 'Nobody touches him,' which is, of course, nonsense, since he's been blown away. The killing of Murphy [Peter Weller] was also cut. The killing was absolutely agonizing the first time. It was unwatchable, I would say. I mean, it wasn't unwatchable, but that's probably how you would feel if you saw it. It was so power-ful, it was so mean, that I think it had more impact even for the rest of the movie. His death is memorable, and it's still agonizing in the film, but in the original cut, it threw a shadow over the whole movie that never left you."

Still, *RoboCop* is "violently" effective. Unfortunately, the film was followed by two sequels (*RoboCop 2* in 1990 and *RoboCop 3* in 1993, neither directed by Paul Verhoeven), an animated TV series, and a live-action one. The sequels never lived up to the standards and the style established by Verhoeven in the original. *RoboCop 2* was particularly—and absurdly—savage, but the plot-less and characterless narrative proved one more time that screen violence, without a strong story line and convincing heroes, simply has no redeeming value.

RoboCop . . . The future of law enforcement is as bleak as its present. (Orion Pictures, photo by Deana Newcomb)

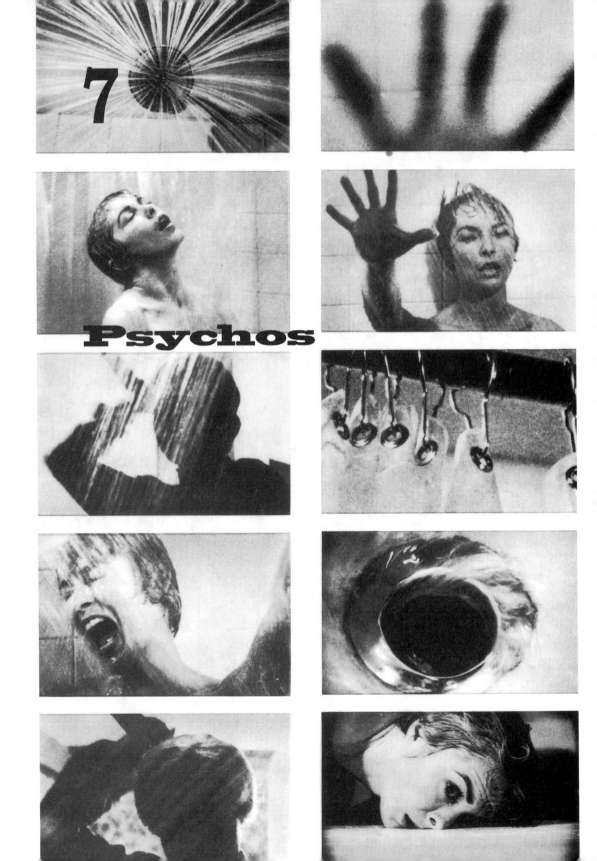

7

Psychos

Psycho

Undoubtedly one of the most violent scenes ever filmed is the shower sequence in Alfred Hitchcock's *Psycho* (1960). Based on a novel by Robert Bloch, the film is about a young man, Norman Bates (Anthony Perkins), who, having murdered his mother and her lover, develops a split personality. When the mother side takes over, he kills. In Bloch's novel, Marion Crane (Janet Leigh's character) was also murdered in a shower, but instead of being stabbed to death, she was beheaded with a butcher knife:

> Mary started to scream, and then the curtains parted
> further and a hand appeared, holding a butcher knife.
> It was a knife that, a moment later, cut off her scream.
>
> And her head.

This, of course, would have been impossible to film at the time; the censors would have never allowed it. In adapting the novel, screenwriter Joseph Stefano conveyed the murder with precaution:

> A hand comes into the shot. The hand holds an enormous bread knife. The flint of the blade shatters the screen to an almost total, silver blankness.

The slashing:

> An impression of the knife slashing, as if tearing at the very screen ripping the film. Over it the brief gulps of screaming. And then silence. And then the dreadful thump as Mary's body falls in the tub. [Marion Crane was originally Mary Crane until Hitchcock found out there was a real Mary Crane living in Arizona.]

It took Hitchcock between seven and eleven days to shoot the murder in the shower. Instead of filming the killing from just a few angles, as most directors would have, Hitchcock created about seventy different setups. *Psycho*'s pictorial consultant, Saul Bass, always made the claim that he, not Hitchcock, directed the shower sequence. Janet Leigh, on the other hand, doesn't even remember Bass being present on the set. In any case, the editing, the crunching sound of the knife striking at the victim, Bernard Herrmann's inspired score (although originally Hitchcock had intended the scene to be shown without music), all added to the impact and to the violence of the murder. The scene was so effective that most people in the audience thought they saw the blade actually stabbing the actress, whereas in fact it never touches her.

"Now, I don't take showers, I take baths, and if I have no choice, I always do it with the curtain open," actress Janet Leigh has declared. "Obviously, the bathroom gets very wet, but I sincerely have become phobic about showers. The scene didn't truly affect me when I shot it, but when I saw the film, it absolutely frightened me. I remember having nightmares for a while after that." And so did audiences around the world.

While the film is today considered a masterpiece, reviews were mixed in 1960. *Time* magazine called the shower sequence "one of the messiest, most nauseating murders ever filmed. At close range, the camera watches every twitch, gurgle, convulsion, and hemorrhage in the process by which a living human becomes a corpse." Others found *Psycho* plainly sickening, too violent, and in bad taste.

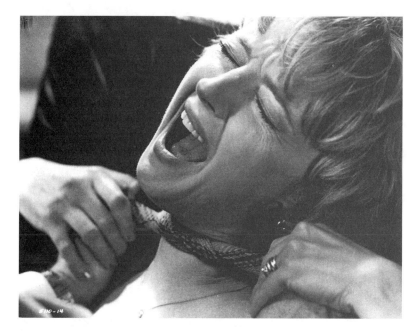

Equally jolting was the killing of Arbogast (the late Martin Balsam), who comes to interrogate Norman Bates's "mother." He climbs the stairs in the motel, and suddenly a figure appears at the top and slashes his face with a knife. He stumbles down the stairs and falls. The killer then stabs him repeatedly. Controversial because of its violence—and the partial nudity in the opening sequence of the film between Janet Leigh and John Gavin—*Psycho* opened a new door and showed that even violence could be exploited in an artistic and creative way.

Six years after its release, the movie was still controversial. When the scheduled CBS broadcast of *Psycho* in 1966 was postponed after the tragic slaying in Chicago of twenty-one-year-old Valerie Jeanne Percy, daughter of Charles H. Percy, the Republican senatorial candidate from Illinois. Although having already deleted nine minutes from *Psycho*, the network judged it would be in poor taste to show the film after such a tragedy. Today, of course, faced with similar circumstances, the network might have commissioned a bloody made-for-TV film based on the crime.

In 1983, three years after Hitchcock died, Universal produced *Psycho II*, directed by skilled Australian director Richard Franklin. Then came *Psycho III* (1986), directed by Anthony Perkins himself, and *Psycho IV: The Beginning* (1990), directed by

185

Mick Garris, from a script by Joseph Stefano. All sequels were produced (or executive produced, as in the case of *Psycho IV*) by Hilton A. Green, who began working with Hitchcock on the unmatched original. The level of violence and nudity increased, and at times the sequels seem more spin-offs rather than homages to Hitchcock's masterpiece. "My objection to *Psycho II*," Janet Leigh said, "was that it was too graphically violent. You see, it went totally against Hitchcock's concept. But on the other hand, I guess it matched today's mentality." One wonders how Hitchcock would direct *Psycho* today. Judging by the violence of the rape scene in *Frenzy* (1972), we can easily assume that if the director was working today, he'd probably want to go as far as possible.

Halloween

John Carpenter's *Halloween* (1978) stands out not only because it was a well-made, if low-budget, film but also because, like *Psycho*, it established the murderer as superstar. After *Halloween*'s Michael Myers, could Jason, Freddy Krueger, or Chucky the Doll be far behind?

Halloween has a very simple plot. A deranged killer, Michael Myers, who had murdered his sister when he was a child, escapes from the asylum where he's been held for many years. He returns to his hometown and terrorizes the neighborhood. Michael brutally kills several horny teenagers on Halloween night and then comes after Laurie (played by Jamie Lee Curtis, daughter of *Psycho* victim Janet Leigh), a virginal baby-sitter. Ultimately, Donald Pleasance, Michael's doctor, tracks down his patient and saves Laurie's life. Although he's been shot several times and has fallen through a window, Michael is still running. "You can't kill the Bogeyman. . . ."

Producer Irwin Yablans got the idea for a movie he wanted to call *The Baby Sitter Murders* and shared the concept of the story with Joe Wolf, his partner, and Moustapha Akkad, a Syrian director-financier. He then contacted director John Carpenter, who had just directed a well-crafted "cheapie" entitled *Assault on Precinct 13* (1976). Carpenter eventually teamed up with Debra Hill, then his sweetheart, to write what became *Halloween*. The film was shot in twenty-two days with a budget of $300,000; it

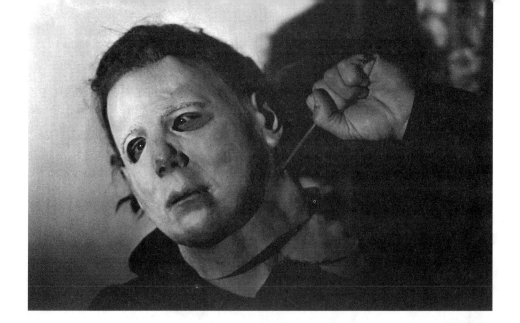

"Michael Myers," *Halloween*'s psycho-killer. (Compass International)

grossed $5 million within two months. To date *Halloween* has grossed well over $65 million, about two hundred times its original cost. Carpenter's concept for the film was to confuse the mythology of Halloween with real horror. On the one hand, there is Laurie, an innocent young teenager; on the other, her friends, who are openly experimenting with drugs and sex. The film was criticized because Laurie, who is a virgin, survives, while the other girls, who are having sex, are murdered.

Carpenter and Hill always resented this analysis and claimed that the victims are murdered because they're too busy to notice what else is happening. Like Hitchcock, Carpenter didn't want to show sex but tried to convey vulnerability—and the violence of being vulnerable without really exploiting it. The director's philosophy on the set was Don't gross out the audience or you'll lose them; "If you don't gross them out, don't show the meat when the knife goes in, don't cut to the blood going everywhere; then all of them will stay with you. If you suggest it, they'll do it right up here, in their heads."

As a teenager, John Carpenter went on a trip to a mental institution and saw a boy who he felt had the look of pure evil. The boy just stared at him, and it terrified him. That description is used by the doctor played by Donald Pleasance in the film when he talks about meeting Michael Myers for the first time. Carpenter almost never shows Myers's face. The killer wears a mask (a modified mask of Captain Kirk) throughout the film. Myers was played—in all but a couple of scenes—by Nick Castle, who later became a director whose credits include *The Last Starfighter* (1984), *Dennis the Menace* (1993), and *Mr. Wrong* (1996). Castle's father was a choreographer, which might explain why the actor managed to create a very distinctive, almost robot-ic-like walk for his character. One of the most violent scenes in the film shows Myers grabbing a teenage guy, lifting him up, and stabbing him to the wall. (The sound of the knife stabbing the guy was added during a dubbing session using a knife stabbing

Trick or treat? (Compass International)

a watermelon.) After killing the victim, Myers just stands there, staring at his victim with a sick fascination, but with a childlike, almost innocent posture.

"What scares me," declared Carpenter, "scares every human on the planet. We're all aware of the forces of darkness, of evil, of loss, death. We know this as little children. I think all of this is dealt with in *Grimm's Fairy Tales*. I think it's dealt with in horror movies. Horror is the universal language."

The horror genre has changed a great deal since *Halloween*

was made, and so has our society. What seemed shocking and violent in 1978 looks tame today. Coproducer and cowriter Debra Hill agrees with this notion and said that whereas it used to be that art was imitating life, today it's the other way around. Life is imitating art. "We sort of have to censor ourselves by showing less graphic violence, by showing more human drama, and also by showing less graphic sex. I think we have a responsibility to the changing times with violence everywhere; with AIDS prevalent everywhere, we just have to take the responsibilities and try to find stories that are driven by characters who find some sense of good in people and some sense of fairness in life and should present those characters as role models."

At the same time, John Carpenter feels it's important to know that there is the possibility of evil out there. "All children should be told that the world can be bad and dark and dangerous but with a little luck and awareness you can survive." Horror films have a job to do, and it could be to prevent violence by offering an "entertaining" vision of it. "If you can scream and be frightened in a theater in safety," Carpenter said, "you come out into the real world and sleep peacefully. You've had a catharsis, you've had an experience that's made you a little bit better. You can survive. You can survive the terrors of the world." And yet screen violence in itself and the possibility that it might have a negative influence on certain individuals do not really concern Carpenter: "I grew up with violent movies, and I didn't turn out bad, so I have a hard time believing that violent movies can have a strong influence on children. But I'm more concerned at the fact that people watch seven hours of television a day; it always comes back to the parents, who need to be more responsible."

Although there is very little gore in *Halloween*, it was criticized for being too violent and antiwoman until Tom Allen, in the *Village Voice*, observed: "*Halloween* is a sleeper that's here to stay. It can stand proud alongside *Night of the Living Dead* and Hitchcock's *Psycho*." Siskel and Ebert gave the film "two thumbs up," saying that "artistry can redeem any subject matter." *Halloween* was followed over the years by *Halloween II* (1981), *Halloween III: Season of the Witch* (1983), *Halloween IV: The Return of Michael Myers* (1988), *Halloween V: The Revenge of Michael Myers* (1989) and *Halloween VI* (1995). Carpenter was only involved in the first sequel—and later said that he felt he was Xeroxing the original, only this time there was more blood, more gore, more violence. "It's sad," Carpenter commented simply.

Dressed to Kill

Brian De Palma's *Dressed to Kill* (1981) was highly influenced by *Psycho*. In fact, over the years, many critics have condemned De Palma as a Hitchcock copycat. *Dressed to Kill* is about Kate Miller (Angie Dickinson), a sexually repressed housewife. She complains to her psychiatrist, Dr. Elliott (Michael Caine), about her husband's pathetic performances in bed and tests her sexual appeal by trying to seduce him. Elliott turns down the proposition. Kate then picks up a stranger in a museum and lives out her wildest fantasies with him. Before she leaves her one-afternoon stand, she discovers that the handsome stranger has a venereal disease. Kate rushes out of the apartment but has to go back up after she realizes she's forgotten her wedding ring. When the elevator doors open, she is attacked and slashed to death by a blond woman with dark glasses. Liz Blake (Nancy Allen), a "Park Avenue whore," is the only witness to the murder and becomes at once the prime suspect as well as the killer's next prey. Liz is saved by Peter (Keith Gordon), Kate's son,

Margot Kidder in De Palma's *Sisters, hates* her birthday. (American International Pictures)

who is determined to unmask the killer, since Marino (Dennis Franz), the detective in charge of the case, is being totally uncooperative. Peter discovers that the killer is one of Dr. Elliott's patients. Liz decides to seduce the shrink in order to check out his appointment book and finds out that Elliott himself was Bobbi, the murderess. Liz is saved by a female undercover cop. It turned out Elliott was a transsexual with a split-personality syndrome; each time he was aroused by a woman, Bobbi—his female alter ego—took over and killed.

When *Dressed to Kill* was submitted to the MPAA, Brian De Palma was informed that his film was likely to receive an X. De Palma declared at the time that this decision took him totally by surprise. This was not the first time he had depicted gruesome murders. In his film *Sisters* (1973), Margot Kidder savagely stabbed a man in the face and in the groin. In *Carrie* (1976), one of the most violent sequences showed Piper Laurie being stabbed to death by flying kitchen utensils. In *The Fury* (1978), De Palma literally blew John Cassavetes to pieces. De Palma argued that there were many other films—possibly including some of his own—that received an R and were as explicit as *Dressed to Kill*. Dr. Richard Heffner of CARA (Classification and Rating Administration) referred to the film as a "masterwork" but nevertheless declared that the administration had to give it an X because it had just too much sex and violence. At the time, Brian De Palma had this to say about the MPAA: "I sense a repressive era begin-

ning in the country again. I always gauge these things by who's headed for the White House."

The controversy around *Dressed to Kill* came at the time director William Friedkin, producer Jerry Weintraub, and United Artists were caught in a battle with the MPAA over their film *Cruising* (1980), which dealt with the world of S and M homosexuals. De Palma had at one point written an adaptation of *Cruising*, based on the novel by Gerald Walker, and had created for the story the character of a sexually repressed housewife. When De Palma abandoned *Cruising*, that character became the departure for *Dressed to Kill*. He felt that his film was a direct victim of the controversy that surrounded *Cruising*. De Palma was forced to make some strategic cuts in the opening shower sequence, in the murder scene in the elevator, and in the nightmare sequence at the end of the film. He also had to replace some of the dialogue in the scene during which Liz (Nancy Allen) comes on to Dr. Elliott (Michael Caine.) De Palma finally got an R rating after submitting *Dressed to Kill* three times to the MPAA.

The critics either loved the film and saw De Palma as Hitchcock's legitimate successor or thought it was an obvious rip-off of *Psycho*. But even more ruthless than the critics and the

MPAA were feminists who viewed the violence in *Dressed to Kill* as an incitement to real violence against women. They also felt that critics who liked the movie—and encouraged audiences to go see *Dressed to Kill*—were as dangerous as De Palma. About fifty people, organized by the group Women Against Violence Against Women (WAVAW), demonstrated against the film in front of the Hollywood Pacific Theater in Los Angeles. The group was created in 1976 around a movie entitled *Snuff*, which showed real deaths and mutilations. At the time *Dressed to Kill* came out, the group had about one thousand members nationally. "A movie like *Dressed to Kill* encourages and perpetuates violence," Stephanie Rones of WAVAW said, "and pairs it with sexuality by showing vicious acts instead of loving and caring. Film critics have enormous responsibilities and often write about what they see in a very narrow sense, reviewing only the artistic relevance and ignoring the social relevance. Is a woman being slashed in an elevator funny or erotic or entertaining? Critics should look at films on a broader level."

San Francisco Chronicle reviewer Judy Stone had this to say about WAVAW's comments and its attack on movie critics: "Filmmakers have a right to do an honest representation of violence and not clean it up. Real violence is bloody, shocking and disturbing. I don't think much of what this WAVAW group has to say. They know nothing about criminal behavior. And women do indeed have fantasies; women are being killed. Art has a duty to show it." WAVAW even wrote a letter to *Los Angeles Times* critic Sheila Benson: "We are shocked and greatly dismayed that anyone would find *Dressed to Kill* elegant, sensual and erotic, a directorial tour de force. We are especially disturbed that a woman would enjoy this film. . . . to glamorize [violence] on the big screen is deplorable. And to praise such a film as brilliant is totally irresponsible." Benson, who had marched in demonstrations against *Cruising*, was shocked by the accusation: "I don't think *Dressed to Kill* tried to depict murder either as attractive or anything to emulate."

WAVAW's Stephanie Rones, who at the time worked with battered women, said the film preyed on the fear of women who go out at night. "The title of the movie itself suggests women can bring on rape by how they dress, that women can be dressed to be killed." According to Rones, another objectionable scene showed Nancy Allen being harassed by a group of black men in the subway. "We all know black men want to rape white women," said Rones, herself a black woman. "The movie perpetuates a myth. And Angie Dickinson fantasizing about being raped. That women subconsciously want to be raped is a myth also. With rising rape statistics, there are still these kind of movies. Another point. Most violent crimes are committed by heterosexual men; this one shows a transsexual man. It's only for prurience's sake. The movie represents aggressive and vicious models to men that women are to be used violently." While encouraging a boycott of the picture, Rones said that, on the other hand, the organization was not advocating censorship. "We object to violence in all forms. There are men in our organization. It's just that violence seems so much more legitimized when aimed at women, that it's okay. Women are victimized more often than men. We're easy targets. We simply feel there's a correlation between what people see and how they act. *Dressed to Kill* is not a documentary. It entices, eroticizes, and perpetuates violence."

Coming to the defense of the film was its star, Angie Dickinson, who felt that *Dressed to Kill* was an honest and true representation of life and that denying such facts as violence against women was more damaging than showing it on the screen. The actress said that feminists want to see an idealistic version of life, not reality; unfortunately, De Palma's vision is to show life as it exists. As for the fact that the film might influence certain individuals to commit violence against women, Dickinson claimed that "if you have violence in your soul, you'll get it out one way or the other. Seeing a movie won't make a difference."

Finally, years after making *Dressed to Kill*, Brian De Palma, on the set of *Casualties of War*, had this to say about the issue of violence in his films: "When someone attacks me, they write about Angie Dickinson getting sliced up by a razor or Debbie Shelton in *Body Double*. [The actress gets run through by a power drill.] Geez, I had Margot Kidder murder a guy with a butcher knife in *Sisters*, a man get cut up with a chain saw in *Scarface*, and we just blew Al Pacino to bits in that one. They never mention that. I say it's pretty much equal-opportunity mayhem in my films."

Basic Instinct

In 1992 *Basic Instinct*, directed by Paul Verhoeven, caused a big uproar in the gay community. As with *Cruising*, activists thought the film was dangerous because it portrayed lesbians as killers. In *Basic Instinct*, Michael Douglas investigates a murder and gets involved with the prime suspect, a bisexual woman played by Sharon Stone. Blinded by lust, the Douglas character ends up losing his partner on the force and his former girlfriend, who gets blamed for the murders, and still believes in the end that the madwoman is innocent.

This particularly gruesome shot was deleted from the American version of Verhoeven's *Basic Instinct*. (Carolco/Le Studio Canal, special effects makeup by Rob Bottin)

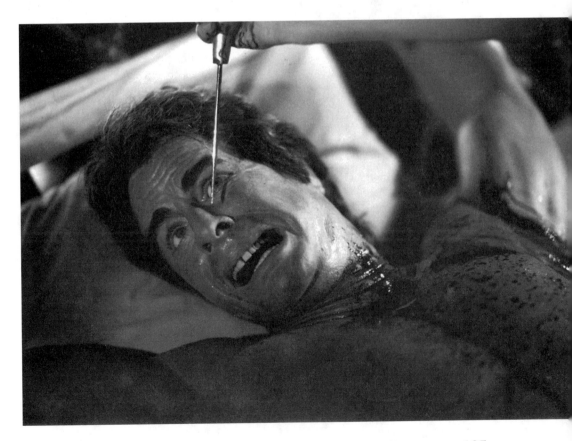

Anthony Hopkins as Dr. Hannibal Lecter in Jonathan Demme's *Silence of the Lambs* gave psycho-killers a good name. (Orion Pictures, photo by Ken Regan)

Gays tried not only to stop production but to have director Verhoeven and screenwriter Joe Eszterhas change the script. All their attempts failed. The MPAA found the film (a) too sexually explicit and (b) too violent and gave it an NC-17. The opening sequence has a woman stabbing a man with an ice pick; another murder scene takes place in an elevator, as in *Dressed to Kill*. Both scenes, along with some of the most erotic moments, had to be changed. *Basic Instinct*, however, was released completely uncut in Europe; "The murder [in the opening sequence] in the European version is, I think eight seconds," Verhoeven said. "It's about seven seconds in the U.S. version. So timewise it's practically the same scene, but the impact of it is gone. The close-up of the ice pick going through his [the victim's] nose and the full body shot where you see the blood and her [the killer] stabbing on top of him have all been taken out. The shock of the scene in the European version is—you're really like blown away. It's what I wanted. It's strange because it's so short. It's not twenty seconds, it's eight seconds! I mean, it's probably shorter than the shower sequence in *Psycho*, but it's so powerful. I wanted it to be that shocking because for a very long time after that scene nothing really happens. And later, when we have a bed scene again and you see her [Sharon Stone], you should know that this might happen again, and it's horrible."

Both *Basic Instinct* and *Dressed to Kill* are now available uncut at local video stores.

196

Henry: Portrait of a Serial Killer

In 1988 I was doing feature-film development for a New York independent producer and received the tape of a yet-to-be-released movie, entitled *Henry: Portrait of a Serial Killer* from a talent agency. The company I worked for had optioned the rights to a horror novel, and we were looking for a writer-director to adapt it. According to the agent who had sent us *Henry*, John McNaughton, the cowriter, coproducer, and director of the film, was the man for the job. So I sat through *Henry*, and what I saw disturbed me so much that I remember having to stop the film several times. I confess having fast-forwarded through several scenes that were simply too violent. Although most of the violence took place offscreen, McNaughton was forcing you to follow the film from the point of view of a serial killer. It's almost as if he dared you to sympathize with him or to become fascinated with the nuts and bolts of serial killing. In fact, the film, which was shot on a very low budget, looked like a snuff movie in which real people were being killed. Today *Henry* has reached cult status; you can even buy T-shirts with the film's logo on them. The critical success of the film might explain why *The Silence of the Lambs* (1992), a grand-scale version of *Henry* directed by Jonathan Demme and starring Jodie Foster and Anthony Hopkins, became so popular. We're all familiar with the *Lambs* story; FBI agent Foster seeks the help of a legendary serial killer behind bars (Hopkins) named Hannibal Lecter, to crack a case involving another serial killer. She succeeds, but Hannibal escapes. Unlike *Henry*, *Lambs* doesn't follow the story from the point of view of a killer, which makes the film far more accessible to a mainstream audience. Also, although being scary and suspenseful and suggesting a few violent moments, it doesn't compare to the shock that *Henry* elicits from audiences. It's okay to like Hannibal, because he is, after all, Anthony Hopkins, and that's Hollywood. But Henry is another story.

McNaughton's film begins with a montage of Henry's victims; they're all women. We see dead bodies, but we hear the sounds of the killing. Henry (Michael Rooker) shares an apartment in Chicago with Otis (Tom Towles), his former cellmate.

Otis divides his time between working at a gas station, selling drugs to high school boys, trying to seduce them, and visiting his parole officer. We know what Henry does. Becky, Otis's sister (Tracy Arnold), comes into the picture. She has left her daughter and her abusive husband and has come to live with her brother. Our three characters have survived a sordid childhood; Otis and Becky were raised by a drunken father who beat them both and sexually abused his daughter. Henry was in jail for fourteen years for the murder of his mother, a prostitute who forced him to wear women's clothing and watch her having sex with her customers. There've been many killings ever since.

Becky immediately finds herself attracted to Henry; curiously, he is kind to her and treats her well. But Otis gets jealous, and to compensate, Henry decides to spend more time with his friend. One night while driving around, they pick up two prostitutes. Henry is in the backseat with one of them and snaps her neck. When the one up front screams, he nonchalantly snaps her neck, too. He disposes of the bodies in a trash heap. Otis is horrified; Henry explains that he's killed many women, always in a different way. That's why he hasn't been caught; the police think the murders are unrelated. From that point on, Henry becomes Otis's murder mentor.

In a horrifying scene, Henry and Otis invade the home of a couple and decide to film their crime with a stolen video camera. The husband is gagged, and as Otis prepares to rape the wife, the couple's teenage son returns home from school. The kid tries to run, but Henry catches him and kills him. The father and the mother are next. Gradually, the "friendship" between Otis and

Henry gets a little tense, and one night, Henry finds Otis attempting to rape Becky. A fight ensues, and Becky kills her brother by stabbing him through the eye with a comb. Henry and Becky dispose of the body and head west. It seems for a while that Becky is going to change Henry, but she doesn't. Henry ultimately murders her and leaves her dismembered body in a suitcase on the side of the road.

Henry was commissioned in 1985 by Chicago-based MPI home video. The owners, brothers Waleed B. and Malik Alie, chose John McNaughton, who had directed for them *Dealing in Death*, a documentary on Chicago gangsters. McNaughton had been doing documentaries and industrials, and he immediately jumped at the chance of directing a feature film. Aware of the market's constant demand for horror films, MPI wanted McNaughton to turn a low-budget slasher film (the budget they had in mind was $100,000) into a big profit for the company. While McNaughton accepted the offer, he refused to make a bad film, even at a low cost. He brought in actor-playwright Richard Fire to work with him on a script. Together they wondered how they could create a new kind of horror film, one that would break tradition and demand that audiences identify with a serial killer in a new and audacious way.

The catalyst for *Henry* was a piece on ABC's *20/20* on real-life serial killer Henry Lee Lucas, who claimed he had murdered between 120 and 360 people. "Henry [Lee Lucas] was slow-talking and kind of strange looking," McNaughton said, "but he had this sort of dumb charm. And it was because he had this sort of charm that he had been able to get close enough to people to slaughter them. So I immediately thought: Here was a real-life horror. And, anyway, we had no budget for chain saws and special effects and monsters." McNaughton had realized while watching the *20/20* segment that true horror was right here with us, next to ordinary people, but mainly he realized that our feeling of security might just be an illusion and that our world wasn't safe. "We tried to make it something more than junk. We didn't try to lay in a very specific theme, only that it's a crazy, dangerous world. These people, killers, are out there, and if it's your turn. . . ." The filmmakers sold MPI on their intentions to do a fictionalized portrait of a serial killer.

At first, McNaughton and Steven A. Jones, his producer, had thought of making a semidocumentary movie, "a sort of week in the life of a serial killer." Writer Richard Fire gave the film more of a narrative and, with McNaughton, also planned to explore the fact that it is human nature to want to watch violence; don't we all stop to watch the victims of car accidents? "There's always a gapers' block when somebody's lying slaughtered along the side of the road," Fire said. "It's human nature, and to deny it is false. To admit it, I think, is some small victory—you have a little more understanding of humans." The writer was from the Organic Theatre Company, one of Chicago's top off-Broadway-type groups, as were both Tom Towles, who played Otis, and Tracy Arnold, who played Becky. In an eerie coincidence, some of Henry Lee Lucas's victims had been friends of Tracy Arnold's family.

"I couldn't find a Henry until our effects man suggested Michael Rooker, who was then between engagements and painting houses for a living," McNaughton recalled. "The minute he started reading for the part, we knew he was it [Henry]. Michael's from a dirt-poor hillbilly family from Alabama that settled in Chicago when he was a boy." Rooker has since been in such films as *Sea of Love* (1989), *The Music Box* (1989), *Days of Thunder* (1990), and *Cliffhanger* (1993). "You might have noticed in *Henry*," McNaughton said, "that every time he kills someone he takes his jacket off first—he [Rooker] wore his own clothes in the movie. He only owned one jacket then and didn't want it stained." Michael Rooker had this to say about his character: "Henry is a paradox. He is at once a cold-blooded killer and a gentle giant. This synthesis of emotions is what fascinated me about the character and continues to fascinate me about the acting process." Rooker gave Henry a face, and the personality of the actor helped McNaughton accomplish his goal: "Without doubt, Henry was a very damaged person," McNaughton said. "But I wanted viewers to explore how different he is—or isn't—from the rest of us. It's healthy to poke around in ourselves, even if it makes us uncomfortable. Human beings are capable of horrific violence." It was difficult to get Henry to challenge the audience's desensitization to violence. At one point, Henry kills a rude salesman. As with the Rambo movies, the audience is supposed to say: "Yeah, get him, Henry!" Immediately after, however, Henry and Otis murder an innocent family. That's when reality hits and when *Henry* becomes an uncomfortable experience for the viewer.

The film was shot in 1985 and 1986 in four weeks on 16-mm color negative stock which eventually was blown up to 35 mm. "*Henry* was the most artistically realized thing we could do," coproducer Steven A. Jones said, "but it was also a dark, brutal experience. I figured they'd either flock to our door or put us in jail." When the filmmakers organized a screening of *Henry* for MPI, their comments were: "Where's the blood and where's the tits? You've made a goddamn art film. What are we going to do with this?"

When MPI started to search for a theatrical distributor, Vestron was interested, but it also wanted to own the video rights. Atlantic Releasing was also interested, but on one condition: that the film receive an R rating. Of course, it didn't; the MPAA gave *Henry* an X, finding basically the whole film objectionable and unsuitable for children. Who could disagree? No one except maybe the producers, who would see their possible profit shrink to nothing if the film came out with an X. "I don't have a problem with the ratings system itself," McNaughton declared. "Children shouldn't see certain things—that's okay in my book—but it shouldn't be penalized in the marketplace so severely."

Unfortunately, since releasing *Henry* with an X would kill the film, Atlantic bowed out. So the film was shelved until 1988, when a man named Chuck Parello was hired by MPI as publicity director. He made it his mission to get the movie into theaters.

Henry ran in late shows in one theater in Chicago, and later, one screening was arranged in New York by artist Joe Coleman. *Village Voice* critic Elliott Stein saw the film and put it on his Top Ten list of 1989. In September of that year, Errol Morris (the acclaimed director of *The Thin Blue Line* [1988], a documentary in which Morris set out to prove that a convicted hitchhiker did not kill a Dallas policeman) was a guest programmer at the Telluride Film Festival in Colorado and decided to show *Henry*. The audience, critics, and exhibitors were split— and shocked by the film. About 15 percent of the audience walked out; others were simply nailed to their seats. In any case, everyone was talking about *Henry*, and during the second screening, no one walked out. The film was subsequently shown at the Boston Film Festival, and it finally got a distributor, Greycat Films, a company headed by two former executives from Vestron Pictures. The rating was still a problem; sometimes the MPAA will give filmmakers an indication of what could be cut to make the product acceptable, but in the case of *Henry*, the ratings board seemed to think that everything about the movie was tainted. "What I want to know," MPI's Waleed B. Ali declared, "is how in *Indiana Jones and the Temple of Doom* [1984] a man sticks his hand into the chest cavity of another man and pulls out a bleeding, beating heart and the movie gets a PG rating. And our movie, which has nothing like that, gets an X?" The producers of *Henry* sued the MPAA, charging the ratings board with treating their movie in a discriminatory fashion by refusing to grant it an R even though it has less graphic violence than most R-rated movies. What the producers were overlooking was the intensity of the film; had they forgotten about the scene of the brutal murders of an entire family which Henry and Otis capture on videotape? McNaughton himself considered this moment the key scene in the film and decided to use video to shoot it. "With film you believe in the surface illusion, but with video you don't. We knew that by using that video image, it would make that act seem absolutely, terriffyingly real." At that point, the film completely turned inside out. "You think this is graphic," McNaughton said, "but you're sitting here watching it, waiting to be entertained. Now what do you think about yourself, and what do you think about watching this kind of violence on the screen?"

The MPAA did not find their X rating of *Henry* unfair; at the time MPI challenged their decision, the board issued a statement that basically said that it was quite confident that the courts would continue to agree that the rating system is providing a proper and useful system to parents while protecting the creative freedom of filmmakers. *Henry* was finally released unrated, but the controversy surrounding it was one of the factors that forced the MPAA to replace the X with a new adult category called NC-17. When the film came out in selected theaters, *Henry* was already a favorite among critics. "Of all the slasher movies made in the 1980s," Jay Carr wrote in the *Boston Globe*, "only two have been worth seeing. One was Joseph Ruben's *The Stepfather* [1987], and the other is John McNaughton's *Henry*. The inky fatefulness in this story of a killer among us will haunt you." "The movie takes a sinister, unabashed look at violence in America," John M. Glionna said in the *Los Angeles Times*, "featuring a disturbing home invasion scene and others in which Henry—the epitome of the urban bogeyman—snaps necks, wields a screwdriver, and decapitates a dead victim with a kitchen knife . . . when it was over, I needed instant therapy." Michael Rooker also received glowing reviews: "Rooker manages

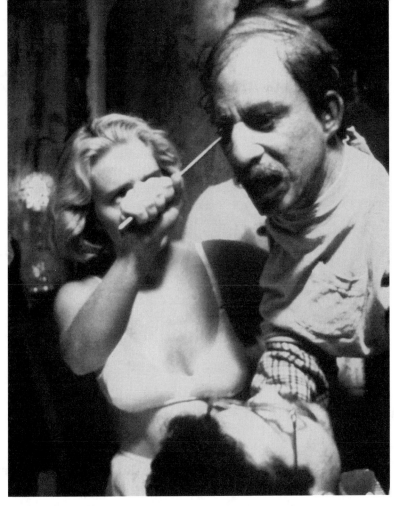

An eye-catching scene from John McNaughton's *Henry: Portrait of a Serial Killer.* (MPI Video)

to make even his muscular torso appear a symptom of psychosis," Henry Sheehan found in the *Hollywood Reporter*, "though his conventional good looks help suggest that soupçon of liability that the film hinges on." The funkiest review came from Joe Bob Briggs of the *San Francisco Examiner.* "Fourteen dead bodies. Two breasts. Multiple neck snapping. Rat-tail comb through the eyeball. Head carving. TV screen kicking. Drive-in Academy Award nomination for Tom Towles, as Otis, for saying, 'I'd like to kill somebody,' and 'You want a beer?' and John McNaughton, the director, cowriter, coproducer, for having Otis say, 'Where you going?' and having Henry answer, 'Nowhere—you wanna come?' Four stars. Joe Bob says check it out."

"The device was to pull the fantasy out and make it real," John McNaughton said. "If you make it real, they'll believe it.

When you leave the theater after *The Texas Chainsaw Massacre*, you may have nightmares, but you don't really believe that Leatherface is going to come flying around the corner and chase you down the street with a chain saw. You can have your thrill and walk away from it. With *Henry*, there's nowhere to run." The director explained how we all have a murderous urge but that there is a little gate that keeps us from crossing the line. Obviously, Henry doesn't have the gate. "There always will be people like him. We've been criticized for not 'explaining' why he kills. That's ridiculous. We're a long way from being able to explain such things. Of course, you could say it was his mother's fault, or society's, or he was abused, he was in jail, but then he could have had a twin brother who became a heart surgeon."

Man Bites Dog:

*M*an Bites Dog (1993), a cross between *Natural Born Killers* and *Henry*, is a low-budget black-and-white film from Belgium, directed by Remy Belvaux, André Bonzel, and Benoit Poelvoorde. The story is about Ben (Benoit Poelvoorde), a serial killer who is quite proud of his crimes and jumps at his chance for immortality when a crew of filmmakers approach him to do a documentary on his exploits. Ben proves to be a poet-philosopher who comments on everything from personal hygiene to architecture. He goes as far as to offer financial backing for the documentary when he discovers that the crew is operating on a shoestring. The crew meets Ben's friends, his family, his girlfriend. Then the killings begin, and during an exchange of fire between Ben and a gunman, the soundman is shot. But the show must go on; the victim is replaced. Ben attacks a family and kills everyone, including a young boy.

Later on, Ben takes the crew around a derelict mansion where he hides what he steals from his victims; suddenly, they're ambushed, and the new soundman is killed. Ben goes after the intruder and shoots him down. It turns out that the man was Ricardo Giovanni, a gang member. Ben also kills a rival film crew making a documentary on Giovanni. Another soundman is hired, and filming resumes. One night, they all get drunk and rape and murder a girl and her partner. Meanwhile, the Tavier gang sends death threats to Ben's family; Ben decides to ignore this, and while training in a boxing ring, he is knocked out and sent to the hospital. His return is celebrated with a birthday party; the film crew gives him a gun holster, which Ben tests by shooting Bobby, his trainer. When trying to dispose of the body, Ben finds out that his other victims have been uncovered. He is arrested but manages to escape. Ben learns that his mom and his girl-friend have been murdered, and then, while returning to the mansion, Ben and the entire film crew are shot down by un-known assailants.

"The thing about Ben," declared Benoit Poelvoorde, "is that most of the time he is not physically violent and that he actually becomes more murderous because of his fascination with being on camera." Still, despite the fact that *Man Bites Dog* was meant as a spoof on reality television, it is a descent into hell, at times barely watchable and yet fascinating. The film starts off as a harmless cinema verité documentary and quickly turns into snuff moviemaking. Most of the killings are cut in a few edits, but a scene when a woman is carved open after she's been raped by Ben and the film crew really tests one's tolerance for screen violence. It was suggested that this sequence be deleted for the U.S. release; actually, when the film opened in San Francisco, the American distributor, who also owned the theater where the film was being shown, took out the scene. The filmmakers were outraged and insisted that the rape scene be in it even though they had received an NC-17, limiting the distribution of the pic-ture. "I think the viewer really becomes the camera because it's always the point of view of the camera," declared codirector-writer André Bonzel. "That's why in the rape scene, when the cameraman gets in, it's even more disturbing, because it's like you are going to do it."

Man Bites Dog (its Belgian title is *C'est Arrivé Près de Chez Nous—It Happened in Our Neighborhood*, in reference to the local news section of a newspaper) received fairly good reviews and became a favorite on the festival circuit. Like *Henry*, however, its subject matter dramatically reduced audience appeal. Ella Taylor of *L.A. Weekly* wrote: "Either my boss is a sadist who delights in assigning me to review films so gruesome they make me want to throw up—or violence has become the motor that drives the movie biz." And yet, in the same article she concluded: "Yes, you should see it—if you can stand its escalating brutality, which culminates in a rape scene that almost did me in."

In Europe, and particularly in France, the original poster showing Ben shooting a baby offscreen, with blood and a pacifier flying in the foreground, had to be changed; the pacifier was replaced by false teeth.

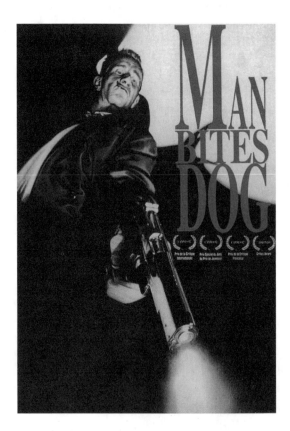

"It's all right to kill old people but not babies," said Bonzel, who admitted being surprised at certain negative reactions the film received. "Violence is there in society even if we don't show it. And maybe, if you do show it on-screen, you don't have to be violent in real life. But I agree that the violence you show should be honest and make people think. Our film is not like *Rambo*, where you have black-and-white villains and the hero just shoots lots of people up and you're meant to cheer along with it. That's obscene." And on the influence of screen violence: "People assign too much responsibility for violence to films and filmmakers. You never get people saying the same thing about writers and painters and artists. And to tell the truth, we never really thought our film would be very offensive. TV is far more offensive."

The Bad Lieutenant

In Abel Ferrara's *The Bad Lieutenant* (1993), Harvey Keitel portrays a corrupt cop who deals drugs, humiliates women, and lives a scummy existence until a nun is brutally raped by two hoods. Although she knows who they are, he is outraged by the fact that she won't talk. He continues to sink into a world of filth, making enemies, and soon realizes that his badge doesn't necessarily protect him anymore. By coincidence, he meets the two rapists, and instead of killing them, he lets them go. But it's too late for redemption, and the bad lieutenant is shot in his car.

Ferrara, mostly known for his underground films (*Driller Killer* [1979], *Ms. 45*, [1981], and *King of New York*, [1990]), brought us, with *The Bad Lieutenant*, a nasty, rude, and raw movie, at times almost embarrassing to watch. After all, who wants to see Harvey Keitel masturbating on the hood of a car while he forces two young women to scream obscenities at him? *The Bad Lieutenant*'s profane and offensive nature caused it to be released with an NC-17. "I don't even want to get into the mind-set or terminology of censors," declared Ferrara. "I don't even know what NC-17 means. I like the look of it on the poster, but I don't know what it means. And they don't, either. If people want to see my movies, they'd go, anyway. Why would they give a shit?" According to Ferrara, *The Bad Lieutenant* is about personal violence: "People can lay violence on each other just with words. You don't have to shoot somebody to really hurt 'em." That's true; you can do it with words . . . and with images.

207

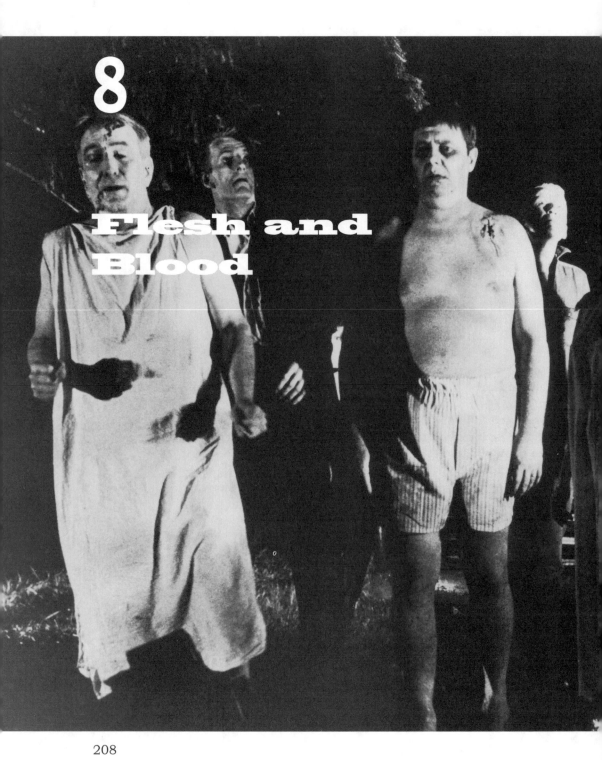

8

Flesh and Blood

Night of the Living Dead

Violence doesn't necessarily need to be shown explicitly to be shocking and effective. Most slasher and horror films make exception to the rule, and yet, as we've seen with Alfred Hitchcock's *Psycho*, some of the most violent and terrifying sequences worked on audiences not because of what they saw but because of what they thought they saw. George A. Romero's *Night of the Living Dead* (1968) and Tobe Hooper's *Texas Chainsaw Massacre* (1974) are two groundbreaking horror films that showed very little screen violence but presented extremely violent situations. These movies marked new turning points in the horror genre and unfortunately spawned not only forgettable sequels and remakes but also many clones and bad imitations.

Made on a shoestring budget by filmmakers from Pittsburgh, *Night of the Living Dead* begins as a young woman named Barbara (Judith O'Dea) and her brother visit their father's tomb. They are suddenly attacked by a stranger. Barbara runs away

209

and finds refuge in a farmhouse. Outside, the house is besieged by frightening-looking ghouls. Ben (Duane Jones), a young salesman, manages to escape from the creatures and fights his way into the house. We find out that a freak molecular mutation caused by atomic research has transformed these corpses into living-dead zombies and that the only way to kill them is to smash their brains out (not an easy task). Moreover, a wound from a zombie can infect a living person with the same flesh-eating disease. Ben and other fugitives try to fight the ghouls, but some of them become zombies, and soon the attackers grow stronger. Only Ben survives the night, but in the end, irony of ironies, he is mistaken for a zombie and dies at the hands of men who have come to the rescue.

Unofficially inspired by Richard Matheson's novel *I Am Legend*, in which biological warfare results in the dead returning to life, *Night of the Living Dead* was written by George A. Romero and John Russo. Nothing quite like it had ever been put on film before. In addition, the cheap black-and-white look of the film added to its realism and value, bringing a certain authenticity even to the most stylized sequences. Director Romero used black-and-white photography in the hope that it would give the film a Gothic and murky ambience, and it did! "We felt that films aren't usually made this graphic," Romero declared. "But why not? You know what's happening. Why cut away when you know exactly what's going on? We got the intestines, and we showed the ghouls going at them, and we said, 'Well, we're just going to leave that stuff in.' "

The film was an enormous success, with a campaign directly borrowed from famed producer-director William Castle that offered a $50,000 life insurance if you died of fear while watching the movie. "The film's horrific specifics are remarkably detailed," observed movie scholar R. H. W. Dillard. "Walking corpses fighting over and eating the intestines of the film's young lovers, a close shot of one of them eating her hand, a child's stabbing of her mother on camera fourteen times or gnawing on her father's severed arm, to say nothing of the countless rekillings of the living dead, the bashing in of their skulls. One of the film's backers was reputedly a butcher, and its footage shows much evidence of his enthusiastic support." Although it is now considered a classic, when it was released, many were appalled by its violence. Some wondered if it had some kind of message and intellectual underlying subtext. "Certainly the film's open-eyed detailing of human taboos, murder, and cannibalism has had much to do with its success," Dillard pointed out. However, some critics felt that Romero had gone too far; "Censorship isn't the answer for something like this—it never is," critic Roger Ebert wrote. "But what are parents thinking when they dump their kids off to see a film titled *Night of the Living Dead*?" *Variety* was even more concerned about the film's impact:

Romero's remedy for fast headache relief in *Dawn of the Dead*. (United Film Distribution)

> Until the Supreme Court establishes clear-cut guidelines for the pornography of violence, *Night of the Living Dead* will serve nicely as an outer-limit definition by example. In a mere ninety minutes, this horror film (pun intended) casts serious aspersions on the integrity and social responsibility of its Pittsburgh-based filmmakers, distributor Walter Reade, the film industry as a whole and the exhibitors who book the picture, as well as raising doubts about the future of the regional cinema movement and about the moral health of filmgoers who cheerfully opt for this unrelieved orgy of sadism.

Of Romero's movie, Stephen King wrote in his book *Danse Macabre*:

> A lot has been made of the film's graphic violence, but one of the film's most frightening moments comes near the climax, when the heroine's brother makes his reappearance, still wearing his driving gloves and clutching for his sister with the idiotic, implacable single-mindedness of the hungry dead. The film is violent, as its sequel, *Dawn of the Dead* [1979]—[there was also another sequel entitled *Day of the Dead* (1985) and a remake of the original in 1990]—but the violence has its own logic, and I submit to you that in the

horror genre, logic goes a long way toward proving morality.

Night of the Living Dead was remade in 1990 by gore make-up artist Tom Savini, from a script by George Romero. Although this time the film was in color, it lacked the impact of the original and proved to be a useless effort at outgrossing the first version.

The Texas Chainsaw Massacre

Tobe Hooper's *Texas Chainsaw Massacre* is another film whose violent reputation has become legendary. While on the road with her crippled brother Franklin (Paul Partain) and three other friends, Sally (Marilyn Burns) stumbles across a family of grave robbers-butcher-cannibals, led by chain-saw-wielding Leatherface (Gunnar Hansen), who wears a mask made of human skin. One after the other, the friends are brutally murdered—except for Sally, who manages to escape. Like *Psycho*, the story was inspired by the true crimes of Wisconsin mass murderer Ed Gein; after he was arrested in 1957, the police found in his place lamp shades made of human flesh and human organs simmering in pots on the stove.

Unlike *Friday the 13th*, the violence in *Chainsaw* is more subtle and less graphic; the most gruesome moment shows Leatherface impaling one of his victims on a meat hook, but when he cleaves at Franklin, director Tobe Hooper decided not to show the dismembered body. All we see is the victim's blood as it spurts out on Leatherface's butcher's apron. Much is left to the imagination, although the creepy atmosphere more than compensates.

Chainsaw Massacre, like *Night of the Living Dead*, was shot in 16 mm on a very low budget. The film's frightening realism led critics, such as Linda Gross of the *Los Angeles Times*, to call it "despicable" and a "degrading, senseless misuse of film and time." On the other hand, Vincent Canby of the *New York Times* called the film a shocker that "demonstrates the art that can

rarely be found in horror-film sleaze."
The film was followed, as has become
de rigueur, by three pointless, grue-
some, and unsuccessful sequels: *The
Texas Chainsaw Massacre 2* (1986),
*Leatherface: the Texas Chainsaw
Massacre III* (1990), and *The Return of
the Texas Chainsaw Massacre* (1995.)

Gore Fests

Since *Night of the Living Dead* and *The
Texas Chainsaw Massacre*, most horror films have become as predictable
as pornographic movies. Fortunately, a
few films have survived the carnage.
These include Sam Raimi's *Evil Dead*
series, Stuart Gordon's *Re-Animator*
(1985) and *From Beyond* (1986), and
New Zealander Peter Jackson's *Bad
Taste* (1988) and *Dead Alive* (1993).
The latter set new standards in gore.
The film is so bloody and repulsive
that it practically makes the viewer
gag. Forget Romero's flesh-eating zombies; the living dead in *Dead Alive* are

Tobe Hooper's
*Texas
Chainsaw
Massacre*
. . . Hangin'
with the
homeboys.
(Bryanston)

a lot more voracious. With a climax which includes a diversity of
mutilations and all kinds of gruesome "gags," *Dead Alive* pushes
the envelope on screen violence. Still, the comedic overtone of
the picture, which can be seen in the *Evil Dead* sequels and in
Stuart Gordon's films, makes the whole experience almost bearable. Very few of these films are meant to be taken seriously.
Interestingly enough, the most violent sequence filmed by Peter
Jackson is not in *Bad Taste* or *Dead Alive*, but in his *Heavenly
Creatures* (1994), in which a young girl, with the help of her best
friend, brutally murders her mother with a brick. More frightening is the fact that *Heavenly Creatures* was based on a true
story. Despite its extreme violence, the film avoided the critical
lambasting associated with horror-and-splatter-genre movies.
Peter Jackson was nominated for an Academy Award for the
screenplay of *Heavenly Creatures*.

213

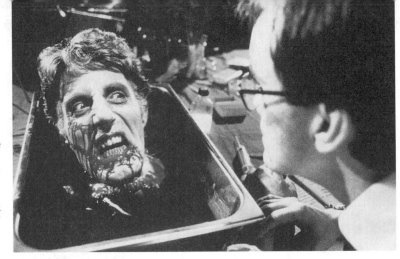

Stuart Gordon's *Re-Animator* gave new meaning to the expression "Having your head delivered on a silver platter." (Empire Pictures)

Friday the 13th

Directly influenced by *Halloween*'s success, *Friday the 13th* (1981) proved that ultraviolence and gore galore could translate into loads of cash at the box office. The film concerns a psychotic woman (Betsy Palmer) whose son Jason is drowned because a camp instructor was screwing around instead of doing his job. She eliminates a group of teenagers who have come to reopen the camp, but in the end she loses her head—literally—when the sole survivor decapitates her. *Friday the 13th* became an enormous success and led to *Friday the 13th Part 2* (1981), *Friday the 13th Part 3* (1982), *Friday the 13th Part IV: The Final Chapter* (1984), *Friday the 13th Part V: A New Beginning* (1985), *Friday the 13th Part VI: Jason Lives* (1986), *Friday the 13th Part VII: The New Blood* (1988), *Friday the 13th Part VIII: Jason Takes Manhattan* (1989), and *Jason Goes to Hell: The Final Friday* (1993), plus a TV series and several spoofs.

"I had been working in Connecticut, where I lived for a number of years, and I had made a horror movie with Wes Craven called *The Last House on the Left* (1973), which became kind of a cult classic," director Sean S. Cunningham recalled. "It's very easy in this business to get pigeonholed in that sort of genre; people see you as someone who can do something disgusting and do it cheap! But I decided to stay away from the horror genre, although I felt that sooner or later I could get back to it if I needed to. In 1977 I made a little kids' movie called *Manny's Orphans*, which I did with private money. The guy who wrote that script lived down the street from me; his name was Victor Miller. As it turned out, the film got picked up by United Artists; they wanted to make it into a TV series. We made some test screenings; the film was well received, but people didn't seem to like the title. So, as you often do, you sit down, trying to figure out titles. Out of frustration, at one point, I wrote down on my list of titles *Friday the 13th*. I said, If I could call this film *Friday the 13th*, I could sell that. And I just let it go, but it kept coming back to me. Then I started thinking of a television spot where just the title comes from infinity to the center of the screen and as it hits the screen it shatters like a mirror and a voice off would say, '*Friday the 13th*, the most terrifying film ever made.' Something like that. I thought it was great. I ended up going to a graphic artist, still in Connecticut, and I had him do a full-page ad in *Variety* that said: 'From the producer of *Last House on the Left* comes the most terrifying film ever made. *Friday the 13th*.' The title was breaking glass. I ran the ad in the July Fourth issue of *Variety* to see what would happen. Well, the phone started ringing off the hook; everybody wanted this movie which didn't exist. So I called Victor Miller. He came over, and we sat around the kitchen table, and I asked him: 'Did you ever write a horror film?' He said no, and I said: 'Let's try to figure it out, because it looks like we're going to have to make this movie somehow.' And we started asking ourselves what would be really scary, and slowly the story came together."

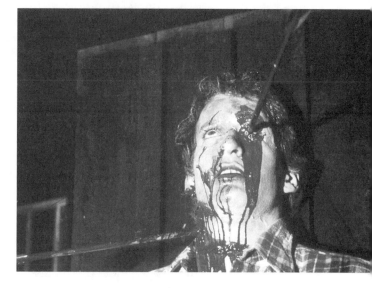

Sean Cunningham's *Friday the 13th* . . . Follow the arrow for gore. (Paramount)

The independently financed film began shooting in September in New Jersey. "When we finished editing the film," Cunningham said, "we showed it to some of our friends, and the picture worked extremely well. We showed it to distributors, and even those guys who've seen it all, basically, jumped out of their

215

seats, especially at the end of the film. [Jason bursts out of the water and grabs the heroine, who is lying in a boat. She wakes up screaming; it was only a nightmare.] As it turned out, we quickly ended up in a bidding war between Paramount, United Artists, and Warner Brothers. United Artists dropped out, and Paramount took the film for the United States and Canada and Warners for the rest of the world. What happened was that Frank Mancuso [of Paramount] had decided that he would take a chance with an independently produced movie, with no stars and with nothing except the title *Friday the 13th*, and treated the film as if it were a major movie and released it nationally. That kind of commitment was unheard of. He also picked a date in early May [1980], 'between the raindrops,' as he said. He just guessed right, and the picture was a huge success."

When working on the screenplay, Cunningham didn't necessarily try to find ways to gross out the audience; "I was more like a naughty kid trying to scare his friends, saying, 'Boo,' from behind the bushes. It's not any fun to gross people out. The metaphor that I was using when I was working on the film and afterwards was that of a roller coaster. I was trying to create a roller coaster with hills and valleys. That metaphor works, especially when you watch the film with an audience. Like with a roller coaster, it's a social experience. If you see a horror film in an empty theater, it's just ugly and grim; there's no fun. But if you go with four hundred kids laughing and screaming, it's a different experience. There's also that whole date thing going on; the guy has his arm around the girl, who is hiding her face."

Tom Savini, also from Pittsburgh, was hired to do the special-effects makeup on the film. At the time, none of that "stuff" was very advanced, and the filmmakers had to be extremely well prepared before shooting started. With script lines such as "She goes into the bathroom, and then she dies," Savini had to have an enormous amount of imagination to create interesting ways of killing the victims in the film, and his work on *Friday the 13th* is one of the reasons for its success. As a result, *Friday the 13th* and its sequels are extremely violent, but none of it affected Cunningham. "It's always so silly. It's only disturbing in context. It's like Halloween; everyone is giggling. The only disturbing moment on the set was when we killed a snake for real. Everything else was make-believe except for the snake, which was chopped up with a machete. It's an important moment in the film, it's a tone setting, but it was very upsetting to everyone,

216

including myself, that we actually killed that snake. The reality of it was disturbing. The movie has no emotional impact on me at all. It's all plumbing. The characters were at best thin. In fact, much later on, when I made a movie called *DeepStar Six* [1989] with a big ensemble cast . . . after three or four weeks came the time when there's an explosion and some of the characters die, and I was just depressed because there was more substance to them."

Surprisingly, Cunningham only had minor problems with the MPAA. "The violence happens very quickly. . . . It comes in and goes," the director explained. "On the other hand, because of the film's impact, there were a lot of imitators who kept pressing the envelope when they submitted their films to the MPAA; they would say: 'But in *Friday the 13th*, this and that . . .' and as a result when I went back to get a rating on my subsequent films, it was much tougher for me. I don't know if it's because of what happened after *Friday the 13th* with other horror films, but they take a very careful look at my films."

Friday the 13th was a huge box-office success, and its impact on audiences was enormous. Jason, who mainly appears as a character in the sequels, became, like Freddy Krueger, the psychopath from the *Nightmare on Elm Street* series, a landmark name. "What makes Freddy and Jason so attractive is that they're so strong," Cunningham explained. "They have such an agenda, and nothing will stop them. 'I'm coming through! You're putting up a wall? I'm still coming through. You got a gun? I'm still gonna get you!' So the kids say: 'Yeah! That's the guy! I want him on my side!' Their single-mindedness is what the kids really respond to. Evidently, the kids don't want to be mass murderers; they just want to get what they want!" Cunningham was involved with the first two *Friday the 13th* sequels mainly because his wife edited them; he had no interest in making the same film over and over again, although eventually Cunningham bought the rights back and directed *Jason Goes to Hell* for New Line. He eventually wants to make a Jason and Freddy Krueger movie, something along the lines of *King Kong versus Godzilla.*

Sean Cunningham doesn't feel that slasher movies are dangerous to audiences. "People do horrible things to each other all over the world all the time whether they see movies or not. The notion that people are pure until they're exposed to something really bad and that children are really innocent and that if you keep them away from violence, for instance, they'll never do any-

Jason, the indestructable villain from the *Friday the 13th* series. (Paramount)

thing bad is to deny the essence of human nature. We are a mixture of good and bad. I think that horror movies, if they're done right, function the same way fairy tales do. At least that's what we tried to do with *Friday the 13th*. In fairy tales you try to acclimate a child to the real world, and you do that by putting faces on the things he's really afraid of and by dealing with the fears in the context of a story. By bringing it out of the recesses of the subconscious, you get to look at it, and it all seems a little less scary. The operative fear in horror films is the fear of untimely death. Every high school class has a kid who is in a motorcycle accident. That's devastating, because kids live in a state of invulnerability. Therefore, the randomness of the killings and the violence in *Friday the 13th*, [set] against perfectly happy and nice kids who look like they stepped out of a Coke commercial, is scary. That's why kids are interested in horror films, not older people. Fear of untimely death is no longer an issue for me; timely death is! When you stop being afraid of all of your initial fears, these movies become boring."

Are there then any limits to screen violence? There is what Sean Cunningham calls "a self-imposed" limit that directors of horror films establish, because "at the end of the day people are just grossed out, as opposed to being entertained. What's really important in a film is the story. You can enhance your story by the judicious use of violence, like they did in *Interview With the Vampire*, but by itself violence is pointless. It's not a big trick to chop somebody's head off on-screen; it's a big trick to make the audience care about it."

218

A Nightmare on Elm Street

The success of *A Nightmare on Elm Street* (1984) also came as a big surprise to director Wes Craven. In the story, a group of small-town teenagers have the same terrifying nightmare and are horribly murdered by the dream's lead character, a disfigured psychopath named Freddy Krueger (Robert Englund) who was burned alive by the kids' parents. Like Carpenter and Cunningham, Craven shares the exact same views not only on the function of horror and violence in film but also on the influence of such entertainment on kids. "If I really knew, I would do it again!" Craven answers when asked how he explains the success of Freddy Krueger. "I have, however, a lot of different theories. I think the film struck a nerve in people's mind; it made a unique statement, explored an uncovered territory. The movie was about the exploration of dreams as part of our everyday life. People usually dismiss dreams; they say they don't dream or forget about them, never try to explore them. In fact, we all have the knowledge of that other level of consciousness. Dreams are very primal; they're like visions, basically; they're like horror films. When people saw *A Nightmare on Elm Street*, they were intrigued and fascinated by that world. Dreams are like the most ancient theater we have if you think of early theater, with simple icons and images."

Wes Craven wondered for a long time why kids found the character of Krueger appealing; he came to three conclusions:

"Number one: If you look at any primal society, they would always choose the most ferocious beast as their icon, as their symbol, as their God. It was their way of protecting themselves from the rest of the world. When a kid wears a Krueger mask or collects posters of him, he is basically saying: 'Don't mess with me. If I can deal with Krueger, I can deal with anyone else.'

"Number two: A kid once told me that the reason why he liked Freddy was because he was so honest. Krueger cuts through the bullshit. I found that comment quite profound. Many things in our world are

phony. Commercials are phony; the government constantly lies to us. Kids feel like they're drowning in phoniness, in falsity. So their instinct tells them to hang on to someone that represents truth. Krueger is what he is, and he kills anyone who doesn't understand what's going on. Kids today are desperate for the truth.

"Number three: Eighty percent of the rock music you listen to is pessimistic and extremely cynical. There's something about a character that destroys innocence, because, as even rock music spells it, you can't afford to be innocent in today's world. Facing a character like Freddy helps kids deal and understand the reality of our society. It's sad and chilling, but it's the truth."

While most parents believe that the violence in horror films can be damaging to their children, Wes Craven thinks that these accusations are merely a front for a deeper issue. "Many, many things are dangerous in our world. To raise kids on a Disneyish kind of mentality is dangerous; certain religious beliefs pushed to a limit are dangerous; commercials and TV are dangerous, and so is the world of sitcoms. All these things are more dangerous than horror movies, but nobody does anything about them because they're turning in a lot of dollars. I don't think that horror films are dangerous. In the *Rambo* movies, they're basically telling you it's easy to have a solution to all your problems; you just have to pick up a gun. In order to understand why kids liked gore so much in horror films, I had to take myself back to my youth. I remembered that the first thing I wanted to do with appliances was to take them apart. Gore is about our primal instinct. We cover up what we're made of with fashion, makeup, etc., but we're bodies, we're flesh, blood, and guts. Horror films tell us what we're made of, and they show it. The adult world constantly tries to distract kids away from the real world; but the reality is that if our president gets shot, the world will stop. I just saw on television a kid in Bosnia that had been shot by a sniper. It was horrifying. Now, if you put that in a film, they tell you it's a bad thing. People refuse to see that life is a blood-and-guts show."

For Wes Craven, the most violent sequence in *A Nightmare on Elm Street* is the death of a teenage girl who gets thrown against the wall and up to the ceiling. "It's quite bloody, but it also presents a reversal of gravity. Gravity is one of our rules, and if that rule ceases to exist—like it does in that particular scene—then it's terrifying." Incidentally, that scene was a problem for the MPAA, and Craven had to trim down the moment where the girl falls from the ceiling onto the bed in a big splash of blood. "I also had to take out a shot of the blood in Johnny Depp's bed after he's been murdered. Curiously, they didn't have any problem with *New Nightmare* [in which Freddy Krueger enters the real world of the filmmaker, his cast, and their families] despite the fact that the film dealt with a child in jeopardy. I have a low opinion of censorship of any kind. To me, they're violating the right to artistic freedom."

A Nightmare on Elm Street was quite dark, as was *New Nightmare* (1994). The characters were solid, and therefore the violence done to them worked on an emotional level. The sequels, however, took a comic book–like approach to the story. *Freddy's Revenge* (1986), *The Dream Warriors* (1987), *The Dream Master* (1988), and *Freddy's Dead: The Final Nightmare* (1991) were a lot bloodier and at times more violent than the original film, but they also had a sense of parody. They (and the later TV series) managed, however, to establish Freddy Krueger as a cult figure and as one of the most famous villains in film history, alongside Dracula, Frankenstein, Leatherface, Jason, and a nasty little doll named Chucky.

Robert Englund as Freddy Krueger . . . Just don't call him pizza face. (New Line Cinema)

Child's Play

In Tom Holland's *Child's Play* (1988), a young boy's favorite doll, Chucky, is possessed by the evil soul of a mass murderer who now wants to be human again and enter the body of the kid. After several unexplained deaths, mother and son team up to destroy Chucky. Two sequels were made: *Child's Play 2* (1990) and *Child's Play 3* (1991). The third installment in the series created quite an uproar when it was alleged that the film had induced two young English kids, Robert Thompson and Jon Venables, to murder a two-year-old toddler.

In the film *Child's Play 3*, the killer doll is chased along a railway line in an amusement park and dies after being spattered with blue paint and badly mutilated. In the real-life British tragedy, the victim was also splashed with paint and beaten up near a railway line and was then left lying on the tracks. Three weeks before the murder, the father of one of the killer boys had rented a tape of *Child's Play 3*, and the tabloids in England and America immediately assumed that the film had influenced the boys to commit murder. Later, the murder of a young woman by a gang of drug-addicted thugs was also pinned on Chucky; supposedly, the killers chanted the catchphrase from the film "I'm Chucky. Wanna play?" as they tortured their victim.

Writer Don Mancini, who penned the three *Child's Play* movies, was shocked when he heard about the murders. "I felt terrible, because nobody wants to feel responsible for something like that, not even indirectly. My feeling then and now, however, remains that a filmmaker's responsibility ends with the R rating. That's why we have a rating system. This movie is not for children; it's rated R for a purpose. Society in general, parents in general, and in particular the parents of the two boys who murdered that kid don't want to feel responsible for that behavior; it has to be due to something else. It turns out that both boys come from abusive families. But a crime like that is so atrocious, the idea that kids could commit such a crime is so horrifying, that no one wants to suggest that it could have something to do with our parenting. I later found out that the case was all trumped up, anyway; it wasn't even true that the boys had seen my movie and copied something out of it. It was completely made up by the tabloids. I was relieved.

The tabloids accused Chucky of inspiring real-life violence. (Universal Pictures, photo by Peter Iovino)

But you know, it's inevitable that some people are going to abuse the right to drive a car. Some people are going to drink and drive; some people are going to drive recklessly. Does that mean that carmakers are responsible? Does that mean that we shouldn't have cars at all? No, because society at large benefits from having cars. I'm not saying that *Child's Play* is as indispensable a commodity as a car, but in the abstract it is true that people benefit from entertainment, even if it's a horror movie. But because of *Child's Play 3*, they've made it illegal in England to rent R-rated movies to children.

When I'm writing, I only think about the story and about the dramatic impact. But I don't ignore the issue of responsibility; for example, I don't mix sexuality and horror. I understand why it's done in certain horror films, and I've enjoyed some of them. Personally, I know that even though my films are rated R, some kids will see them, so I try to avoid mixing sex and violence. I don't have that correlation between sex and violence in my own mind."

In *Child's Play*, a young actor (Alex Vincent) played the kid in jeopardy; back when *The Exorcist* (1974) was released, controversy surrounded the fact that Linda Blair, who was then only a teenager, could have been damaged by the role she played. Don Mancini doesn't necessarily agree and has mixed feelings about this particular issue; "Kids in our culture play cowboys and Indians, cops and robbers, every day; they enact violent scenarios that involve death all the time. So, I don't think to have a kid

223

in a horror film was ever an issue. Alex Vincent, who played the young boy, even admitted being bored on the set because of all the mechanical effects involved with trying to get Chucky to do his thing. For that reason, on a movie set, the line between fantasy and reality is very clear. On the other hand, when I saw *Pet Semetary* [1989] and you have a two-year-old kid walking around holding a knife and saying, 'I'm gonna kill you, Daddy,' that sort of gave me pause. I don't think that a two-year-old can distinguish between fiction and reality. Also, in *Kindergarten Cop* [1990] you had a disturbing scene with a crazy father putting a gun to the head of his own son; if I were a parent, I wouldn't want my kids to watch this film. In the *Child's Play* movies the kids are never the sources of evil, and we never harm the kids, either. The kids always escape."

The early draft of *Child's Play*, which at the time was entitled *Blood Buddy*, was a lot more disturbing—and had stronger implications—than what ended up on the screen, after director Tom Holland had worked on the script. "The original idea was that rather than being possessed by the soul of a serial killer and therefore being an uncomplicated villain as in the movie, the doll was the manifestation of the boy's subconscious," Mancini explained. "It was his walking id basically. The boy lives with his single working mom [Catherine Hicks] and spends a lot of time alone. He loves his mom, but he also feels a lot of anger toward her because she is never home. She is torn because she needs to make a living. So after one of their arguments she gives him the doll. It temporarily solves the problem. The doll has a synthetic red liquid inside it; so if you're playing with it, the latex skin may break, and it will bleed, and you have to buy these Good Guys Band-Aids. Like a rite of brotherhood, the boy cuts his own thumb and the doll's thumb and mixes the blood. After that, the doll comes to life when the boy is asleep, just to further underline the fact that this is the boy's subconscious. In the original script, the doll was always striking out at the kid's enemies, and that's why ultimately he goes after the mother, because the boy has this rage against her for not being there for him. I thought this concept was very interesting, a little complex and disturbing, because children do have these feelings. I think that the complexity of the story might have scared film executives because it almost suggests that the boy is a bit guilty."

After the murders in England, Martin Amis wrote an article in the *New Yorker* saying that "Americans are demanding relief from the violence that has come to define our society." In turn, Amis asked the question "But are the movies a part of the problem or the solution?" Finally, Amis rented *Child's Play 3* and declared that after the film was over, he felt no urge or prompting to go out and kill somebody. "And I knew why, too. It's nothing to boast about, but there is too much going on in my head for Chucky to gain sway in there. Probably the worst that Chucky could do to me is to create an appetite to see more Chucky or more things like Chucky." And appeasing our appetite for "things like Chucky" is exactly what Hollywood is doing.

Hellraiser

When Stephen King said, "I have seen the future of horror . . . and it is named Clive Barker," he wasn't exaggerating. Writer-director-producer-artist, Clive Barker has surfaced with his *Hellraiser* film series as a new leader and true visionary in the horror genre. His movies are brutal, violent, and graphic, but they also have style and stand on their own as quite unique and "hellbreaking." Barker directed the first *Hellraiser* (1987) and based the script on one of his short stories, "The Hellbound Heart." Larry Cotton (Andrew Robinson) and his wife, Julie (Clare Higgins), move back to the old family house. Through flashbacks we find out that Julie had an affair with Larry's brother, Frank (Sean Chapman). While moving, Larry injures himself, and his blood drops on the floor of the attic. The blood somehow brings Frank back from an unknown territory which he entered willingly through a magical cubical box. But before he can escape from this other dimension and from the Cenobites (a bunch of weird-looking dudes with their notorious leader, Pinhead—whose skull and face are covered with pins), he must be whole (he is just raw flesh for now), and he asks Julie to provide him with bodies. Guided by lust, Julie accepts and becomes Frank's partner in crime until Larry's daughter, Kristy (Ashley Lawrence) discovers what her stepmother is up to. Kristy escapes with the box, unleashes the dark forces, and promises the Cenobites Frank in exchange for her life. Meanwhile, Frank kills his brother and, using his skin, becomes whole again and is reunited with Julie. Kristy confronts the ultimate evil, and during

a final struggle, Julie is killed and Frank destroyed.

Hellraiser has been so far followed by *Hellbound: Hellraiser II* (1988), directed by Tony Randel; *Hellraiser III: Hell on Earth* (1992), directed by Anthony Hickox; and *Hellraiser: Bloodlines* (1995), directed by Alan Smithee (the pseudonym used by a member of the Directors Guild of America when he wishes his name to be removed from the credits) with Clive Barker as executive producer. In addition to his novels and short-story collections, Barker wrote and directed *Nightbreed* (1989) and *Lord of Illusions* (1995). He wrote the stories for *Candyman* (1993), directed by Bernard Rose, and *Candyman: Farewell to the Flesh* (1995), directed by Bill Condon, which Barker also executive produced.

> "We are a violent species. We are attracted to, excited, and aroused by acts of violence."
> —Clive Barker
> (New World Pictures)

An Interview With Clive Barker

Laurent Bouzereau: What is a horror film?

Clive Barker: Horror movies for me have to contain the element of the fantastic. In other words, there are movies that horrify me that are not fantastical and that I would not call horror movies. *Schindler's List* is a good example. A movie like *Taxi Driver* is not a horror movie. I know that David Cronenberg would take issue with me because when asked to name his favorite horror movies, he named *Taxi Driver* among them. For me, horror films have to do with taboo subjects, the problems of the flesh, insanity, obsession, death, the things that horrify us. For a horror film to work, Wes Craven said that you have to feel that you're in the hands of someone who will do anything to you. You have to have that sense that you're giving power to someone who is not quite sane. Horror movies are image driven, not performance driven; in westerns, in social dramas, in comedies, you think of characters and performances.

226

LB: What do you think of the way horror films are perceived, mainly by critics? They don't seem to be able to look beyond the gore and the violence . . .

CB: One of the reasons that I take issue with reviewers on their disparagement of horror movies is that they don't look deep enough into the subtext of horror movies. Obviously, horror movies work on some subconscious or primal level which requires decoding. One of our problems is that we don't have a far enough sight historically. The world in the nineteenth century was extremely violent; public executions took place. Sure, today we have access to all of this imagery through TV and movies, but less than a hundred years ago, this same imagery would have been within walking distance of us at any given time. I think that saying that our society has become violent because of movies doesn't really work. We are a violent species. We are attracted to, excited and aroused by, acts of violence. When we watch violent movies, we know it's fiction; we have a safety net. . . . We know that Pinhead [one of the Cenobites from the *Hellraiser* series] or Candyman are actors.

LB: For me, the most violent scene in *Hellraiser* is when Julie grabs a hammer and repeatedly smashes a man's skull with it. What's disturbing is that it seems so real, whereas the other graphic and bloody sequences are part of a fantasy world.

CB: Horror movies should constantly go back and forth between reality and fantasy. There's a very simple scene in *Lord of Illusions* in which somebody kneels on top of somebody else and he is holding a scalpel and cuts the inside of the other guy's lip. You see nothing at all, but it seems completely real. There are other violent sequences in the picture, but none of them have this simple power over the audience. You had a similar situation in John Carpenter's *The Thing* [1982] when Kurt Russell opens his thumb with a scalpel to draw some blood. The biggest audience response in *Hellraiser* is when the nail makes a gouge on Andrew Robinson's hand because it's happened to all of us and we can relate to the pain.

LB: In your movies, there seems to be a strange link between pleasure and pain, between beauty and violence.

CB: That's actually where my film work overlaps with a literary tradition. The sexual arousal and arousal in the face of violence have great similarities. The sensation of pleasure taken too far

227

can turn into pain, and the pain, if offered under the right circumstances, can be the greatest pleasure. What's interesting about good horror movies is how much ambiguity there is in them. Bad horror movies, on the other hand, don't have any ambiguity at all; there's nothing in them but "Boo!"

LB: Is there a distinction between gore and violence?

CB: I don't know what the term "gore" really means. I know that there are gross images in movies which have no blood in them. Linda Blair puking on the priest in *The Exorcist* is a good example. It's gross, not gory. A lot of Cronenberg images are not necessarily gory, but they're gross; the gun that becomes a hand in *Videodrome* [1983] is a very obvious one. There are a lot of images that movies use to gross out the audience, but that's not the same as gore. The head exploding in *Scanners* [1981] or the body coming apart at the end of *Hellraiser*, that's a very different thing; there we're being shown the autopsy image, the slaughterhouse image. . . . We're being presented something which is really about blood and body parts. Clearly, the blood and body parts are gross, but they're also violent images.

LB: Do you find the amount of blood and violence in a film like *Dead Alive* excessive? Do you think it's comparable to the function of pornography?

CB: My feeling is that just like pornography has its place in our lives, there is a kind of honesty about a movie which is unapologetically, mindlessly, violent. I love very good food, but once in a while, I'll eat junk food. There are all kinds of horror movies, and one of our great curses is to create a hierarchy. As consumers, we have moods; sometimes I want to see *Queen Margot* [1994], and sometimes I want to see a great B movie. Moral assumptions have been made about horror and fantasy movies, very often by reactionary forces who feel they have a bad influence. "Helter Skelter" was a Beatles song, and Charlie Manson found motive for murder in it. I think that for the overwhelming bulk of people, horror movies, especially "fantastical" horror movies, are actually a fun, therapeutic way to discharge anxieties. On the other hand, vigilante pictures, to my mind, make heroic a certain type of behavior, and Sly Stallone killing two hundred Commies with a machine gun is a much more dangerous image than Freddy Krueger because it celebrates the idea of a mindless avenger.

LB: What are your feelings about the MPAA?

CB: Part of the problem is that there are no rules. I'm constantly amazed, when I show my pictures to the MPAA, at the things that do bother them and at the things that don't bother them. Most often, the things that do bother them are things I didn't think about, and things that I thought they'd worry about they pass over. My dealings with them have been increasingly comfortable. They know where I'm coming from, I know where they're coming from . . . vaguely. I believe that people who can be sent to war should be able to see what the fuck they like on the cinema screen; I assume that they believe that if certain images are put into people's heads, they will go out and bring our civilization to ruin. There's a very genuine concern in our society about lawlessness, about a drop in moral standards, about the fact that eleven- year-old boys are bringing guns into schools. People want to find out what's causing all this, and they look at television, movies, comic books, and they say, "It's got to be these things." I don't for one moment think it's those things. I believe it's important for people to have something to point to, and horror movies stand right there as perfect targets for this kind of simpleminded association of ideas. The fantastic images in horror movies do not seem to me to have significant influence on the headlines; I have yet to find any stories of people who [after watching *Hellraiser*] filled their heads with pins. . . . What I do find is a lot of disgruntled postal workers who go into work and shoot their colleagues. What people are responding to is a general atmosphere of violence in popular art which has always been there. You can go around the great churches of Spain where there's a tradition of meticulously realistic painted crucifixes. Lenny Bruce has this wonderful joke about the fact that it's a good thing that Christ wasn't execcuted today, because we'd all be wearing little electric chairs around our necks. Of course, the crucifix is an image of sacrifice and redemption through death as opposed to an image of graphic violence enjoyed for its own sake,

Writer-director Clive Barker with one of the creatures from *Lord of Illusions.* (United Artists Pictures, Inc.)

and as special effects have become much, much more sophisticated, it's been possible to look at these images for longer on the screen, and the longer you look at them for their own sake, the more they seem to exist for their own sake. And many movies, like John Carpenter's *The Thing*, are entirely predicated around special effects.

LB: What is the most violent image you ever put on-screen?

CB: It think it's gotta be the death scene with the swords in *Lord of Illusions*, which is a double trick because it turns out to be an illusion. The character is a magician who is so terrified of the man who gave him the power to perform magic, who he then murdered, coming back to get him that he decides to disappear from public's sight, and so he stages his own death in the most public way he can. He dies onstage in front of two thousand people in what seems to be a trick that has gone horribly wrong. He is tied to this wheel, and swords are dropping off, and he is supposed to escape, but he fails. For the next hour of the film, we think he's dead, and then it turns out to be a trick. What's interesting about it is that the audience has no clue that this is an illusion. What's interesting for me as a filmmaker was staging an illusion which was supposed to be real but was, in fact, an illusion. It's a trick within a trick within a trick. You're trying to do something that's very showy, like a piece of theater, and you equally want to make it as violent and as gut wrenching as you possibly can, but you also want the moment when the audience realizes it was a trick. I think that's the most violent moment [in *Lord of Illusions*] because it goes on for a long time, and the MPAA had problems with that. The swords keep falling, and the guy tries to get off the wheel, and another sword falls.

LB: What would be the most violent image you ever saw?

CB: The most violent image I ever saw was actually in a special-effects man's collection of photographs. Most of them, as you know, have reference photographs. One of them had a photograph that I sort of wish I could forget in a way, which was a man who had been tortured somewhere in South America and his corpse was being taken to a communal burial ground and his face had been removed. Everything else was intact. What was violent about it was the implication of what had happened to the man and the implication about the people who had done this to him.

Afterword

In the few years since the original publication of this book, there have been very few movies that have had the impact of *Taxi Driver*, *Natural Born Killers*, or *Pulp Fiction*. In fact, Tarantino's latest, *Jackie Brown* (1997), was tame in comparison to his previous *Reservoir Dogs* and *Pulp Fiction*, and hardly anyone went to see Oliver Stone's *U-Turn* (1997). Of course, we've had our share of violence in action movies such as *Con Air* (1997), *Face/Off* (1997), and the grand guignol sci-fi flick *Starship Troopers* (1997); and let's not forget *Air Force One* (1997), starring Harrison Ford who, as the president of the United States, didn't turn the other cheek; to the contrary, he kicked ass like everyone else. And we, the audience, cheered at each punch, each explosion, and were gratified by this display of entertainment.

The problem in today's action films is a lack of character development; screen violence, as pointed out by French director Bertrand Tavernier to the *Hollywood Reporter*, has become another special effect, another spectacle. Tavernier explored the theme of screen violence and its consequences in real life in *L'Appat* (1995), a movie about a pair of young men obsessed with Brian De Palma's *Scarface*. Tavernier explains: "It's not only a

231

matter of the violence, it's a matter of the result—of the reverse shot. Now, in many films you don't have the reverse shot on the people who are subjected to violence. In one John Woo film, a woman is thrown from a plane. Okay, it's an incredible, beautiful shot. Exciting. But where is the effect of her death? Where is the body of the woman? Raoul Walsh or Sam Peckinpah would have had a shot to show it's a woman who was killed. In today's films, there's a lack of reaction shots."

In all fairness, the absence of such shots is partially due to the conventions set by the ratings board—although it's interesting to note that of all the films to receive the restrictive NC-17 rating, most of them had strong sexual content, not violence. *Con Air,* in which a man is incinerated in exacting and colorful detail, received an R rating while the highly sexually-charged *Showgirls* (1996) was slapped with an NC-17.

The debate is very much about the difference between gratuitous violence and violence expressed as part of a narrative art form. Robert Redford has taken issue with the use of violence for exploitative reasons, but other than that the actor-director of *The Horse Whisperer* (1998), which features an extremely disturbing and graphic accident, says: "I accept it [violence in film] from a guy who has been raised in the streets and he's making a film about the ghetto. His world is violent. Violence has a lot to do with frustration in film. People become frustrated when they lose hope. Their frustration produces violence in films."

When directing his Oscar-winning epic drama, *Braveheart* (1995), Mel Gibson felt he had to depict the battles as realistically as possible: "I don't feel I violated any kind of moral code with what I portrayed as thirteenth-century battles," Gibson told the *Hollywood Reporter.* "I went for realism, and it was harsh. I'm not going to have 'em go up and hit each other with pillows. Or cut it out. That robs you of the impact of the true hell it must have been. I didn't make it attractive. It was ugly." Gibson, who has starred in the *Lethal Weapon* and *Road Warrior* series, points out that violence has existed in drama at least since Shakespeare and that the issue over the influence of violence in film is a debate that you can't win or lose: "I have found certain things disturbing, and they're meant to be that way. It's not gonna make me run out and gun down a bunch of people in a post office or anything. There are people, I guess, who have that mind-set where it may affect them.

It may blur the line between reality and whatever else it is that they're going through in their mind. It's just a very hard debate. A play like *Hamlet,* for instance, is probably one of the most violent things. There are killings and stabbings and poisonings, all kinds of things happening, and people don't rail at that. Well, what's the difference? I mean that's art, you know?"

The difference may be in the choice filmmakers have between showing acts of violence, suggesting them, or simply showing the results of violence. Films like *Seven* (1996) and *L.A. Confidential* (1997) serve as good examples of what I'd call postmortem violence. The discovery of the victims of a serial killer in David Fincher's *Seven* is possibly as disturbing as being a witness to the murders. (Kevin Spacey kills his victims according to the seven deadly sins, with results bound to make saints out of everyone who saw the film.) Curtis Hanson accomplished the same discomfort for audiences in his brilliant 1950's police drama *L.A. Confidential.* The film is bulleted with gunfights, brawls, and torture scenes, but the most disturbing images show the violence after the fact: a young man is found lying in a pool of blood in a cheap motel, his throat freshly slit; a cop finds several dead bodies in the men's room of a restaurant and his partner discovers the decomposed corpse of a man under the foundation of a house, his face eaten by rats, etc. What makes *L.A. Confidential* possibly more powerful than *Seven* is the fact that several of the most disturbing events in the film are based on facts and set in a brutal reality, depicted at greater length in the novel by author James Ellroy. Having experienced the effects of extreme violence when he was just a boy (his mother was murdered and the crime remains unsolved to this day), Ellroy recreates in his work an era just as corrupt, as savage, and as fierce as ours. And yet this was a time when movies didn't depict crime graphically; it was the era of *Dragnet,* not *N.Y.P.D. Blue.*

As we're about to celebrate the end of one millenium and the beginning of another, it seems that the end of the nineties has been marked by a return to the seventies; disaster films have made a crashing comeback culminating in the mega-worldwide success of James Cameron's *Titanic,* but the most unexpected genre to resurface is horror and more particularly, slasher films. It all began—again—with the surprising popularity of Wes Craven's *Scream* (1995); the film was originally titled *Scary Movie* and was written in three days by then-struggling screenwriter Kevin Williamson. The idea for *Scary Movie* came while watching a Barbara Walters special on the Gainesville murders. Williamson recalls: "I was housesitting and got so scared that I freaked out. I called a friend and he kept saying, 'Kill, kill, kill, don't you remember the garage scene in *Halloween*?' That gave me the kernel for the opening scene," in which Drew Barrymore is harrassed and eventually brutally murdered by an anonymous caller, obviously obsessed with classic slasher films such as Craven's own *Nightmare on Elm Street*. Williamson continues: "If you ask me what movie put me into this industry, it was *Halloween*. I'm sorry, but *Citizen Kane* didn't do it. I was ten years old, sitting in the theater and watching people scream and jump. I wanted to do that, I wanted to make people respond." Williamson thought: "What if I wrote a story about all these kids who grew up next to Blockbuster and know Freddy and Michael and Jason like the back of their hand? What would they do if they were in a real situation with a guy with a knife?" The answer became *Scary Movie,* a parody of slasher movie cliches featuring a bunch of teenagers who are, as *Newsweek* put it, "Smart enough to acknowledge horror-movie chestnuts (sex equals death, never drink or do drugs, never say 'I'll be right back') and dumb enough to break those rules as an equally horror-hip killer hunts them down."

Once Williamson finished his script, he delivered it to his agent and a bidding war between several filmmakers and major and independent studios began. Even Oliver Stone was interested. "By the end of the day," Williamson recalls, "it was Stone and Bob Weinstein [of Dimension, Miramax's horror division] fighting into the late night." Stone offered more money but only wanted to produce it, not direct it. Weinstein, on the other hand, promised he'd get the film started right away. So Williamson decided to trust his guts—pardon the expression—and went with Dimension. Less than a year later, the movie was done and eventually grossed a total of $103 million at the box office. Danny Boyle *(Trainspotting),* Anthony Waller *(Mute Witness),* and Robert Rodriguez *(El Mariachi)* were initially approached to direct the film. They all turned it down, as did veteran horror director Wes Craven. The original screenplay had lots of offbeat dialogue but not enough scares. Ironically, Kevin Williamson had purposely toned down the horror stuff, fearing that the script wouldn't be taken seriously. Luckily, the next draft was dead-on (and how!) and Craven finally committed to the project, as did name actors like Drew Barrymore (who, not unlike Janet Leigh in *Psycho,* is

brutally murdered), Skeet Ulrich, and TV's Courteney Cox
(Friends) and Neve Campbell *(Party of Five)*.

Scream was not an instant hit and received mixed reviews; *Variety* predicted that the film's underlying mockish tone would not please die-hard horror fans. But in fact, the clever blend of genre convention and sophisticated parody eventually built good word of mouth, even among non-horror fans, and the film proved to have long staying power. It became the ultimate date movie for a new generation, who has, for the most part, experienced the great horror classics on video.

Scream was almost immediately followed by *Scream 2* (1997), an equally clever sequel also directed by Wes Craven. Strangely enough, Craven's parents were baptist fundamentalists who thought movies were the tool of the devil. "They really believed that the bulk of material coming out of Hollywood was too sexual, too violent, and too anti-Christian for their children to see. Very, very few people in our church went to the theaters." Around the same time Craven got divorced, he began his career in film with the controversial cult-horror film *Last House on the Left* (1972); as a result of both his personal and career choices, Craven barely talked to his family more than once or twice a year. To this day, his ninety-year-old mother, who has never seen any of her son's movies, still asks: "Well, why do you always do these horrible subjects?" Craven comments: "It's a valid question, and I don't have a pat answer for it. But there was stuff I needed to work out. And I don't know if it was rage from a youth that was so oppressed."

Amidst all the mockery and parody of the *Scream* movies, there is a message, or more exactly, a question summarized in the opening of the sequel. The scene takes place at a movie theater on the opening night of *Stab,* a film based on the events that took place in *Scream.* Actress Jada Pinkett is stabbed to death and, in her last moments, manages to climb on stage. The audience within the film thinks it's part of the show and cheers. In a disguised way, Wes Craven is warning us not to confuse the very thin line between screen violence and the real world. Or has it already happened? Is the warning a little late? In 1996, lawyer and bestselling author John Grisham began a crusade—and a lawsuit—against Oliver Stone when a friend of his was murdered by teenagers who cited *Natural Born Killers* as inspiration. In response to the accusation, Stone replied, in brief, that art should not be a scapegoat for holding up a mirror to society. And on January 15, 1998, a *Los Angeles Times* headline read: "Son, Nephew Inspired by *'Scream'* Movies Kill Woman, Police Say."

In the wake of the success of *Scream,* Kevin Williamson took on the adaptation of a young-adult horror thriller by Lois Duncan entitled *I Know What You Did Last Summer* (1997) and turned it into another box-office hit, inevitably to be (at some point) followed by a sequel. *I Know What You Did Last Summer* is about four kids who accidentally hit a man on the road, dump his body off a pier, and split; a year later, a hook-wielding killer, possibly the victim, comes after them for revenge. "I made it very clear when I took the first meeting that I was not going to make a slasher film," *Last Summer* director Jim Gillespie told *Drama-Logue.* "Therefore, it was never an issue. What I then had to do was deliver on my promise that I could make it exciting and scary and not be graphic in terms of the blood count. I think the film works on a suspense and scare level. It is actually a strong character piece and the ensemble cast pulls it off. That's what sucks the audience into the film. Understanding the characters, wanting to know what's going to happen to them. So the need to keep enough of the scares going becomes critical. Otherwise you lose the tension. Younger audiences need it to keep going."

I Know What You Did Last Summer, which starred Jennifer Love Hewitt of *Party of Five* and Anne Heche in a standout supporting role, was distributed by Sony Pictures. The film was marketed toward the fifteen-to-twenty-five-year-old date-crowd (hence the clever casting of young and hip television actors in both *Scream* movies and in *I Know What You Did . . .*). Although Kevin Williamson is now also known as the creator of the teen-hit television drama series *Dawson's Creek,* his name is still associated with slasher films and sells tickets. But he claims he is no horror boy: "If you look at what my work has in common, it's teenagers. Instead of a John Carpenter [the creator of *Halloween*], I'd say I'm more of a John Hughes [the creator of *The Breakfast Club* and *Pretty in Pink*]. A wicked, warped, demented John Hughes."

Horror is hip again. A genre that was dead, or at least had become unprofitable for general theater release, has been resucitated. The fever has caught on and look who is back: Chucky, the killer doll in *Bride of Chucky,* Michael Myers and Jamie Lee Curtis in *Halloween VII* (also known as *H207*). Even Norman Bates, the most popular of all serial killers, strikes again, not in another *Psycho* sequel, but in a remake of the Hitchcock masterpiece, directed by *Good Will Hunting*'s Gus Van Sant. *Bride of Chucky* screenwriter Don Mancini had this to say about the fourth chapter in his *Child's Play* series: "This new film is overall more comedic and one of the reasons why the studio wanted to make this film is because *Scream* was perceived not only as a horror movie but also as a comedy. The title alone, *Bride of Chucky,* carries an element of humor but it is of course also an homage to *Bride of Frankenstein. Bride of Chucky* stands in relation to the previous Chucky movies in much the same way that *Bride of Frankenstein* stands in relation to the original *Frankenstein.* At the same time, we haven't sacrificed any of the horror, but when Hong-Kong director Ronny Yu was hired to make the film, it became clear that we didn't want to do another slasher movie. We wanted the violence to be stylized, rather than entrails in your face. A good example of that is a sequence in which one of the characters is electrocuted in a bathtub. I always thought this would make an interesting scene; in fact, it was in my original screenplay of *Child's Play* but it was never filmed. It's a violent scene and it's also beautiful and extremely stylized. It's been more than twenty years since *The Exorcist* and slasher films like *Halloween* and *Friday the Thirteenth* and audiences are a bit jaded. But the good news is that movies like *Face/Off* are emerging and offer a lot more than violence; we're back to telling intelligent stories with strong and interesting characters. I don't think we could push the envelope on violence any further than we already have unless we go into virtual reality!"

As long as violence exists in the world, and just as much as there is love, or laughters and tears, the screen will continue to imitate and recreate, for better or for worse, who we are. The issue of violence in film is not about Hollywood; it's about the human race and the world we live in. For a preview of coming atttractions, just turn on the six o'clock news.

Bibliography

Adler, Dick. "Film Script Upsets Author." *Los Angeles Times*, December 1, 1975.

Amis, Martin. "Blown Away." *New Yorker*, May 30, 1994.

Andrew, Geoff. "Shoot to Kill." *Time Out*, December 12, 1992.

Ansen, David. "Pulp, Passion, Petty Hoods." *Newsweek*, October 26, 1992.

———. "The Redemption of *Pulp*." *Newsweek*, October 10, 1994.

Associated Press. "Dole Tells Hollywood to Clean Up Act." *Atlanta Journal*, June 1, 1995.

Barra, Allen. "Brian De Palma's Latest Outrage." *Village Voice*, August 22, 1989.

Batchelor, Ruth. "Critic's Corner." *Hollywood Reporter*, March 17, 1976.

Bennetts, Leslie. "Do the Arts Inspire Violence in Real Life?" *New York Times*, April 26, 1981.

"Bill Holden's Ghost Story!" *Hollywood Citizen News*, May 25, 1968.

Bishop, Jerry. "Experts Say Films Can Prod the Disturbed." *Wall Street Journal*, April 2, 1981.

Blaire, Nancy. "Cutting to the Chase." *L.A. Village View*, April 9–15, 1993.

Blevins, Winfred. "*Straw Dogs*: Terror and Threat." *Los Angeles Herald Examiner*, December 19, 1971.

"The *Bonnie and Clyde* Caper." *Time*, March 22, 1968.

"Bonnie and Clyde Captured at Century City." *Century City News*, March 14, 1968.

"The Boyz of Bloodshed." *Newsweek*, July 22, 1991.

Brennan, Judy. "*Natural Born* Flap Over, Yes, Violence." *Los Angeles Times*, July 3, 1994.

_____. "Warners Giving *Born Killers* a Light Promotional Touch." *Los Angeles Times*, August 12, 1994.

Broeske, Pat H. "The Curious Evolution of John Rambo." *Los Angeles Times*, October 27, 1985.

Burk, Greg. "Bullets Over Hollywood." *L.A. Weekly*, June 23–19, 1995.

Busch, Anita M. "*Killers* Doesn't Go Better With Coke." *Variety*, August 29, 1994.

Canby, Vincent, "How Should We React to Violence?" *New York Times*, December 11, 1983.

_____. "*The Wild Bunch.*" *New York Times*, June 26, 1969.

_____. "When a Tame Film Inspires Violence." *New York Times*, March 4, 1979.

_____. "*Death Wish* Exploits Fear Irresponsibly." *New York Times*, July 31, 1974.

_____. "Is the *Bunch* Too Wild?" *New York Times*, July 20, 1969.

_____. "*Orange* Disorienting but Human Comedy." *New York Times*, July 31, 1972.

_____. "Scorsese's Disturbing *Taxi Driver.*" *New York Times*, January 15, 1976.

_____. "Which Version Did You See?" *New York Times*, July 20, 1969.

Cantwell, Mary. "It's Only a Movie." *New York Times*, June 18, 1993.

"Catholics and Film Office Neutral on R-Rated *Wild Bunch.*" *Variety*, July 3, 1969.

Champlin, Charles. "Violence Runs Rampant in *The Wild Bunch.*" *Los Angeles Times*, June 15, 1969.

_____. "Kubrick's Version of *Clockwork Orange.*" *Los Angeles Times*, December 21, 1971.

_____. "Time Bomb Ticks Toward Bloodbath in *Taxi Driver.*" *Los Angeles Times*, February 22, 1976.

Cheshire, Godfrey. "Hollywood's New Hitmen." *Interview*, September 1994.

Christopher, James. "*Clockwork Orange.*" *Time Out*, December 6, 1989.

Ciment, Michel. *John Boorman.* London: Faber & Faber, 1986.

_____. *Stanley Kubrick*, Paris: Calmann-Levy, 1980.

Cooper, Jim. "The True Story of Bonnie and Clyde and Their Pursuer." Dallas *Suburban News*, November 2, 1967.

Corliss, Richard. "Apocalypse Pow!" *Time*, May 10, 1982.

Crist, Judith. "*The Wild Bunch.*" *New York*, June 30, 1969.

Criterion Collection: *Halloween/Taxi Driver* (laser discs with audio commentary).

Crow, Tom. "Writer/Director Abel Ferrar Discusses Blood, Guts and the Church." *Los Angeles Village View*, January 1, 1993.

Dargis, Manohla. "Pulp City." *L.A. Weekly*, October 7–13, 1994.

Darton, Nina. "On De Palma." *New York Times*, November 18, 1984.

Dean, Peter. "Explosive Reaction Follows Link to Toddler's Murder." *Billboard*, December 11, 1993.

Denby, David. "The Gang's All Here." *New York*, March 5, 1979.

"Director Arthur Penn Weighs Balance of *Bonnie and Clyde*'s Yocks and Shocks." *Variety*, August 30, 1987.

Dutka, Elaine. "The Horrors of Filmmaking." *Los Angeles Times*, September 1, 1991.

Ebert, Roger. "Beatty Takes on *Bonnie* Critic." *Los Angeles Times*, October 1, 1967.

Elrick, Ted. "The Woo Dynasty Comes to Hollywood." *DGA Magazine*, November/December 1995.

Elstein, David. "Demonising a Decoy." *The Guardian*, December 22, 1993.

Farber, Stephen. "*The Warriors.*" *New West*, March 12, 1979.

———. "*Scarface* and the Onus of the X Rating." *New York Daily News*, November 20, 1983.

Farrell, Pia. "French Slayings Focus Scope on *Killers.*" *Hollywood Reporter*, October 18, 1994.

Feerick, Lisa. "John Woo: Spaghetti Easterns." *Film Threat Video Guide*, August 1993.

Fine, Marshall. *Bloody Sam: The Life and Films of Sam Peckinpah.* New York: Donald D. Fine, 1991.

Fretts, Bruce. "The Making of a Hitman." *Entertainment Weekly*, November 25, 1994.

Galbraith, Jane. "Sam Peckinpah Meets the Mild Bunch." *Los Angeles Times*, March 14, 1993.

Galloway, Stephen. "The Influence of Hollywood: Violence." *Hollywood Reporter*, 65th Anniversay issue, 1995.

Gardner, Marilyn. "Monsters and Their Keepers." *Christian Science Monitor*, March 19, 1991.

Geff, John. "W7's *Wild Bunch* Top Western, Sights Top BO." *Hollywood Reporter*, June 16, 1969.

Gilliatt, Penelope. "*The Wild Bunch.*" *New Yorker*, July 5, 1969.

Glionna, John M. "No Escaping the Clutches of a Cult Film." *Los Angeles Times*, May 19, 1994.

Goldman, John J. "'I'm Scared,' Jodie Foster Says of Link to Hinckley." *Los Angeles Times*, April 2, 1981.

Goodman, Walter. "Is There a Moral Limit to the Violence in Films?" *New York Times*, December 18, 1983.

Grant, Lee. "Women vs *Dressed To Kill.*" *Los Angeles Times*, September 12, 1980.

———. "New *Warriors* Ad Campaigns." *Los Angeles Times*, February 22, 1979.

Greenberg, Abe. "Meet 'Brownie,' a New Star." *Hollywood Citizen News*, May 31, 1968.

Gritten, David. "The Battle to Avoid the X Rating." *Los Angeles Herald Examiner*, December 9, 1983.

"*Hard Target* Cutting." *Variety*, July 8, 1993.

Harmetz, Aljean. "Movie *Scarface* Receives X Rating." *New York Times*, September 30, 1983.

———. "Toning Down, John Woo Earns His Hollywood R." *Los Angeles Times*, August 15, 1993.

Heffner, Richard D. "X Marks the Film Parents Would Balk At." *Wall Street Journal*, December 19, 1983.

Hoberman, Jim. "*True Romance.*" *Village Voice*, August 30, 1994.

Houston, Penelope. "Kubrick Country." *Saturday Review*, December 25, 1971.

James, Caryn. "Now Starring, Killers for the Chiller 90s." *New York Times*, March 10, 1991.

Kael, Pauline. *For Keeps.* New York: E. P. Dutton, 1995.

Kagan, Norman. *The Cinema of Stanley Kubrick.* New York: Continuum, 1989.

Kaminsky, Stuart M. *Don Siegel: Director.* New York: Curtis Books, 1974.

Kelly, Mary Pat. *Martin Scorsese: A Journey.* New York: Thunder's Mouth Press, 1991.

Keyser, Les. *Martin Scorsese.* New York: Twayne, 1992.

King, Thomas R. "Black Youth Film's Ads Spark Concern." *Wall Street Journal,* January 13, 1992.

Klein, Andy. *"Man Bites Dog II:* The Interview." *L.A. Reader,* April 9, 1993.

Klemesrud, Judy. "What Do They See in *Death Wish?" New York Times,* September 1, 1974.

Knight, Arthur. *"The Wild Bunch." Saturday Review,* July 5, 1969.

Lane, Anthony. "Degrees of Cool." *New Yorker,* October 10, 1994.

Leland, John with Donna Foote. "A Bad Omen for Black Movies?" *Newsweek,* July 29, 1991.

Leydon, Joe. "New Gun in Town." *Los Angeles Times,* January 3, 1993.

Maslin, Janet. "I shall Repay." *New York Times,* August 22, 1982.

_____. "A Night in the Underworld, a Day Pulling a Bank Job." *New York Times,* August 19, 1994.

_____. "Quentin Tarantino's Wild Rise on Life's Dangerous Road." *New York Times,* October 23, 1994.

McCarthy, Todd. *"Scarface* Gets an X Rating: Appeal Planned." *Variety,* November 4, 1983.

McGregor, Alex. "Reservoir Snogs." *Time Out,* September 29–October 6, 1993.

McKey, Keith. *Robert De Niro: The Man Behind the Masks.* New York: St. Martin's Press, 1988.

"McNaughton Redefines Nature of Film Terror." *UCLA Daily Bruin,* April 18, 1980.

"Milestones of Mayhem." *Hollywood Reporter,* November 23, 1992.

Morgan, David. "Return to Cape Fear." *Los Angeles Times,* February 17, 1991.

Morgensten, Joseph. "The Thin Red Line." *Newsweek,* August 28, 1967.

Morrell, David. "The Man Who Created Rambo." *Playboy,* August 1988.

"The MPAA Pistol Whips a Cinematic Milestone." *Los Angeles Village View,* March 26–April 1, 1993.

Murrill, Mary Beth. "Gang War Film Requested." *Los Angeles Herald Examiner,* January 17, 1979.

"Paramount Cancels *Warriors* Ad." *Variety,* January 20, 1979.

Pennington, Ron. *"The Warriors." Hollywood Reporter,* January 12, 1979.

Pizzello, Stephen. *"NBK* Blasts Big Screen With Both Barrels." *American Cinematographer,* November 1994.

Pollock, Dale. "Paramount Offers to Pay Security Tab. . ." *Variety,* February 14, 1979.

_____. "X Excised From New *Scarface." Los Angeles Times,* November 10, 1983.

"Press Violent About Film's Violence." *Variety,* June 24, 1969.

Provenzano, Tom. *"True Romance* Pushing the Envelope on Violence." *Dramalogue,* September 5, 1993.

Rafferty, Terrence. "Artist of Death." *New Yorker,* March 6, 1995.

Rainer, Peter. *"First Blood:* It's Rocky vs the World." *Los Angeles Herald Examiner,* October 22, 1982.

_____. "Putting Violence in Its Place." *Los Angeles Times,* June 24, 1990.

"Rating *Scarface:* A Postmortem." *Motion Picture Product Digest,* February 15, 1984.

Readers. "Where Do You Stand on *Orange*?" *New York Times*, February 6, 1972.

Riddell, Edwin. "*Killers* Slain by UK Censors." *Hollywood Reporter*, October 28–30, 1994.

Riley, Clayton. ". . . Or a Dangerous, Criminally Irresponsible Horror Show?" *New York Times*, January 9, 1972.

Rohter, Larry. "Art Tries to Distance Itself From Life." *New York Times*, August 3, 1991.

Rose, Bob. "Beatty's Side of the Gangster Movie Coin." *Los Angeles Times*, March 3, 1968.

Rosenbaum, Ron. "The Evil Movies Do." *Mademoiselle*, February 1991.

Rosenfield, Paul. "How *Casualties of War* Survived." *Los Angeles Times*, August 13, 1989.

Royko, Mike. "*Bonnie and Clyde*? They Want No Part of It." *Los Angeles Times*, March 3, 1968.

Russo, John. *The Complete Night of the Living Dead Filmbook*. Pittsburgh: Imagine, Inc. 1985.

Sabatini, Vicki. "*Henry* Producers Taking MPAA to Court Over X Rating." *Hollywood Reporter*, May 18, 1990.

Sassone, Rich. "*The Wild Bunch*." *Filmmakers Newsletter*, March 3, 1973.

"*Scarface* Gets X, Appeal Next Week." *Hollywood Reporter*, November 4, 1983.

"*Scarface* Still Bleeding." *Los Angeles Herald Examiner*, March 6, 1984.

"*Scarface* Wins R After MPAA Plea Over Violent Content." *Hollywood Reporter*, November 9, 1983.

"*Scarface* Wins R Tag on Appeal." *Daily Variety*, November 9, 1983.

Schickel, Richard. "Don't Play It Again, Sam." *Life Magazine*, February 14, 1972.

Schiff, Stephen. "The Last Wild Man." *New Yorker*, August 8, 1994.

Schjeldahl, Peter. "Can Blood Baths Make Men of Us?" *New York Times*, February 1972.

Schmidt, William E. "British Test 19-Year Ban on *Clockwork Orange*." *New York Times*, February 6, 1993.

"Schrader Quizzed by FBI." *Rolling Stone*, September 29, 1981.

Schwartz, Emanuel K. "A Psychiatrist's Analysis of *Clockwork Orange*." *Hollywood Reporter*, January 1, 1972.

Scott, Tony. "*Orange* Actresses Part of Arsenal to Combat Ad-Pub Doorslams on Pic." *Variety*, June 13, 1972.

Shaw, Gaylord. "Suspect Sent Love Notes to Actress." *Los Angeles Times*, April 1, 1981.

Shelton, Robert. "Records . . . Sound of *Bonnie and Clyde*." *Los Angeles Herald Examiner*, March 17, 1968.

Sherman, Paul. "McNaughton Creates the Art of Serial Killing in Horror Film." *Boston Herald*, January 5, 1990.

"*Shooting Star: John Woo*." *Time Out*, October 6–13, 1993.

Siegel, Don. *A Siegal Film*. London: Faber & Faber, 1993.

Simmons, Garner. *A Portrait in Montage: Peckinpah*. Austin: University of Texas Press, 1976–1982.

Softley, Jeff. "Two Thumbs Down for *Natural Born Killers*." *Los Angeles Times*, September 12, 1994.

Specter, Michael. "Myths Shape a Movie From Australia." *New York Times*, August 15, 1982.

Stein, Elliott. "Sexual Adversity in Chicago." *Village Voice*, March 27, 1990.

"Stone Answers *Killers* Critics." *Hollywood Reporter*, September 12, 1994.

Sterritt, David. "Hitchcock's *Psycho* Still Influences." *Christian Science Monitor*, July 31, 1990.

Svetkey, Benjamin. "Why Movie Ratings Don't Work." *Entertainment Weekly*, November 15, 1994.

Taylor, Ellen. "Carnage Knowledge." *L.A. Weekly*, April 2, 1993.

Thomas, Karen. "Hollywood Dares You to Watch." *USA Today*, October 26, 1994.

Thomas, Kevin. "Orgy of Violence in *Sudden Impact.*" *Los Angeles Times*, December 9, 1983.

Thompson, David and Ian Christie, eds. *Scorsese on Scorsese*. London: Faber & Faber, 1989.

Thompson, Thomas. "An Outburst of Gratuitous Movie Gore." *Los Angeles Times*, March 11, 1976.

Turan, Kenneth. "Stone Removes the Gloves in *Killers.*" *Los Angeles Times*, August 26, 1994.

_____. "Bloody, Marvelous Peckinpah." *Los Angeles Times*, February 26, 1995.

_____. "Gunfight at the Hokey Corral." *Los Angeles Times*, October 10, 1993.

Varaldiev, Ameliese. "Luc Besson Does New York." *Venice*, November 1994.

"Violence." *Empire*, June 1994.

"Walter Hill Disowns *Warriors*; Goldman Defends Necessary Cuts." *Variety*, October 1, 1980.

Wake, Sandra and Nicholas Hayden, eds. *The Bonnie and Clyde Book*. New York: Simon & Schuster, 1972.

Warga, Wayne. "The *Wild Bunch*'s Fight Against Censor's Scissors." *Los Angeles Times*, October 11, 1993.

Warren, Jonathan. "The *Death Wish* Debacle." *Gallery*, February 1975.

Watkins, Roger. "British Author Burgess Irked by *Orange* Press." *Variety*, August 23, 1973.

Webble, David. *"If They Move, Kill 'em!" The Life and Times of Sam Peckinpah*. New York: Grove Press, 1994.

Weber, Bruce. "Cool Head, Hot Images." *New York Magazine*, August 15, 1989.

Weintraub, Bernard. "An Angry Chorus in Hollywood Dismisses Dole's Harsh Criticism." *New York Times*, June 12, 1995.

_____. "Dole Lashes Out at Hollywood Undermining Social Issues." *New York Times*, June 1, 1995.

_____. "How a Movie Satire Turned Into Reality." *New York Times*, August 16, 1994.

Wood, Peter. *"Dressed To Kill*: How a Film Changes From X to R." *New York Times*, July 20, 1980.

Zimmerman, Paul D. "Rites of Manhood." *Newsweek*, December 20, 1971.

Index

About the Author

Laurent Bouzereau is the author of *The De Palma Cut, The Alfred Hitchcock Quote Book, The Cutting Room Floor,* and *Star Wars: The Annotated Screenplays.* He has also written, directed, and produced documentaries on the making of Steven Spielberg's *Jaws, Close Encounters of the Third Kind, 1941, E. T.: The Extra Terrestrial,* and *Lost World;* George Lucas's *American Graffiti;* Brian De Palma's *Scarface;* Lawrence Kasdan's *Big Chill* and *Silverado;* and Alfred Hitchcock's *Psycho.*

Bouzereau, originally born in France, currently resides in California.